FURNITURE

FOR ALL AROUND THE HOUSE

FURNITURE
FOR ALL AROUND THE HOUSE

Niall Barrett | Bill Hylton | Kim Carleton Graves | Masha Zager
Andy Charron | Anthony Guidice | Jeff Miller

The Taunton Press

The Taunton Press, Inc., 63 South Main Street, PO Box 5506, Newtown, CT 06470-5506
e-mail: tp@taunton.com

The Taunton Press
Inspiration for hands-on living®

EDITOR: Helen Albert
COVER DESIGN AND LAYOUT: Howard Grossman
ILLUSTRATOR: pp. 54–151, 194–281 by Melanie Powell; pp. 2–53, 152–193 by Bob La Pointe
and Mark Sant Angelo
COVER PHOTOGRAPHERS: (front cover, clockwise from top left) Chris Holden, Tom Gerniglio,
Tanya Tucka, Sandor Nagyszalancy; (back cover, top, left to right) Richard Bienkowski,
Chris Holden, Bob Gregson, Robert North; (back cover, bottom, clockwise from top left)
Dennis Griggs, Tanya Tucka, Tom Gerniglio

LIBRARY OF CONGRESS CATALOGING-IN-PUBLICATION DATA
Furniture for all around the house / Niall Barrett ... [et al.].
    p. cm. -- (Woodworking for the home)
  Includes bibliographical references and index.
  ISBN-13: 978-1-56158-853-4 (alk. paper)
  ISBN-10: 1-56158-853-9 (alk. paper)
 1. Furniture making. I. Barrett, Niall.

TT194.F965 2007
684.1--dc22

                                    2006024813

Printed in the United States of America
10 9 8 7 6 5 4 3 2 1

The following manufacturers/names appearing in *Furniture for All Around the House* are trademarks:
Bioshield®, Blum®, Delta®, Ebon-X™, Elmer's®, Festo®, Hydrocote®, Masonite®, Minwax®, Plexiglas®,
Robo-sander™, Sutherland Welles®

WORKING WOOD IS INHERENTLY DANGEROUS. Using hand or power tools improperly or ignoring
safety practices can lead to permanent injury or even death. Don't try to perform operations you learn
about here (or elsewhere) unless you're certain they are safe for you. If something about an operation
doesn't feel right, don't do it. Look for another way. We want you to enjoy the craft, so please keep safety
foremost in your mind whenever you're in the shop.

To Niall, Bill, Kim, Masha, Andy, Anthony, and Jeff,
who put in the extra effort to show other woodworkers
how to build these projects.

ACKNOWLEDGMENTS

THE PROJECTS IN THIS BOOK were drawn from six previously published Taunton books: *Bookcases* by Niall Barrett, *Tables* by Anthony Guidice, *Dining Tables* by Kim Carleton Graves with Masha Zager, *Beds* by Jeff Miller, *Desks* by Andy Charron, and *Chests* by Bill Hylton. Photos for Niall's book were taken by Chris Holden, and for Anthony's book by Tom Cerniglio. In Kim and Masha's book the photos were taken by Richard Bienkowski with the exception of those taken by Bob Skalkowski. Photos for Jeff's book were taken by Tanya Tucka, for Andy's book by Robert North, and for Bill's book by Donna Chiarelli, with the exception of those taken by Bob Gregson.

CONTENTS

PART ONE
BOOKCASES

Simple
Short Bookcase

My three-year-old son loves two things: trains and books. It follows that he especially loves books about trains. What more perfect gift for him than a bookcase to hold his growing collection of books, trains, and especially his books on trains?

Looking around our house for a location to put it, I realized that the bookcase had to be less than 3 ft. wide to fit a wall in his room. Also, it could be no more than 4 ft. high or I'd have to build a stool so my son could reach the top shelf. And like most things I build for my home, it had to be really easy and fast. So I came up with this project, the Simple Short Bookcase.

This is an instructional bookcase, which means that I chose its attributes in part to clearly illustrate basic techniques. It's built of solid butternut, uses traditional joinery, and has fixed shelves. The sides have a gentle taper from 9 in. at the bottom to 7⅛ in. at the top. The sides also extend past the top shelf, making it a little more interesting and actually a little easier to build. A small (2-in.) radius at the top front edge of each side completes the package.

The case is quite easy to build, and only took a couple of days, including finishing. By the end of a weekend, my son was proudly taking his train books off the shelves (and when reminded, putting them back).

Simple Short Bookcase

This very simple bookcase is joined together with rabbets, dadoes, and glue. It has fixed shelves and a plywood back. The use of solid butternut, the tapered sides, and the radius top on the sides add considerably to what would otherwise be a plain piece.

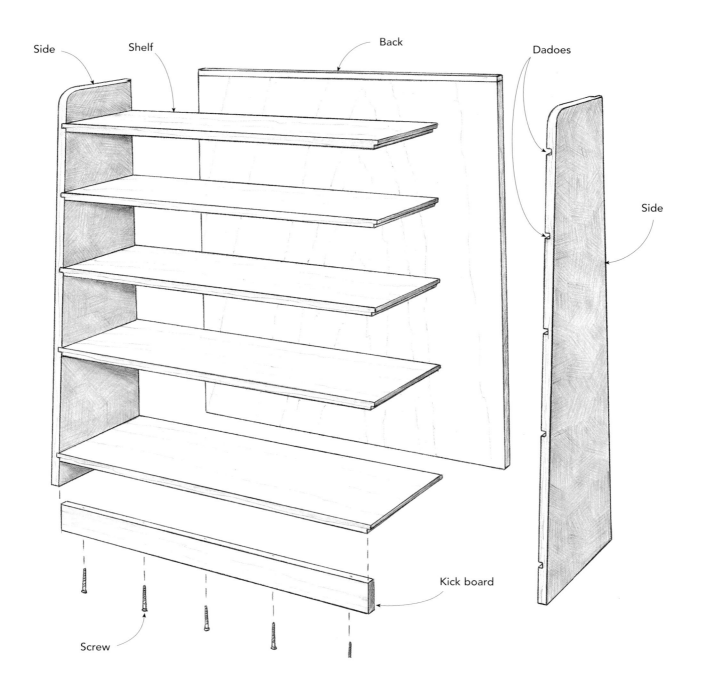

Side

Shelf

Back

Dadoes

Side

Kick board

Screw

FRONT VIEW

SIDE VIEW

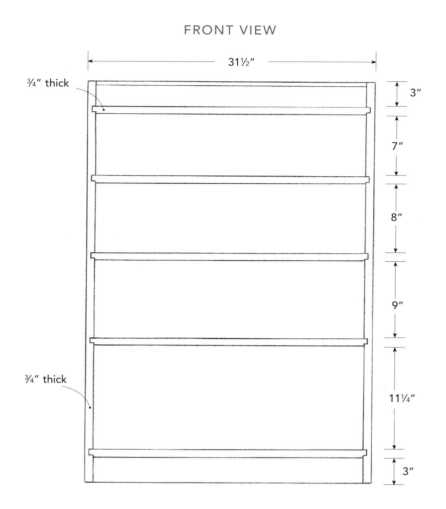

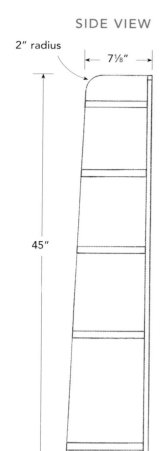

¾" thick

31½"

3"

7"

8"

9"

11¼"

3"

¾" thick

2" radius

7⅛"

45"

9"

CUT LIST FOR SIMPLE SHORT BOOKCASE

Carcase and Shelves

2	Sides	45 in. x 9 in. x ¾ in.
5	Shelves	30¾ in. x 9 in. x ¾ in.
1	Edging for top of back	30¾ in. x ½ in. x ¾ in.
1	Kick board	30 in. x 3 in. x ¾ in.
1	Back	30¾ in. x 44¼ in. x ½ in.

Hardware

5	Screws	3 in. x #8

All parts are solid butternut except the back, which is ½-in. maple plywood.

BUILDING THE BOOKCASE STEP-BY-STEP

THE JOINERY in this bookcase is a little fussy, but the scale is such that all the parts are easy to manage. This allows me to do almost all the work on the tablesaw, which is by far the quickest way to cut this joinery. In fact, once the tablesaw is set up, the joinery goes very quickly, and you're on to the more fun aspects of furniture making—shaping and styling. Some simple jigsaw, router, and sanding work completes the bookcase.

PREPARING STOCK

A cut list and drawing

1. Make a drawing of the bookcase to give you a look at scale and proportion and to allow you to work out construction details.
2. Write up a cut list with rough dimensions and final dimensions (from the cut list on p. 7). A good rule of thumb to figure rough dimensions is to add 1 in. to the width, 3 in. to the length, and 25 percent to the thickness for rough solid stock. Vary these additions depending on the condition of the stock. Don't apply the rule to sheet goods like plywood.
3. Pick out your stock using the rough dimension list. It will help keep the parts straight, and ensure that you have enough to work with when you shape the parts.

Milling to thickness

1. Flatten and thickness all the stock at one time since the bookcase is small and there are only nine solid wood pieces.
2. Size the parts to the rough-dimensions cut list. You can work faster at this stage by milling to the numbers (see **photo A**).
3. Rip the parts to finished width and crosscut them to length.

Photo A: Rough-dimensions cut lists help you keep track of the parts before they are recognizable as you mill them to size.

CUTTING THE JOINERY

Laying out the joints

Because the sides continue past the top shelf, you can use the same joint, a shallow dado, to connect all the shelves.

1. Butt and clamp the sides together with their ends flush.
2. Mark the location of each dado across both sides on their inside faces. This ensures that the shelf spacing will be exactly the same.
3. Mark the bottom and back of each side so you don't mix them up later.
4. Mark the location of the tenons on the shelves and clearly mark the top face of each shelf (see "Layout of Dadoes and Stub Tenons").

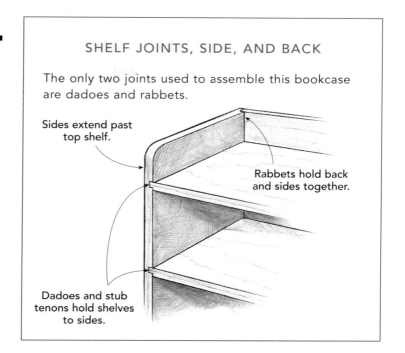

SHELF JOINTS, SIDE, AND BACK

The only two joints used to assemble this bookcase are dadoes and rabbets.

Sides extend past top shelf.

Rabbets hold back and sides together.

Dadoes and stub tenons hold shelves to sides.

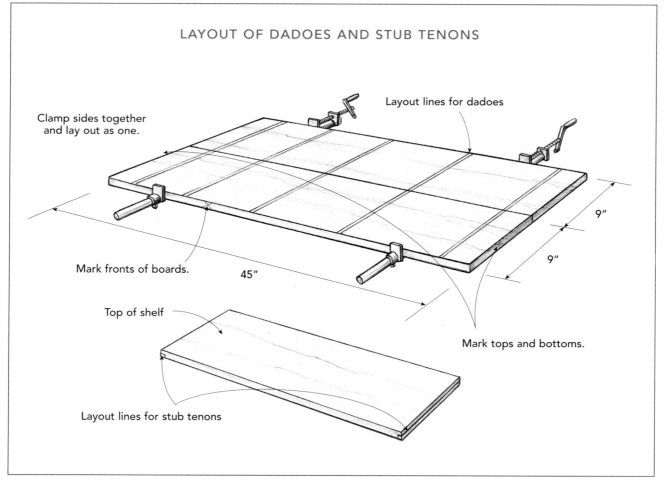

LAYOUT OF DADOES AND STUB TENONS

Layout lines for dadoes

Clamp sides together and lay out as one.

Mark fronts of boards.

45"

9"

9"

Mark tops and bottoms.

Top of shelf

Layout lines for stub tenons

Tip: *Don't taper the sides before you cut the dadoes because working with square boards is a lot easier.*

Photo B: **A short stop block positioned at the back of the fence helps keep the dadoes consistent and reduces the risk of binding the board in the cut.**

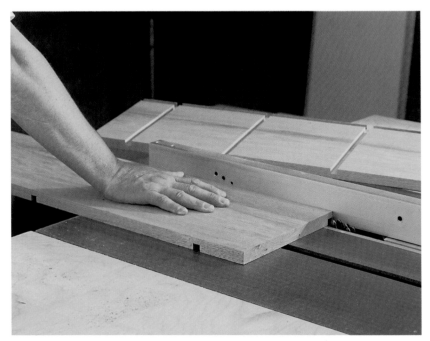

Photo C: **The same dado blade at the same height setting will cut the rabbets for the back.**

Cutting the dadoes in the sides and the rabbets on the shelves

You can use the tablesaw to cut all the joints because the sides and shelves are so small. On a larger bookcase, you would have to bring the tool to the wood and use a router or a plow plane to cut the joints.

1. Clamp a stop block to the back of the saw fence to register against the end of each side. The stop block keeps the workpiece from binding between the blade and the fence.

2. Set the fence to cut one set of opposite dadoes in each side. Then reset the fence to cut another set of dadoes (see **photo B**).

3. Cut the dadoes with a ½-in.-wide dado head using the miter gauge to guide the sides. The exact depth is not critical, but should be consistent. Cut no deeper than half the thickness of the stock, or to ⅜ in.

4. Start cutting the dadoes from one end in toward the middle of the side. When you cut the middle shelf dado, turn the board around and work back the other way to avoid having too little stock resting on the miter gauge.

The stock must be straight and square for this method to work. If it's not, errors will accumulate, and misaligned shelves and a twisted bookcase will result.

5. Set your rip fence so it just clears the dado head and leave the dado head set at the same height.

6. Rip-cut the rabbets on the inside rear edge of the sides (see **photo C**). This joint will house the back. You may have a little whisper of wood on the edge of the joint. If it doesn't just fall off, hit with a sanding block.

Cutting the stub tenons on the shelf ends

Because the shelves aren't very long you can cut the stub tenons with the same dado head and a shopmade carrier that rides on your fence and holds the shelves on end. If you don't have a carrier like this or don't wish to make one, Delta® sells a tablesaw tenoning jig that works as well. The joint can also be cut with the workpiece horizontal on the tablesaw or with a router and rabbeting bit.

1. Test the carrier's setup with scrap pieces until you get it cutting the right thickness.
2. Test-fit the scrap pieces in the side dadoes. The fit of this joint is crucial to the strength of the piece as a whole. The tighter the joints, the stronger the case. You should have to apply some pressure to assemble a dry joint, but you shouldn't have to hammer it home.
3. When the dado head is set up properly, run the shelf ends over it, making sure that the same side of each shelf is facing the fence. Use a piece of scrap to back up the exit point of the dado head (see **photo D**).

Photo D: **A simple shopmade carrier will guide the shelf ends over the dado blade to tenon the ends.**

Photo E: Draw the profile of the bookcase directly on the board in heavy pencil lines so you can clearly see where to cut.

SHAPING THE PARTS

Laying out the profile of the sides

The profile of the sides is composed of two simple shapes: a gentle taper from the bottom up and a 2-in. radius at the top.

1. Draw the taper with a straightedge from top to bottom.

2. Scribe the radius at the top with a compass. To find the center of the radius, spin the dividers from two points, one that is 2 in. down the taper from the edge, and the other that is 2 in. in from the taper line. The intersection of these arcs is the center of the radius (see **photo E**).

3. Cut to within ⅛ in. of the line with a jigsaw (see **photo F**).

4. Put a smooth edge on the sides, using a board with a straightedge as a guide and a router fitted with a top-bearing straight bit, also called a pattern bit (see **photo G**).

5. Smooth the radius portions by hand with a sanding block.

Ripping angles on the front edge of the shelves to match the sides

The taper of the sides requires that the front edges of the shelves be ripped at the same angle, in this case at about 2 degrees.

1. To determine the angle, you can measure it off the drawing using a protractor or, to be extra certain, off the sides.

2. Rip the angle first on all the shelves, making sure the same side of each shelf is up (see **photo H**).

3. Fit the shelves in their grooves with the front edges flush with the sides, and then mark the back edges at the rabbet to get their respective depths.

4. Rip the shelf backs to width, remembering to readjust the sawblade to 90 degrees.

Photo F: A jigsaw is the quickest and simplest way to cut the taper and the radius in one operation.

Photo G: With a straight plywood board to guide the router, trim the edge of the case side with a straight bit. Don't worry about smoothing the radius this way. It's best done by hand later.

Photo H: Rip the small angle on the front edge of the shelves on the tablesaw.

Tip: Wait until you have the rest of the bookcase dry-fit together to cut the back to size. This way, you can measure the real dimensions you need.

Photo I: **Use biscuits to align the solid butternut strip on the top of the back.**

Cutting the back to size

The plywood back should run the full height of the bookcase. It fits into the rabbets in the sides and butts up against the back edges of the shelves.

1. To cover the top edge of the plywood, attach a ½-in. by ¾-in. strip of butternut with #10 biscuits and glue (see **photo I**). The biscuits help align the strip and keep it in place during clamping.
2. Cut the back to size.

ASSEMBLY

Pre-assembly
1. Sand all the parts that will be difficult to reach after the bookcase is assembled. These include the shelves and the inside faces of the sides and back.
2. Be careful not to sand the ends of the shelves that fit into the grooves unless you need to adjust the thickness to fit better.
3. Dry-fit the whole bookcase. This is your chance to make any minor corrections in joint fit and alignment. It's also a chance to make

Tip: It's a really good idea to sand everything smooth before assembly because it's far easier to sand parts that are flat than to sand into and around corners.

DRY-RUN ASSEMBLIES

Yellow glue sets very quickly—in a matter of minutes. This makes it good to know how long a glue-up will take, especially if it could be longer than the open time of the glue.

To make sure, I often do a complete dry-run assembly. I apply all the clamps that will be necessary during actual glue-up to make sure all the joints close up tight and so I can position clamps where they're needed. I also normally mark the mating tenons and dadoes. If they get mixed up during glue-up, it's a mess to pull things apart and get them in the right places.

I sometimes go so far as pretending to apply glue. This may sound funny for a professional woodworker, like a politician practicing how to lie; but if there is a lot of glue area, knowing how much time it will take to spread the glue can be a big help. If it is too long, you'll need to break your glue-ups into two parts. This bookcase is so small that glue-up time isn't an important issue, but in larger projects it will be.

Photo J: An acid brush is small enough to spread glue evenly in the dadoes of the sides.

sure you have everything you need for glue-up and can work quickly and smoothly within the open time of the glue (see "Dry-Run Assemblies").

Final glue-up

1. Gather all the clamps, glue, rags, and other tools and supplies you will need. You don't want to be looking for something during glue-up.

2. Lay out both sides with dadoes and rabbets up and back to back.

3. Spread glue into the joints with a small acid brush (see **photo J**). Don't just squeeze a bead of glue from the bottle into the dadoes. You won't get a good indication of how much glue you're using. Don't put any glue on the tenon or on the shoulder; it doesn't add any strength and ends up just making a mess.

4. Work from one side, inserting tenons in dadoes, one at a time, and aligning the back edges with the rabbet for the back before pushing them home. In a well-fitting joint it may be impossible to slide the shelves sideways once fully inserted.

5. Use a dead-blow hammer for extra persuasion when necessary. A hammer and a block of wood are just as good—except that you need an extra hand to hold the block.

6. Lay the second side on top of the open shelf tenons (see **photo K**). By this time, any glue brushed into these grooves has had a chance to set just enough so it won't run when you place this side.

Photo K: Glue-up can be a hectic time, so make sure you have all the clamps and pieces ready to go and proceed in a quick but orderly fashion.

Photo L: After you've clamped up the whole case, check the diagonals for overall square. If one diagonal is longer than the other, apply light clamp pressure across the long diagonal.

7. Draw the joints tight with clamps. On a case this small, two clamps per shelf should be all you need. Sometimes a caul may be necessary to put pressure on the center of the joint.

8. Check the case for square by measuring the diagonals once everything is well clamped and the joints are tight.

9. If the case is out in any direction (i.e., shaped like a parallelogram), apply a clamp over the longer diagonal until the glue dries (see **photo L**). Minor out-of-square issues can usually be taken care of when the back is installed, provided the back is square and fits just right.

10. If you have a lot of glue squeeze-out, try to scrape most of it off when it's a little rubbery. A clean, damp cloth should take care of the remainder.

11. Remove any remaining glue squeeze-out with a sharp chisel when dry.

12. Sand any spots you smeared with glue during cleanup, or the glue will hamper the penetration of the finish.

Attaching the back and the kick board

1. When the glue is dry, unclamp the carcase and attach the last two pieces: the back and the kick board.

2. Screw the back to the rabbets and to the backs of the shelves with 1-in. trim-head screws. Trim-head screws are thin screws with a very small head, about 3/16 in. in diameter. I use these to attach the back because the rabbet is only 3/8 in. wide, and larger-head screws are just too big.

3. Butt-fit the base piece, or kick board, tight between the sides and screw it in place through countersunk holes into the bottom shelf (see "Attaching the Kick Board").

ATTACHING THE KICK BOARD

The kick board is simply screwed through countersunk holes into the underside of the bottom shelf.

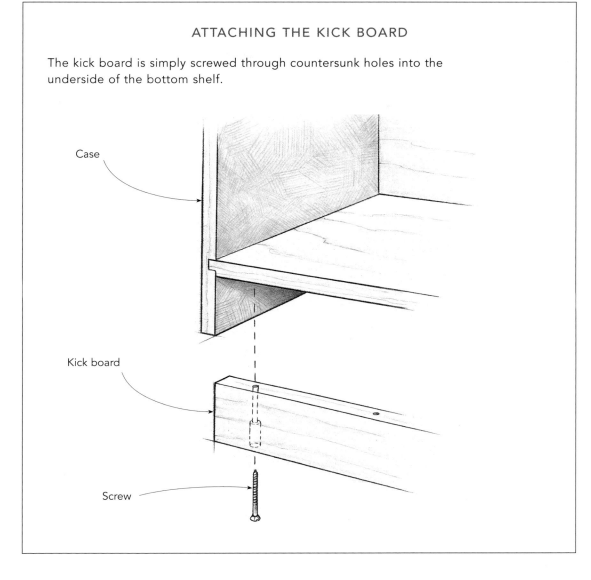

Case

Kick board

Screw

Tip: Breaking the edges is important because otherwise you risk having the edges splinter.

FINISHING UP

Final sanding and finish application

1. When the glue is dry, sand the outside of the bookcase to 180 grit.

2. Break all the edges by lightly sanding them with 180 grit. It may seem as if you'll lose some definition, but that's only a risk if you go overboard.

3. Remove the back to make finishing easier.

4. Apply the finish. I recommend a simple wax finish for this project. It's a very under-rated and underused finish. It looks and feels wonderful, and for applications like a bookcase, it's more than adequate protection. A wax finish takes a lot of elbow work, but it's almost impossible to do wrong—if you apply too much, it can be hard to rub out to a good shine, but that's about the worst that can happen. I used butcher's wax. It adds only a small amount of color, is easy to find, and is self-stripping. This means it dissolves itself when a new coat of wax is reapplied, so it doesn't build up and dull the finish you are trying to shine.

Simple Tall Bookcase

My wife and I have a room we call our office. It isn't really "ours" but hers. I do my writing in my shop. The dust is a little rough on the computer, but it's my space. Anyway, "our" office used to be what we called the junk room. You know, every house has one. It's the place where everything that doesn't have a place ends up, generally in piles on the floor.

The junk-room conversion, however, was never really completed to "our" office because there was still a certain amount of stuff, mostly magazines, piled here and there. As the magazines were all mine, it was my job to get them up off the floor. So, I designed and built a tall, simple bookcase, which I gave the catchy name of Simple Tall Bookcase, to get all the magazines off the floor.

This bookcase is similar to the one on pp. 4–17 in that it's very basic in design but different in a number of important ways. First of all, it's made from edge-banded plywood, not solid wood. I used biscuit joinery to put it together and added adjustable shelves above and below a fixed central shelf. I sized it to fit a sliver of wall between two doors and to hold my entire collection of back issues of *Fine Woodworking, Fine Homebuilding,* and *Home Furniture* with room left over. It's simple to build, and it holds a relatively large amount of stuff. It also doesn't look too bad.

Simple Tall Bookcase

THIS BOOKCASE HAS a very simple boxlike shape, with shelves, top, and bottom all looking essentially identical. The interest is in the details, which include the five adjustable shelves in between the top and bottom fixed shelves, and a center fixed shelf for support. The construction is very simple, using only biscuits, even on the kick board.

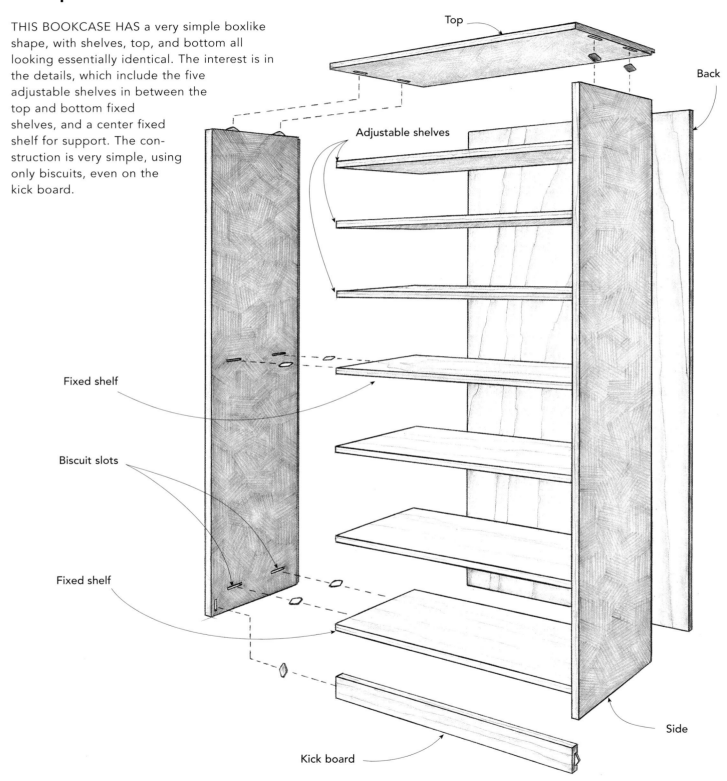

Top

Back

Adjustable shelves

Fixed shelf

Biscuit slots

Fixed shelf

Side

Kick board

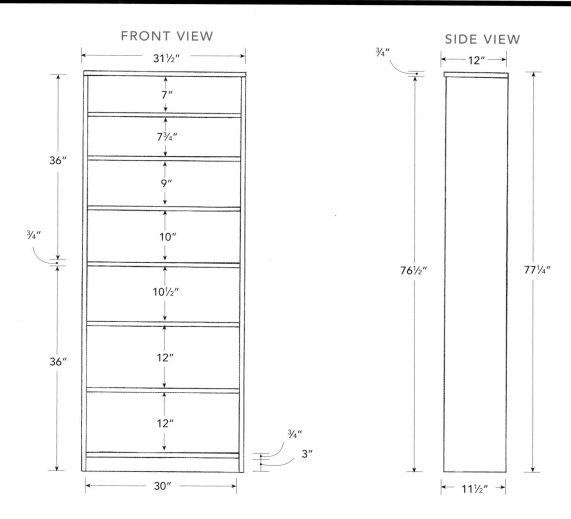

FRONT VIEW

31½"

36"

7"

7¾"

9"

10"

10½"

36"

12"

12"

¾"

¾"

3"

30"

SIDE VIEW

¾"

12"

76½"

77¼"

11½"

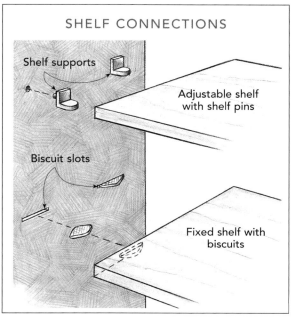

SHELF CONNECTIONS

Shelf supports

Adjustable shelf with shelf pins

Biscuit slots

Fixed shelf with biscuits

CUT LIST FOR SIMPLE TALL BOOKCASE		
Carcase and Shelves		
2	Sides	76½ in. x 11½ in. x ¾ in.
1	Back	76⅞ in. x 30¾ in. x ½ in.
7	Shelves	30 in. x 10⅞ in. x ¾ in.
1	Top	31½ in. x 12 in. x ¾ in.
1	Kick board	30 in. x 3 in. x ¾ in.
	Edge-banding	35 ft. x ⅞ in.
Hardware		
20	Shelf pins	

All parts are ¾-in. maple plywood except the back, which is ½-in. maple plywood.

BUILDING THE BOOKCASE STEP-BY-STEP

BOOKCASES OF THIS type are the workaday bookcases we all need in our lives to organize our stuff. They won't win any design contests, but I rather like their honesty. What will set this bookcase apart from the unpainted-furniture-store variety is attention to detail. Treat these simple cases the same way you do all your furniture, keeping the fit and finish as crisp as you can. This is a piece with strong edges. It's all veneer and edge tape. There's nowhere to soften it, so it has to be just so. Just because it's simple doesn't mean it should be built with any less care. People will notice!

LAYING OUT THE PLYWOOD PARTS

The size of this bookcase, 31½ in. wide by 77¼ in. high by 11½ in. deep, takes into account the size of a sheet of plywood and its design limitations (see "Designing with

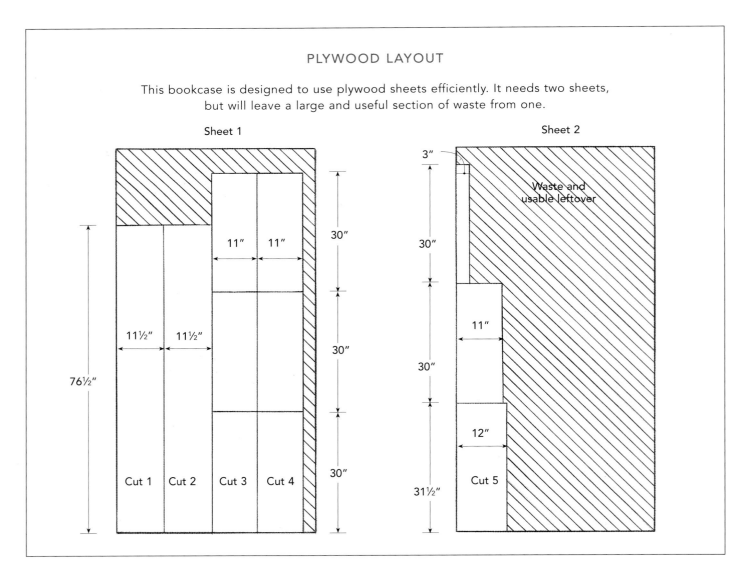

PLYWOOD LAYOUT

This bookcase is designed to use plywood sheets efficiently. It needs two sheets, but will leave a large and useful section of waste from one.

Sheet 1

Sheet 2

Plywood"). The 11½-in. depth of the piece is sized to be cut efficiently from two sheets of ¾-in. plywood. My magazines also happen to fit it quite nicely. And it has no vertical span longer than 3 ft., beyond which the plywood might bow.

1. Prepare a drawing and cut list, and then lay out the parts on the sheets of plywood (see "Plywood Layout").
2. Always add ⅛ in. to the thickness of your lines to compensate for the thickness of the sawblade. Also don't measure in exactly from any of the edges. Add ⅛ in. or more so that you can later trim the factory edge, which is usually a little uneven or beat-up in some way.

MAKING THE PARTS AND CUTTING THE JOINERY

Cutting parts to size
Rip and crosscut the plywood parts to finished sizes. For information on how the application of edge tape will affect overall dimensions, see "Designing with Edge Tape" on p. 24.

Rabbeting for the back
1. Cut the rabbets for the plywood back along the inside edge of the sides and rear edge of the top. Use a router fitted with a ½-in. bearing-guided rabbeting bit (see **photo A**).
2. For the sides, run the rabbet all the way from end to end.
3. For the top, stop the rabbet short of both ends about ⅜ in. This dimension is not critical—judge it by eye. Just be careful not to rout through to the edges since they show.
4. Don't square up the rounded end in the rabbet with a chisel just yet. Wait until after the case is assembled (but before you fit the back).

DESIGNING WITH PLYWOOD

Plywood has many advantages. You don't need to mill it to thickness, it generally doesn't have serious warps or twists, and it's strong in every direction, unlike solid wood.

Its limitations, though, are often overlooked. One, it comes in sheets no longer than 96 in. If you want a 97-in.-tall bookcase made of plywood, you're out of luck. Its width poses the same problem. Making plywood bookcases demands that you design with 96 in. by 48 in. in mind at all times. To get the most out of a sheet, you don't want to design a bookcase with 25-in.-wide by 96-in.-tall sides because you will only be able to get one side out of a sheet and have 23 in. of waste.

Photo A: **Cutting the rabbet in the sides is easy with a router and a ½-in. piloted bit. It's especially useful for the stopped cut on the top edge.**

Laying out and cutting the biscuit slots

There are 28 biscuit slots in this bookcase. They are not all the same type of slot and fall roughly into three categories: slots on the edges of a board, slots at right angles to an edge, and slots in the middle of a board's face (see "Three Basic Biscuit Joints" on p. 26).

1. Work out the location of the fixed shelf if you need shelves spaced differently than shown. An inch or so in one direction won't really compromise the structure, but don't go more than a few inches either way.

2. Lay out and cut the biscuit slots according to the rough locations in "Biscuit Slot Layout." Mark the slots with a simple line centered where you want the biscuit. Leave

---

DESIGNING WITH EDGE TAPE

Applying edge tape to the parts will add some thickness, but I don't compensate for it when I rip parts to size. There is a method to my madness.

First, edge tape is usually less than $1/16$ in. thick, which is an almost meaningless increment in a bookcase of this kind.

Second, most of the parts will have this $1/16$ in. added in the same plane. For example, both the sides and shelves will have tape applied to their front edges, so their relationship doesn't change.

Third, there are two places where the added edge tape stands proud, and in both cases it is to the advantage of the design. The top will become $1/8$ in. wider than the case ($1/16$ in. on each side), giving a little definition to the otherwise featureless sides. Also the kick board ends up recessed an extra $1/8$ in. To get this effect, however, you have to remember to cut the biscuit slots before you edge-tape.

These are minor details, but thinking through the whole design before you lay out the parts is a good habit to get into. Well practiced, you can clear up confusing details, find solutions, and prevent mistakes.

Biscuit Slot Layout

The entire bookcase is held together with biscuit joints. All centerline measurements for biscuit layout are made from the back of the shelves and from the edge of the rabbet on the sides and top. This is because the shelves are set back $1/8$" from the front of the case.

UNDERSIDE OF TOP

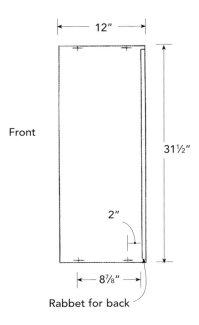

12"

Front

31½"

2"

8⅞"

Rabbet for back

End   2"

KICK BOARD   Front   Face

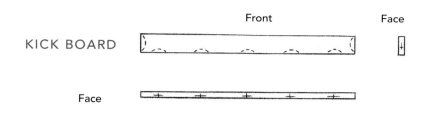

Face

CENTER FIXED SHELF

Front

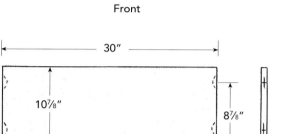

UNDERSIDE OF BOTTOM FIXED SHELF

End

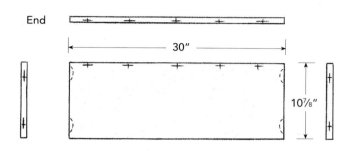

INSIDE OF RIGHT SIDE

Front

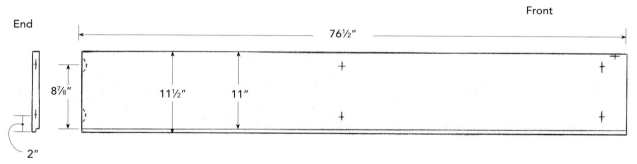

End

INSIDE OF LEFT SIDE

End

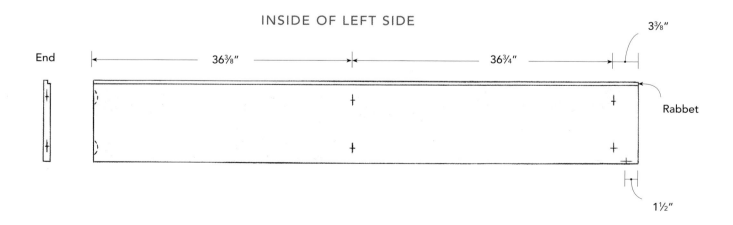

Photo B: **Cut biscuit slots in the ends of the fixed shelves and at the top of the sides.**

enough room on each side of every slot for other biscuits or the edge of the board.

3. Cut the slots in the ends of the fixed shelves, at the top of the sides, and in the kick board (see **photo B**). These are cuts in the edge of a board. Most of the biscuit slots in this project are of this type.

4. Cut the slots in the top piece. These are the only slots you cut in a board's face at the edge (see **photo C**).

5. Cut the slots for the center fixed shelf and base. These slots are in the face of the sides but not near an edge. You must make a temporary fence or stop to register against the base of the joiner. Instead of searching the shop for an appropriate piece of scrap, just use the mating shelf for a stop (see **photo D**).

THREE BASIC BISCUIT JOINTS

Biscuit joinery has revolutionized woodworking in the last 30 years. Biscuit joints are easy to cut, can be very accurate, and are super strong. They have every advantage, and few limitations. There are, however, a few tricks to learn for cutting them. On this bookcase, they fall into roughly three categories.

Slots on the edges of a board

This is certainly the easiest type of biscuit slot to cut, and the one you see used most. With the fence set at 90 degrees and lying flat on the face of the board, plunge into the edge. The machine is no problem to hold, and the plunge is easy to control.

Slots at right angles to an edge

This type of biscuit slot is similar to the first type, but the orientation is reversed. The fence registers against the edge as the joiner cuts into the face. It's the most difficult type of slot to cut because the fence doesn't have much to register against. Make sure the face of the joiner lies flat on the workpiece, and hold it there as steadily as you can in the cut.

An option is to clamp a square block to the opposite side of the board flush with the edge of the workpiece. This will give the joiner more stability. But be careful: If the block is slightly off or out of square, your slot will be as well.

Slots in the middle of a board's face

These types of slots are easily cut, and the fence set at 90 degrees flat on the workpiece is very stable. You must make a temporary fence or stop block, though, to register against the base of the joiner.

The difficulty in cutting these slots is laying them out and keeping track of the direction to cut. You have to be able to measure from the joiner's base to the centerline of the cutter, and then translate that measurement into a location for the stop block so the shelf and the side slots line up just right. Take your time and think about where the shelf and slots should be before marking or cutting anything: There's a bit of Zen involved with biscuit joinery.

6. Cut the slots in the sides for the kick board. As the kick board is set back from the front of the bottom shelf ⅛ in., cut the slots in the underside of the shelf using the ¾-in. setting on the biscuit joiner and cut the slots in the mating edge of the kick board using the ½-in. setting.

7. Cut the slots in the ends of the kick board in the same way as in step 6. Remember the slots in the side have to be set in an extra ⅛ in. for everything to line up.

8. Dry-fit the piece to make sure it goes together properly. Common problems include misalignment of biscuit slots and slots that are cut too shallow.

Laying out and drilling the shelf-pin holes

To cut the shelf-pin holes, I use a Festo® jig and router fitted with a 5mm bit (see **photo E** on p. 28). You can also use a number of other good commercial jigs, or make your own.

1. Locate the jig a specific distance from the front and back edges as well as top to bottom. As a general rule drill holes 2 in. in from the front and back edges of a 12-in.-wide case side (that's one-sixth the total width as a rule of thumb), and leave 6 in. to 8 in. at top and bottom without holes.

Tip: To ensure that the shelves are horizontal (important in my book), be consistent in how you register the layout lines. What you do on one side, do on the other. Otherwise the errors will accumulate.

Photo C: The biscuit slots in the top are cut on the edge but at a right angle. This is a difficult kind of cut to keep stable, so go slowly and carefully.

Photo D: Use a shelf as a stop block, aligned on the edge of where the shelf intersects the side, to support the biscuit joiner when cutting the slots in the sides.

Photo E: The Festo boring jig makes routing accurate holes in the sides quick and easy.

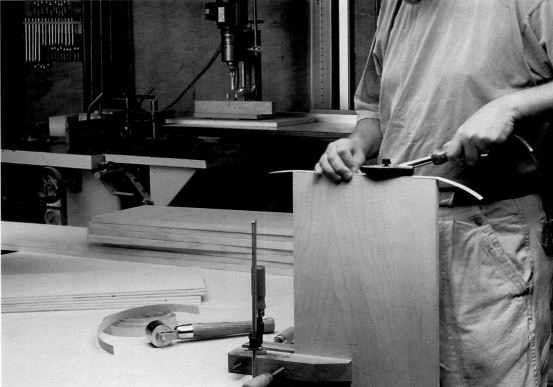

Photo F: With an edge-banding iron, I apply banding to all edges that show.

Tip: To fix mis-aligned slots that won't show, simply glue a biscuit into the slot, trim it flush, and then recut the slots when the glue dries.

2. Drill the shelf-pin holes in the sides. The important thing is to consistently drill two rows of evenly spaced holes on each side that line up with the rows on the opposing side.

Edge-banding shelves

Before assembly you'll want to band all the edges that show, including the front edge of all the shelves, the front edge of the sides, the front edge of the top, and the side edges of the top. I use iron-on veneer tape for this, which is available from many woodworking suppliers. I have an "edge-banding iron" for applying this tape, but a regular household clothing iron set on the dry or no-steam setting works just fine.

1. Break off a piece of tape a little longer than you need and, starting at one end, hold it on the edge and apply heat and pressure until the glue softens under the iron (see **photo F**).
2. Move along the edge a few inches at a time with the iron until the tape is stuck.

3. Trim off the extra length of edge-banding by scoring it lightly on the underside and breaking it off.
4. As the edge tape is slightly wider than ¾ in., sand it with an orbital sander to make it flush to the shelf faces. Then sand the ends flush with a sanding block.

ASSEMBLY AND FINISHING

Preparing for glue-up

1. Sand all the parts up through 150 grit. I find this to be more than adequate surface preparation before spraying the bookcase with water-based lacquer (though there is some debate over how fine a grit one should sand to under a sprayed finish).
2. Double-check that you have everything you need (clamps, etc.) before you put glue into anything.

Attaching the kick board to the bottom shelf

1. Glue up the kick board and bottom shelf before you glue up the case (see **photo G** on p. 29). This cuts down the time and the amount of clamps needed during glue-up.
2. Make sure the ends of the kick board and the shelf are perfectly flush during this glue-up because there is no way to fix this after the fact. If you sand them flush, they will not be as wide as the shelves.

Gluing and clamping the case

1. Glue biscuits into all the face slots on both sides.
2. Lay one side down with the biscuits facing up.

3. Glue and position the bottom shelf/kick board on its mating biscuits, then move to the center fixed shelf, and glue and position it.
4. Attach the other side on top of this assembly and clamp across the case, front and back, at both shelf locations.
5. Check the case for square and adjust clamps, if necessary. Check for square now rather than when the case is fully clamped because the clamp pressure along sides this long will often distort or bow them. Any minor out-of-square problems in the case will usually be corrected when you fit the back.
6. Clamp the top, front and back, on both sides (see **photo H**). Check for square again.

Installing the back

The last part of the assembly stage is to make and fit the back.

1. When the case glue is dry, remove the clamps, clean up any glue squeeze-out with a sharp chisel, and do any touch-up sanding necessary.

2. Lay the case on its face and square up the top corners of the rabbet with a sharp chisel (these were left from the routing earlier).

3. Measure the opening created by the rabbets and cut some ½-in. plywood to fit snugly.

4. Sand the back to 150 grit.

5. Mark out and drill pilot holes around the perimeter and across the backs of the shelves for 1-in. trim-head screws (see **photo I**).

6. Screw the back in place.

Applying the finish

I finished this piece with a clear water-based finish called Resisthane®, which is manufactured by Hydrocote®. I have been using water-based finishes for more than 10 years and am very happy with the results I get from this particular product. There isn't space to get into all the details of applying a spray finish, but if you're interested in trying it and need further guidance, I recommend *Spray Finishing* (The Taunton Press, 1998).

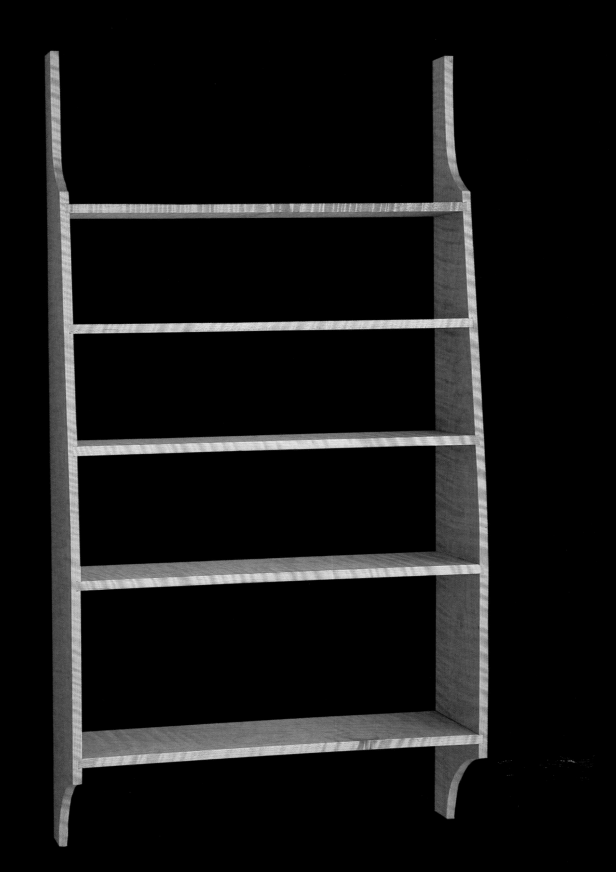

SHAKER-STYLE WALL SHELF

There is an intimacy to small wall shelves. Some woodworkers detail small shelves with ornamentation, turning them into little jewels that could almost be displayed on their own. Others are more subtle, relying on simple but elegant style and flawless execution.

This Shaker-style shelf was originally designed and built by Peter Turner, a woodworker in Portland, Maine. He has one in his kitchen as a spice shelf. In fact, he designed the size and shelf configuration around this application. But Turner gave his shelf a refined design to make it equally at home displaying some special objects.

I have a growing collection of miniature liquor bottles constantly in need of more display space. My plan was to take the best ones and place them on this shelf. Fate had other plans, however: The shelf was sent to be photographed for this book, and it's being used, ironically, as an elegant spice shelf in the photographer's kitchen.

Turner's inspiration to build this piece came from a drawing of a peg-hung Shaker shelf in Ejner Handberg's book, *Shop Drawings of Shaker Furniture and Woodenware* (Berkshire Traveler Press, 1975). The shelf sides in Handberg's drawing are curved on top but straight at the bottom. Peter added another curve at the bottom, experimenting with the curves until he found one he liked. Handberg's shelf also hung from a wall-mounted peg rail.

Shaker-Style Wall Shelf

THIS SMALL SHAKER-STYLE WALL SHELF in curly maple has only seven parts: five shelves and two sides. The shelves join the sides with sliding dovetails. The curves at the top and bottom are determined by eye.

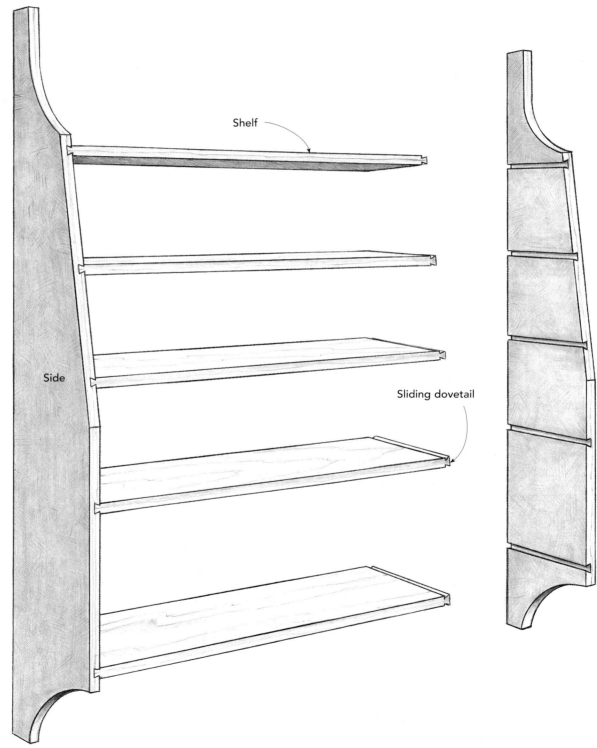

Shelf

Side

Sliding dovetail

ELEVATION

SIDE VIEW

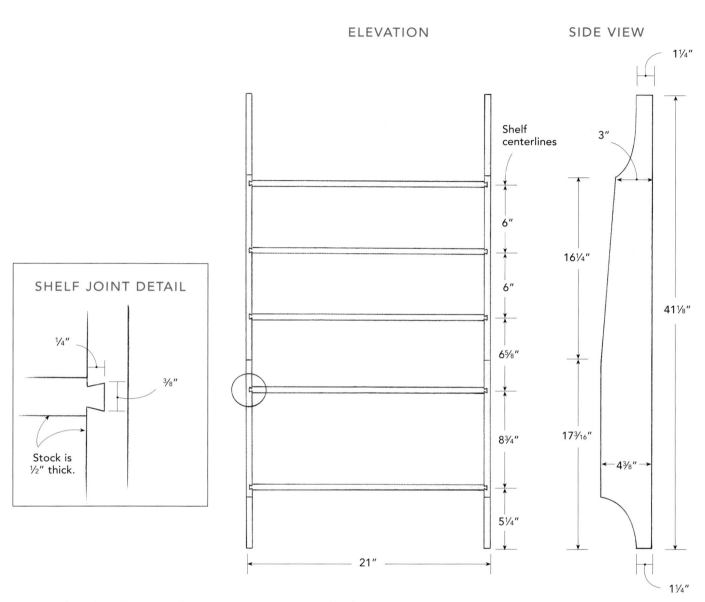

Shelf centerlines

6"

6"

6⅝"

8¾"

5¼"

21"

1¼"

3"

16¼"

41⅛"

17³⁄₁₆"

4⅜"

1¼"

SHELF JOINT DETAIL

¼"

⅜"

Stock is ½" thick.

CUT LIST FOR SHAKER-STYLE WALL SHELF

Carcase and Shelves

2	Sides	41⅛ in. x 4⅜ in. x ½ in.
5	Shelves	20½ in. x 4⅜ in. x ½ in.

Hardware

Shelf hangers

All parts are solid curly maple.

BUILDING THE BOOKCASE STEP-BY-STEP

THIS IS A FAIRLY SIMPLE and quick project. The most difficult aspect (which really isn't) is cutting the sliding dovetails. The Shakers used dadoes, which are simpler, and you can certainly do the same. Dadoes aren't as strong, but in a project like this, it shouldn't matter. Routing the slots in the sides is relatively easy, but the long tails on the ends of each shelf take some patience. I use two router jigs for the process: one for the slots and one for the tails. And I use a plywood pattern and flush-trimming router bit for making identical curves and tapers on the sides.

PREPARING STOCK AND JOINERY

Thicknessing the curly maple parts

1. Mill all the parts at once to ½ in. thick to ensure consistency. For tips on how to work the curly maple, see "Smoothing Figured Wood."

2. Cut the sides to length, but leave them each at least ¼ in. wider than finished width. This will make routing the tails on the ends easier.

Cutting the dovetail slots

Consistency is the key with all sliding dovetail joints. If you start with flat stock of uniform thickness and length, the joinery will flow smoothly. If you don't, you're sure to get joints that are too tight at one end and loose at the other. As there isn't much else holding this shelf together, cutting these joints well is important.

1. Mill ample test pieces out of (non–curly maple) scrap to use before you commit the real pieces to the router bit.

2. Make a jig to cut the small dovetail slots in the sides. (see "Jig for Routing Dovetail Slots"). The jig is simply a piece of plywood with a ½-in. slot, a front fence to register the jig square to the edge of the workpiece, and a rear stop. In order for this jig to work

---

SMOOTHING FIGURED WOOD

Jointing figured wood such as curly maple can be tricky because of the wood's tendency to tear out. The grain doesn't run in one direction, so you can't choose a way to cut that's with the grain. There is, unfortunately, no foolproof strategy to cut curly grain, just a few pointers that will help.

First, the sharper your jointer and planer blades the better. Dull blades will have a much greater tendency to tear out, so if you haven't changed them in a while, do it now.

Second, take many very light cuts instead of fewer deep cuts.

Third, if you're using a handplane, skew it about 45 degrees in the cut. This will make the blade cut with a shearing action that doesn't tear out as much.

Fourth, try dampening the surface to be planed or joined. The water won't penetrate far, but it will create a layer of wet wood that cuts much more easily and won't tear out. Don't get the boards too wet or they'll warp and your planer will rust.

Jig for Routing Dovetail Slots

This plywood jig clamps to the workpiece and has a front fence and a slot that guides a router with a ⅜" top-bearing dovetail bit. You can cut dovetail slots, dadoes, and other types of cross-grain cuts with it.

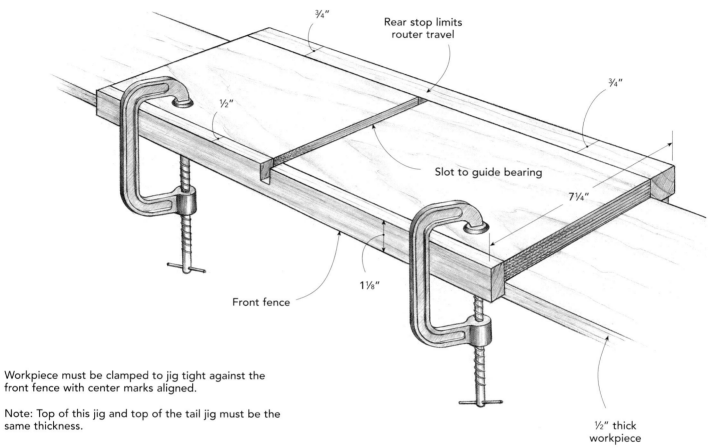

¾"

Rear stop limits router travel

¾"

½"

Slot to guide bearing

7¼"

1⅛"

Front fence

Workpiece must be clamped to jig tight against the front fence with center marks aligned.

Note: Top of this jig and top of the tail jig must be the same thickness.

½" thick workpiece

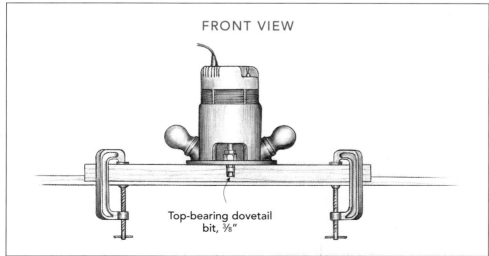

FRONT VIEW

Top-bearing dovetail bit, ⅜"

Photo A: The dovetail slot jig clamps to the workpiece with the centerline on the jig and the workpiece lined up. The slot guides the bearing on the dovetail bit.

Photo B: The jig for routing tails holds the shelf vertical and cuts one side of the tail at a time. It is accurate, if a little fussy to set up.

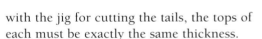

Tip: If you rout the dovetail slots in the sides before you cut their profiles, you don't have to worry about tearout at the ends of the cuts.

with the jig for cutting the tails, the tops of each must be exactly the same thickness.

3. Mark the centerlines for each shelf on both side pieces and transfer them to the back edge. The centerline is used to line up a corresponding centerline on the jig.

4. Fit your router with a ⅜-in. dovetail bit with a ½-in. top bearing, and set it to cut halfway through the piece, in this case ¼ in. deep.

5. Clamp the jig to the workpiece with centerlines aligned and cut the slots (see **photo A**). Because these are very small slots, the router doesn't have to work hard to cut them, and the jig traps the bit so it can't wander. If you were cutting anything larger, you would remove some waste from the slot first with a small straight bit.

Cutting the tails on the shelves

Cutting the tails is not hard, just fussy to set up. This is where those scrap pieces you saved come into play.

1. Make a jig to cut the tails (see "Jig for Routing Tails").

2. Clamp a piece of scrap to the jig, making sure the end of the shelf is tight against the underside of the fence.

3. Adjust the fence to what you think is about right and cut one side of the tail.

4. Turn the piece around, reclamp it, and rout the other side.

5. Check the scrap piece's fit in the slot and make whatever adjustment is necessary to the fence. In this way, creep up on the correct fit. You will see why I call this fussy: The right fit comes down to minute fence adjustments, which can be maddening to get just right. Remember that each adjustment is doubled because you cut both sides of the tail.

6. Once the setting is correct, rout the tails on all the shelves (see **photo B**). Again, don't worry about tearout because the shelves are still wider than their finished width.

Jig for Routing Tails

This jig guides a router at 90 degrees to the end of a
workpiece and will cut sliding dovetails quite well. It is
built of ¾" plywood.

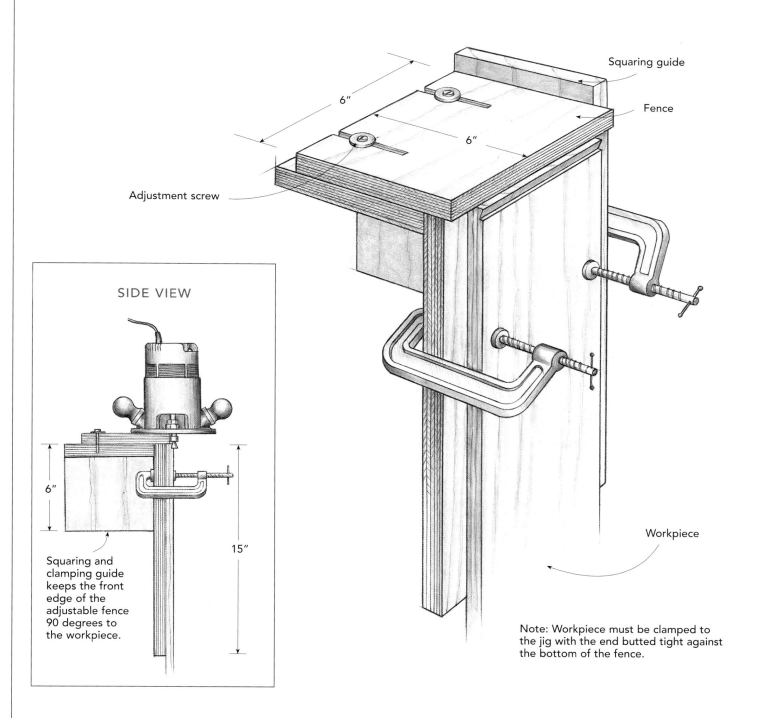

Squaring guide

Fence

6"

6"

Adjustment screw

SIDE VIEW

6"

15"

Squaring and
clamping guide
keeps the front
edge of the
adjustable fence
90 degrees to
the workpiece.

Workpiece

Note: Workpiece must be clamped to
the jig with the end butted tight against
the bottom of the fence.

SHAPING THE SIDES AND SHELVES

Making and using a plywood pattern for the sides

Routing with a pattern to cut the profiles is useful on a number of counts. It ensures a perfect edge and makes both sides identical.

1. Either copy the profile provided or experiment with sketching different curves and angles until you find a profile you like.

2. Make a very precise plywood pattern of the finished shape of the sides.

3. Use a straightedge and a router with a flush-trimming bit for the straight taper and a stationary sander to true the curves. If you don't have a stationary sander, use files, rasps, and sanding blocks to smooth the curves.

4. With the pattern, trace the shape on both sides and cut them on a bandsaw as close as you can to the line (see **photo C**). The less wood left, the less chance there is of tearout when you rout the finished shape.

Using the pattern to shape the sides

1. Attach the pattern to a side using double-sided tape.

2. With a ½-in. flush-trimming bit in the router table, rout the final shape (see **photo D**). Be careful to rout in an anti-climb cut to avoid injury to both self and workpiece (see "Routing the Right Way"). Take very light cuts to avoid tearout.

Cutting shelves to width

1. Rip a clean 90-degree edge on all the shelves, but not to finished width.

2. Rip the two bottom shelves to width, taking the measurements directly from the finished sides. Double ripping will remove any tearout from routing the tails.

Photo C: Rough out the profile of the sides on the bandsaw after you've cut the joinery. Try to cut as close to the line as possible without going over it.

Photo D: The plywood pattern helps you rout a smooth near-perfect edge on the profile of the sides.

3. Because the front edges of the top three shelves are angled to match the tapered sides, transfer the angle to your tablesaw and rip this angle on these shelves.

ASSEMBLY AND FINISHING

Gluing up
1. Sand all the pieces to 180 grit.
2. Slide each shelf halfway into its slot.
3. Carefully brush a little glue on the front of each tail and the back of each slot. It pays to be neat here. If the joints fit well, very little glue is needed. You don't want to be cleaning up a lot of glue on an otherwise finished piece.
4. Starting at the bottom, tap each shelf flush with the front, clamping across each shelf as you go (see **photo E**).

Applying the finish
Finish this piece with Antique Oil Finish made by Minwax®. This is not a particularly hard-wearing oil, but it produces a nice finish. This oil also has just a hint of color to it, which helps bring out the figure in woods like curly or bird's-eye maple.

1. Flood the surface for the first coat and wait about 15 minutes before wiping off the excess.
2. Let the final coat dry at least a couple of hours, and then apply a second coat, wet sanding the wood with 320-grit wet-dry sandpaper.
3. Wipe off any excess again and rub the piece dry with a clean, soft cloth and let it dry overnight. That's it.

Photo E: Clamp one shelf in place at a time, as you go. The clamps don't make the subsequent shelf harder to tap home, and they can help make the shelf square overall.

Attaching the brass hangers
Peter Turner used hangers that were mortised into the back of the shelf. I used some that were surface-mounted, and had to place some clear bumpers on the back of my shelf that stick out as far as the screw heads to allow the shelf to lie flat against the wall. However, any reasonably attractive hanger will do just fine.

ROUTING THE RIGHT WAY

Always run the workpiece against the rotation of the router bit. Otherwise it could pull the piece out of your hands or, worse, pull your hand into the bit. Technically, this is called anti-climb cutting. I call it the "right way," and it's much safer.

Tip: You can give the shelf several coats of oil, but what's the point? The most wear a shelf like this will get is from dusting!

Standing V-Shelf Bookcase

When I first saw the original of this bookcase, it reminded me of similar cases from my childhood and brought back a lot of memories. I can still see my father sitting in a large easy chair next to one of these V-shelves stuffed with books and magazines, a floor lamp shining across his face as he read. Reading was still something that everyone I knew enjoyed. Television was a novelty then, at least in my house. So with the romantic hope that I could inject some of that memory into my life (and banish my color TV), I decided to build this bookcase.

The design of this bookcase is from Peter Turner, a woodworker and furniture maker in Portland, Maine, who modeled it after one that belonged to his great-grandmother. It has V-shaped shelves, which cradle the books.

Turner made his shelf out of cherry; but I chose mahogany to achieve the darker, more subdued look and feel I remember. Also, I had a nice 6/4 mahogany board, large enough for the whole project, that I could resaw and book-match. Otherwise my V-shelf is essentially the same as Turner's.

It's a good style of bookcase to place between a chair and sofa in a living room because it's accessible from both sides, and it's difficult to knock the books out of it. It also has a flat bottom shelf for magazines, which would slither sideways if stored in the V-shelves.

V-Shelf Bookcase for Magazines and Books

WITH NO BACK, the bookshelf is accessible from both sides. The top V-shelf is smaller than the lower shelf, which is an appropriate size for larger books and also gives the bookshelf good proportions. The decorative cutouts on the sides give it some character. The tapered sides and shelves are made from ½"-thick mahogany, joined with #10 biscuits.

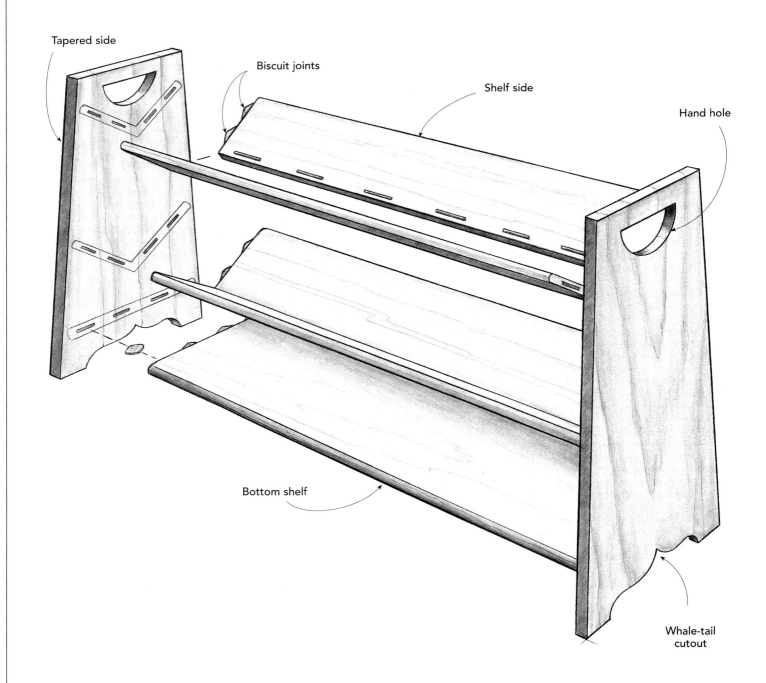

Tapered side

Biscuit joints

Shelf side

Hand hole

Bottom shelf

Whale-tail cutout

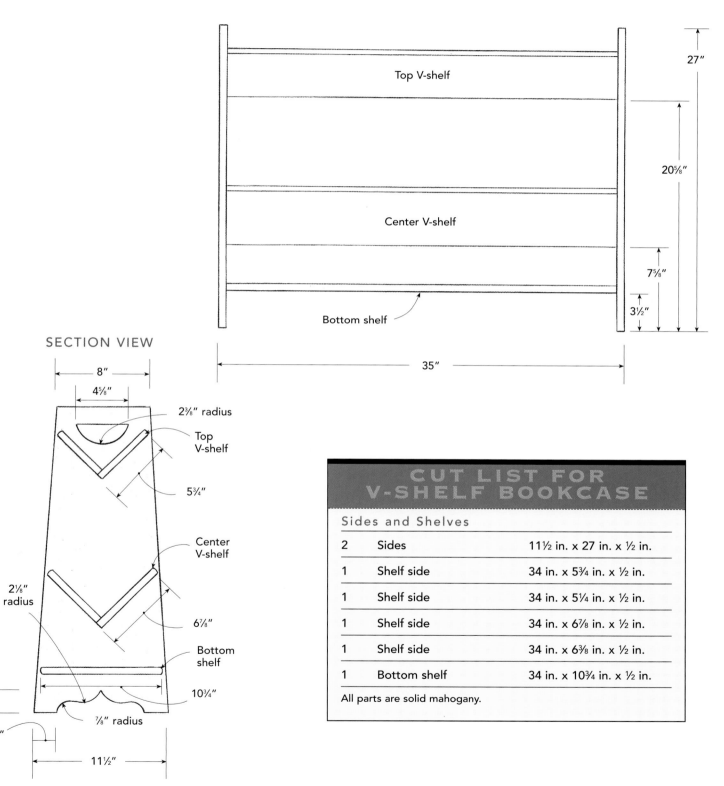

SIDE VIEW

Top V-shelf

Center V-shelf

Bottom shelf

27"

20⅝"

7⅝"

3½"

35"

SECTION VIEW

8"

4⅝"

2⅜" radius

Top
V-shelf

5¾"

Center
V-shelf

2⅛"
radius

6⅞"

Bottom
shelf

2"

10¾"

⅞" radius

2"

11½"

CUT LIST FOR V-SHELF BOOKCASE

Sides and Shelves

2	Sides	11½ in. x 27 in. x ½ in.
1	Shelf side	34 in. x 5¾ in. x ½ in.
1	Shelf side	34 in. x 5¼ in. x ½ in.
1	Shelf side	34 in. x 6⅞ in. x ½ in.
1	Shelf side	34 in. x 6⅜ in. x ½ in.
1	Bottom shelf	34 in. x 10¾ in. x ½ in.

All parts are solid mahogany.

BUILDING THE BOOKCASE STEP-BY-STEP

THIS IS A SMALL, easy-to-build piece with a few simple design details. Using ½-in. solid wood gives the piece a lightness of style that would be lost with thicker boards. The whole bookcase is joined together with biscuits, making the work flow fairly quickly. Spend the time to get the details just right, especially making the edge profiles nice and crisp.

Tip: It's best to plane parts to finished thickness after any edge-joining, but remember that you're limited by the width of your planer.

SHAPING THE PARTS

Preparing the stock

Book-matching the sides and shelves adds a beautiful, though not really necessary, touch to the bookcase. I just happened to have the 6/4 lumber; I probably wouldn't have gone to the trouble to buy it.

1. Flatten, edge joint, and plane flat enough 8-in.- to 9-in.-wide 6/4 mahogany boards for all the parts.

TABLESAW TAPERING JIG

The angled stop positions the bottom of the workpiece at the correct 3-degree angle. The registration block is set on the jig 11½" from the line of cut, which is the width of the bottom of the finished side.

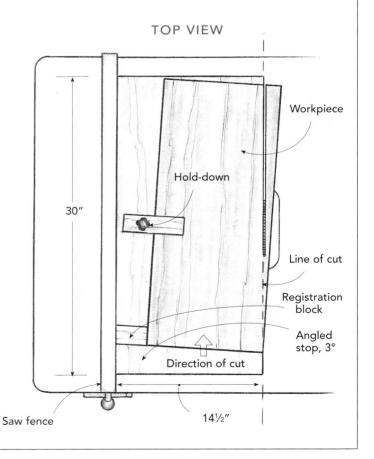

TOP VIEW

Workpiece

Hold-down

30"

Line of cut

Registration block

Angled stop, 3°

Direction of cut

Saw fence

14½"

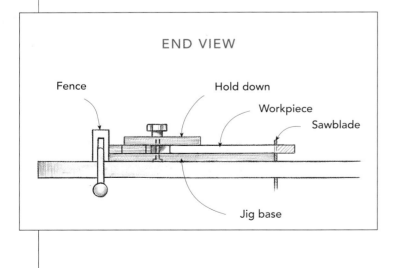

END VIEW

Fence

Hold down

Workpiece

Sawblade

Jig base

2. Resaw the boards on a bandsaw to half their thickness, about ⅝ in., and mark the pairs for the sides and shelves.

3. Plane down all the parts to ½-in.-thick finished stock.

4. If you don't have 6/4 lumber to work with, simply start with 4/4 stock and mill it to thickness. Try to get boards at least 7 in. wide, so you won't have to glue up stock for each half of the V-shelves.

Gluing up the sides

1. Choose the best book-matched boards for the sides. Glue and clamp up the pairs. Keep the glueline in the very center of the boards. Even if you're not book-matching, it will look best.

2. Snug up the clamps just enough to keep things together but still allow them to be moved a little. Slide or tap them even, and then tighten the clamps.

3. Pick the second-best book-matches for the V-shelves and set them aside.

4. Pick out boards to book-match for the bottom shelf last, since a poor match here will be hard to notice. Glue them up like the sides.

Cutting the parts to size

1. Sand the glue joints. Try not to sand too aggressively.

2. Rip all pieces to their final widths on the table saw. Remember that you have to take even amounts off both sides of the glued-up pieces. This will keep the glue joint centered in the finished piece.

3. To rip the V-shelf parts, place the mating edges of the boards together and rip ½ in. from the mating edge of what will be the narrower board.

4. Rip the V-shelf parts to their respective widths on the opposite edge. This will produce a perfectly book-matched face when this board overlaps the wider board to construct the V.

5. Cut the sides and shelves to finished length on a radial-arm saw or a tablesaw with a good miter gauge. All the shelf components must be square and exactly the same length.

Tapering the sides

1. To taper the edges of the sides, first build a taper jig (see "Tablesaw Tapering Jig").

2. Position the jig against the saw fence with the outer edge just touching the sawblade, and lock the fence in place.

3. Secure one of the sides in the jig against the angled stop and up against the registration block.

4. Run the whole assembly through the saw (see **photo A**).

5. Flip the piece over, secure it in the jig, and cut the taper on the other side of the side.

Tip: Be meticulous during glue-up because these boards are finished thickness. Any misalignment will have to be sanded out and cause your boards to vary in thickness—and there is no place to hide this on the piece.

Photo A: A simple taper jig cuts the angle on the side. With the registration block, it also ensures the sides are uniformly wide.

Photo B: A cardboard template with curves made by eye is used for scribing the whale-tail cutout. Use a jigsaw to cut away the waste.

Photo C: Smoothing the whale-tale detail can be accomplished with files, rasps, and an assortment of sandpaper and blocks.

ADDING DETAILS TO THE SIDES AND EDGES

Making the cutouts and shaping the edges

1. Mark out the hand holes with a compass and a straightedge.

2. Drill a large hole on the inside edge of the hole.

3. Using a jigsaw fitted with a fine blade, cut as close to the layout lines as possible.

4. Make a cardboard template to lay out half of the whale tail, as each side is a mirror image of the other. Use a compass or draw the shape by eye and adjust the curves until they look right. Cut out the template with a razor knife (see **photo B**).

5. Cut out the whale tail the same way you cut out the hand hole.

6. To smooth the cutouts, use a combination of rasps, files, and sandpaper-covered blocks and dowels (see **photo C**).

7. Ease the inside edges of the hand holes with a ¼-in. piloted roundover bit. Run it around the inside of the cutouts from both sides.

8. Work with a file and some sandpaper to shape the corners that the router bit can't reach.

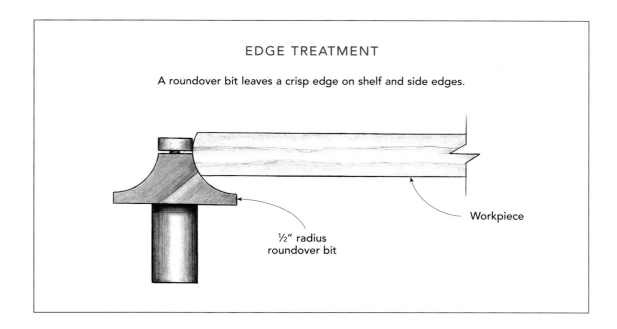

EDGE TREATMENT

A roundover bit leaves a crisp edge on shelf and side edges.

Workpiece

½" radius
roundover bit

Shaping the shelf edges

The long edges of both V-shelves and all edges of the sides should be rounded over. But keep in mind that the roundover looks best when you leave a crisp edge where it meets the edge of the board.

1. Set a ½-in.-radius roundover bit in a router table with the bearing higher than the center of the board so that the blade cuts to the center (see "Edge Treatment").
2. Cut both sides of each board to produce a rounded edge.

CUTTING THE JOINERY

Joining V-shelves

The shelf sides are set against each other at 90 degrees, so there's nothing really special or difficult about this joint.

1. Orient the V-shelf boards correctly for a book-match. It's easy to forget which boards go together.
2. Take the narrower board from each set, and cut #10 biscuit slots in the edge.
3. Cut the corresponding slots in the faces of the opposite board.

HOW MANY BISCUITS IN A GOOD EDGE JOINT?

The number of biscuits to use on a given edge depends on a number of factors and what jobs they're being asked to perform.

For most edge-joint applications, space biscuits between 4 in. and 6 in. apart. If the biscuits are for alignment only and the boards are flat and not prone to warping, I would space them farther apart.

If the wood is not especially flat or prone to warping, bring the biscuits closer together. And if you're concerned about the strength of the joint, add biscuits. There's some debate on how much strength biscuits add to an edge joint (after all, most glues are harder to break than the wood itself in some directions); but I figure a few more biscuits can't hurt.

Photo D: Cut biscuit slots in the edges of the narrower pieces and the faces of the wider pieces. When gluing, put a clamp over each biscuit for even pressure.

Photo E: Cut four biscuits in the end of each V-shelf, registering the joiner off the shelf backs. Leave the layout lines.

Tip: Orient the biscuits in the edge of the thinner board and on the face of the wider board so that the V-shelf has equal-width sides when joined (the longer one tucks under the short one).

4. Glue and clamp the pairs, making sure the clamping pressure doesn't throw the assembly out of square. Use one clamp at each biscuit location and one at each end (see **photo D**).

5. Check to make sure that the ends of both shelf assemblies are exactly even. This joint forms the structure of the whole piece, and it's very visible. It would be very difficult to recut the ends of the shelves to fix any misalignment problems after they are glued together.

Attaching the shelves to the sides

1. Cut four biscuit slots on the ends of each shelf and leave the layout lines. Cut the slots with the fence registering against the bottom of the shelves (see **photo E**).

2. Draw a vertical centerline on the inside face of each side.

3. To locate a V-shelf, place it on end against a side, keeping the apex of the V on the centerline, and move it along the centerline until both edges are inset ⅛ in. from the case side. (see "Shelf Location").

4. Hold the shelf in place and trace along the bottom edge with a pencil (see **photo F**).

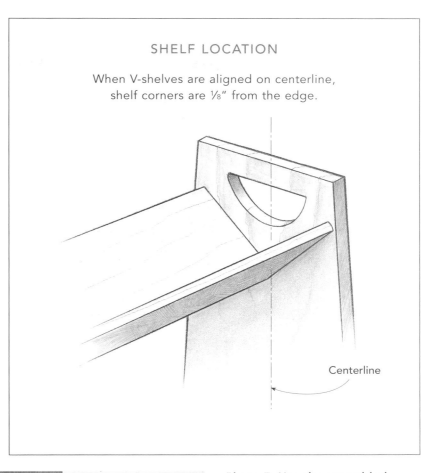

SHELF LOCATION

When V-shelves are aligned on centerline, shelf corners are ⅛" from the edge.

Centerline

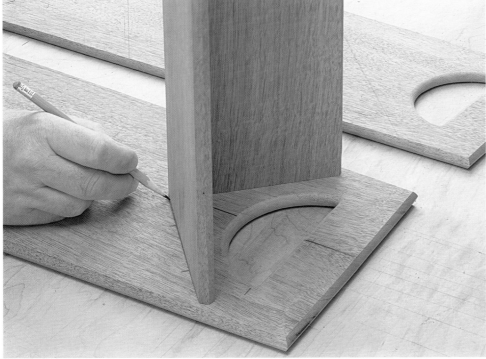

Photo F: Use the assembled V-shelves as marking guides. Scribe a line around the bottom of the shelf to help you align the biscuit joiner in the cut.

Photo G: My biscuit joiner has a plastic adapter plate with an indent on the front edge that acts as a marking gauge. This helps scribe layout lines for the mating slots in the ½-in. stock.

5. Transfer the reference lines for the biscuit slots.

6. To determine how to align the biscuit joiner on the face of the side, draw a line parallel to the line scribed around the shelf bottom that will align the joiner in the right place. The location of this line depends on the distance between your biscuit joiner base and the blade.

For example, my biscuit joiner is designed to cut a slot centered ⅜ in. away from the base, which is too high for ½-in.-thick shelves. The adapter plate for cutting shallow biscuits has a marking gauge built into it for this purpose (see **photo G**). If your machine doesn't, scribe a line at whatever distance is best.

7. Make a plywood fence for the biscuit joiner with index marks for the slot locations and centerline.

8. Lay this fence along the reference line, then place the biscuit joiner against it and cut the slots (see **photo H**).

ASSEMBLY AND FINISHING

Glue-up

1. Before final assembly, sand all the parts to 180 grit and dry-fit the piece.

2. Check if the V-shelves are flush and square at their ends and make any necessary minor adjustments with a low-angle block plane.

3. How you glue and clamp up the piece will depend on the type of clamps you have, but you will find out what you need during the dry-fit stage.

4. Use an additional caul to close up the apex of the bottom V-shelf if it doesn't go together just right.

5. Keep a square on hand to periodically check for square and adjust clamps if necessary.

Applying the finish

I used Sutherland Welles® Polymerized Tung Oil, Medium Luster. It is a relatively difficult oil to apply correctly (make sure you follow the directions on the can), but I recommend it highly.

Peter Turner used Bioshield® Hard Oil #9 finish. It is a linseed oil–based product that contains citrus solvents. The oil is available from the Eco Design Company through the Natural Choice. Peter prefers these products because of their low toxicity, nice satin sheen, and pleasant lemony scent.

Tip: It's easiest to glue and clamp the piece when it's standing upright on its feet. In this position, you can place clamps on most of the joints by using the hand holes and the whale-tail cutouts.

PART TWO
OCCASIONAL TABLES

Arts and Crafts Coffee Table

California woodworker John Lavine places great importance on craftsmanship, sturdy construction, and grain composition. That attitude has produced some very fine pieces, including this coffee table.

This table is unconventional and compelling. The double legs at each corner immediately set the table apart from most, but there are many other thoughtful touches as well. The tabletop's lacewood veneer provides a striking complement to its mahogany frame, which is set off by a black inlaid border. The border extends into decorative squares at each corner, conferring a classic touch to this very contemporary piece. The tabletop's edges bevel upward slightly, providing a visual "lift." The shelf provides visual balance, a platform for books and magazines, and great structural integrity.

The table is easier to make than it appears. The top is simply a veneered 1-in.-thick medium-density fiberboard (MDF) panel framed with solid wood. Lavine sawed his own veneers, but you could use commercial veneers instead. The panel on his table was joined with biscuits to the frame, but I chose to use splines here, although I did use biscuits in the mitered joints.

For the inlay, Lavine used color-impregnated wood sold under the trade name Ebon-X™. Unfortunately it's hard to find these days. You could use ebony instead or wenge, another blackish wood that is less expensive than ebony, or dyed veneer.

Arts and Crafts Coffee Table

THE TOP OF THIS COFFEE TABLE consists of a solid-wood frame glued to a veneered 1"-thick MDF panel. Splines and biscuits help align and reinforce the joints. The border inlay strips are inset into the edge of the frame members before gluing the frame to the panel. The base consists of four leg-and-apron assemblies that intersect each other at half-lapped notches. The legs are glued to the aprons with "floating" tenons and screwed unglued to the shelf.

TOP

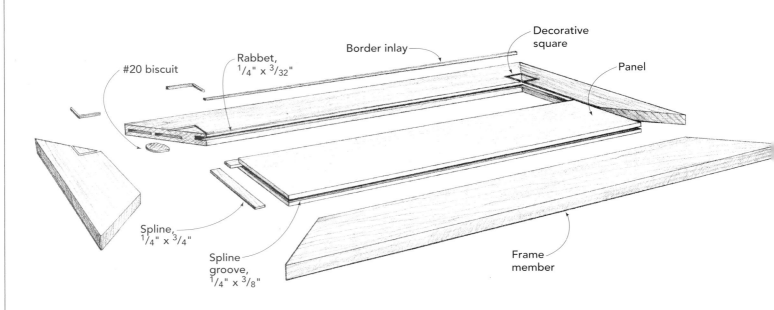

#20 biscuit

Rabbet, $^1/_4$" x $^3/_{32}$"

Border inlay

Decorative square

Panel

Spline, $^1/_4$" x $^3/_4$"

Spline groove, $^1/_4$" x $^3/_8$"

Frame member

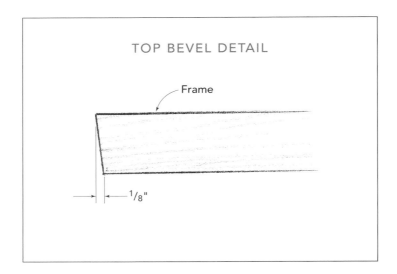

TOP BEVEL DETAIL

Frame

$^1/_8$"

BASE

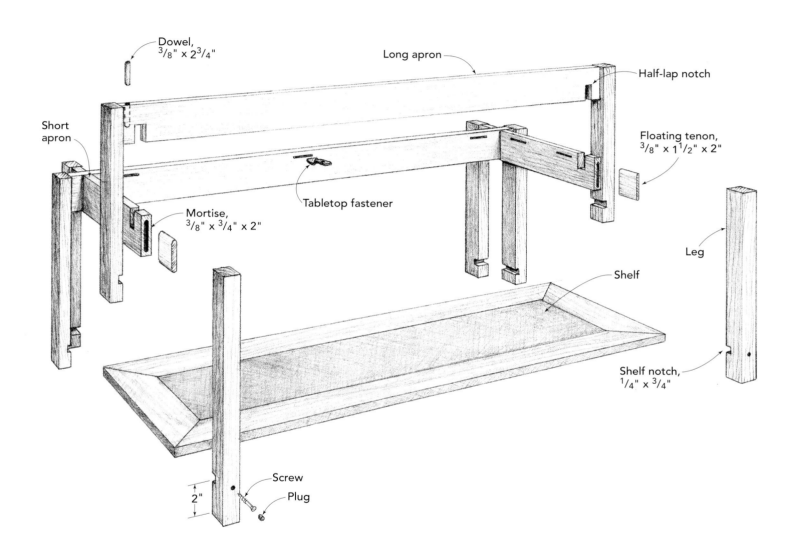

Dowel,
$3/8" \times 2^{3}/4"$

Long apron

Half-lap notch

Short
apron

Floating tenon,
$3/8" \times 1^{1}/2" \times 2"$

Mortise,
$3/8" \times 3/4" \times 2"$

Tabletop fastener

Leg

Shelf

Shelf notch,
$1/4" \times 3/4"$

2"

Screw

Plug

BUILDING THE TABLE STEP-BY-STEP

CUT LIST FOR ARTS AND CRAFTS COFFEE TABLE

Top		
2	Frame members	1⅛ in. x 6 in. x 22 in.
2	Frame members	1⅛ in. x 6 in. x 51 in.
1	MDF panel	1 in. x 10 in. x 39 in.
Shelf		
2	Frame members	¾ in. x 2 in. x 14 in.
2	Frame members	¾ in. x 2 in. x 43 in.
1	Hardwood plywood panel	¾ in. x 10 in. x 39 in.
Base		
2	Short aprons	¾ in. x 3 in. x 13½ in.
2	Long aprons	¾ in. x 3 in. x 42½ in.
8	Legs	1¼ in. x 1¼ in. x 14⅞ in.
8	Floating tenons	⅜ in. x 1½ in. x 2 in.
Miscellaneous		
	Spline stock	¼ in. x ¾ in. (fit to length)
	Inlay strips	¼ in. x ⅛ in. (fit to length)

THE TABLE CONSISTS OF three basic parts: the top, the shelf, and the base assembly. The top and shelf are of similar construction, so build them at the same time. Then make the base, which attaches to the shelf.

MAKING THE TOP AND SHELF

Cutting the pieces to size

1. Dimension the frame members for the top and shelf, cutting the pieces a bit long for now. You'll cut them to final length later, when mitering the corners to fit. It's also best to thickness the shelf frame members to about $^{13}\!/_{32}$ in., so you can plane them flush to the ¾-in.-thick shelf later.

2. Cut the MDF substrate for the top slightly oversize and veneer it.

3. Saw the top panel to the finished size.

4. Cut the hardwood plywood for the shelf to finished size right off the bat.

Installing the inlay border

1. Rout the ¼-in.-wide by $^{3}\!/_{32}$-in.-deep rabbit along all inside edges of the top frame members for the border inlay.

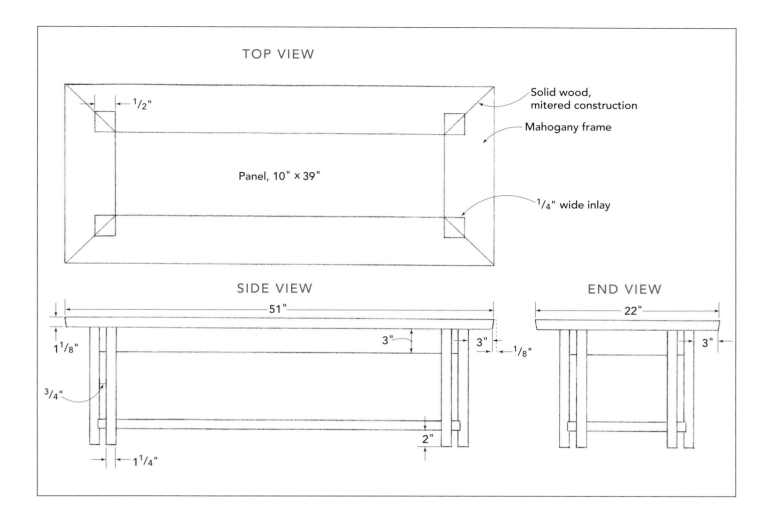

TOP VIEW

Solid wood,
mitered construction

Mahogany frame

$1/2$"

Panel, 10" × 39"

$1/4$" wide inlay

SIDE VIEW

51"

3"

3"

$1/8$"

$1^1/8$"

$3/4$"

2"

$1^1/4$"

END VIEW

22"

3"

2. Saw the ¼-in. by ⅛-in. inlay strips. Make extra for the decorative squares that will be inlayed into the corners of the frame later.
3. Glue the inlay strips into the rabbets on the frame members. You can use masking tape to clamp it in place. After the glue dries, plane the inlay flush to the edges and tops of the frame members.

Making the frame joints

1. Rout or saw a ¼-in.-wide by ½-in.-deep spline groove in the edges of the top and shelf panels. A ¼-in. slot-cutting router bit does a quick, accurate job of cutting the grooves.
2. Cut matching grooves in the frame members so that the frame sits about 1/64 in. proud of the panel after assembly.

3. Rip stock for the splines slightly fat, then plane it to final thickness. The splines should fit snugly, requiring just a bit of finger pressure to push them into their grooves. There's no need to miter them at their corners. You can just butt them, as shown.
4. Cut the frame miters on a tablesaw sled, as shown in **photo A** on p. 63. See "A Tablesaw Miter Sled" on p. 62.
5. Fit a pair of miters at one corner of the frame.
6. Work your way around the frame, carefully marking and cutting the miter on the opposite end of each frame member. As you do this, make sure that the frame members are pulled up tightly against the panel.
7. When the frame pieces fit well, mark them for two #20 biscuits per miter joint and cut the biscuit slots.

A TABLESAW MITER SLED

This shop-built tablesaw sled allows you to cut miters quickly and accurately on your tablesaw. The beauty of this system is that, even if the two fences on the sled aren't positioned at exactly 45 degrees to the blade, you're still assured of a square joint, as long as the fences are square to each other.

1. Cut a piece of ¾-in.-thick hardwood plywood to about 20 in. by 30 in.

2. Mill a couple of 24-in.-long hardwood runners to fit in your tablesaw's miter gauge slots.

3. Place the runners in the miter gauge slots and set your tablesaw's rip fence about 15 in. to the right of the blade.

4. Run a bead of glue on each runner, then set the panel on top of them, butting its right-hand edge against the rip fence.

5. Screw the plywood to the runners.

6. After the glue dries, place the runners back in the miter gauge slots and saw about 11 in. into the panel.

7. To make the fences, rip two 3-in.-wide strips of plywood, making sure that the edges are straight.

8. Miter one end of each.

9. Attach one fence with screws about 8 in. back from the front of the panel and at 45 degrees to the slot you cut.

10. Lay an accurate square against the attached fence, position the second fence along the opposite leg of the square, then screw the second fence to the panel.

11. Attach a thick block of wood behind the juncture of the fences to shield the blade at the end of a cut.

12. To allow easy retrieval of the sled after a cut, attach a Shaker peg or length of dowel at the rear end of the panel.

TABLE SAW MITER SLED

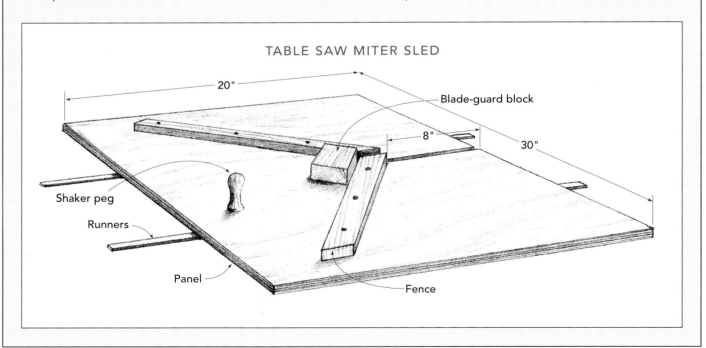

20"

Blade-guard block

8"

30"

Shaker peg

Runners

Panel

Fence

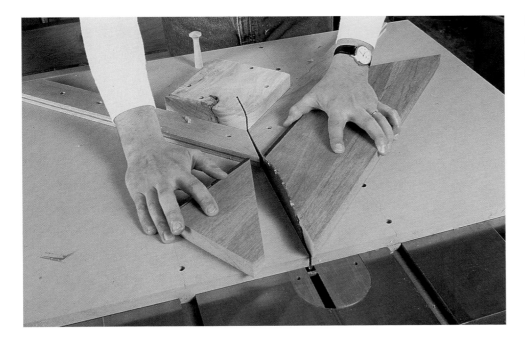

Photo A: A tablesaw miter sled makes quick, accurate work of sawing the miters for the top and shelf frames.

Assembling the parts

1. Dry-fit the top and shelf panel assemblies with their splines and biscuits to make sure that all of the joints mate well and close up with no problems (see **photo B**).

Make certain that the panel doesn't sit proud of the frame. The thin veneer on the panels won't allow you to plane them flush with the frame later. This dry-assembly is also a good opportunity to rehearse your clamping procedures.

2. Glue-up the top and shelf assemblies. I suggest using white glue for this because it allows a longer setting time than does yellow glue and there's a lot to glue-up at once. Have all your clamps, glue brushes, and so on at hand before you start.

3. Apply glue to the spline grooves, the splines, and all joint faces. A good approach is to glue the short frame members to the panel first, making sure that the inside corners of the miters meet the corners of the panel. Then glue on the long frame members. Use ample glue on the biscuit-joined miters. Make sure

Photo B: Dry-assemble all of the top pieces together before glue-up to make sure they fit tightly.

all the joints line up well under clamp pressure and that the veneered panel doesn't sit proud of the frame members.

4. After the glue is dry, remove the clamps and plane and scrape the frames flush to the panels (see **photo C**). Take care not to cut through the veneer.

5. Plane the edges of the top, making sure they meet neatly at the tips of the miters. Then plane a ⅛-in. upward taper on the edges of the top.

6. Lightly "break" the sharp edges on the top and shelf with 150-grit sandpaper.

Inlaying the decorative squares

1. Carefully lay out the lines for the 2½-in.-square corner inlays on the top. Using an accurate square, mark the lines lightly with a sharp pencil (see **photo D**). Go over the lines with a knife, making sure that they meet neatly at the corners.

2. Deepen the knife lines using a wide chisel (see **photo E**).

Photo C: **Use a smoothing plane to level the frame to the panel. To prevent planing through the thin veneer, use a sharp scraper for your final passes.**

Photo D: **Lay out the decorative squares at the corners of the tabletop using an accurate square and a sharp pencil. Then deepen the lines with a knife.**

Photo E: To cut the inlay grooves by hand, begin by carefully chopping the walls of the grooves with a sharp chisel set in your knifed lines.

3. Cut the inlay grooves. Although you can use a router guided by a straightedge for this, I prefer to cut them by hand with a chisel and sharp router plane.

4. Plane out the waste between the lines with a router plane (see **photo F**). Use a ¼-in.-wide cutter, lowering it for each subsequent pass until you reach the final 3⁄32-in. depth.

5. Cut the inlay pieces to length to fit the grooves, then glue them into the grooves, lightly tapping them into place with a hammer (see **photo G**).

Photo F: Using a router plane fitted with a sharp ¼-in.-wide blade, plane out the waste between the groove walls. Take light passes, adjusting the blade downward as you go.

Photo G: Apply the inlay strips into the groove, fitting and gluing one piece at a time to ensure tight butt joints.

Photo H: Use a smoothing plane to cut the inlay flush to the frame.

4. Rout the mortises using a ⅜-in.-diameter straight or upcut spiral router bit in a router outfitted with an edge guide. Clamp scrap pieces to the workpiece as necessary to provide extra bearing surface for the router. To ensure consistent apron setback, always reference the router fence against the outside face of the aprons.

5. Make the floating tenon stock by ripping it slightly oversize and then planing it to final thickness.

6. Test the fit by inserting the stock into a mortise. It should slide in easily, with just a bit of resistance.

7. Rout a ³⁄₁₆-in. roundover on every edge of the tenon stock to match the ⅜-in. diameter at the end of the mortises (see **photo I**). This is most easily and safely done on a router table. Then cut the tenons to length.

8. Using a marking knife, lay out the half-lap joints where the aprons cross each other. But don't cut them yet. Lay the lines out accurately so that the edges of the aprons will meet flush when joined.

9. Install ⅜-in.-diameter by 2¾-in.-long dowels into the top edge of the aprons. The glued dowels help strengthen the short-grain area between the notch and the mortise. The dowel center should be in ¾ in. from the end of each apron.

10. Lay out and cut the notches in the legs to accept the shelf. You can do this with a dado head on the tablesaw or with a handsaw and chisel.

11. Drill for the #6 by 1⅝-in. drywall screws that will hold the legs in the notches. Then counterbore the holes to accept wooden plugs.

Assembling the base

The base assembly is a bit of a Chinese puzzle. For everything to fit, you'll need to assemble the aprons, legs, and shelf in the following specific sequence. Use white glue for a longer open-assembly time and work on a flat surface. Definitely dry-assemble and do a clamping rehearsal in every case before you reach for the glue bottle.

6. After the glue dries, use a sharp smoothing plane to level the inlay flush to the frame (see **photo H**).

MAKING THE BASE

The base is really not that complex to build. You'll make the four aprons and eight legs, cut the mortises, make the floating tenons, then cut the shelf notches in the legs. All that's left is to notch the aprons and assemble the base around the shelf.

Making the parts and cutting the apron-to-leg joints

1. Cut the aprons and legs to size.

2. Lay out the ⅜-in. by 2-in. apron mortises, centering them on the ends of the aprons.

3. Lay out the matching mortises on the legs, starting each one ½ in. down from the top of the leg and centered across the leg's width.

Photo I: After rounding over the edges of the tenon stock and cutting the tenons to length, dry-assemble the leg-to-apron joints. The tenons should fit in the mortise snugly, requiring only a bit of finger pressure to insert them.

1. Glue up the two long apron/leg assemblies. Work on a flat surface and make sure each assembly is flat and square under clamp pressure. Let dry thoroughly.

2. Now is the time to cut out the half-lap notches on the long aprons. If you had cut them before assembling the apron/leg unit, clamping pressure might have broken the short-grain section next to the notch.

3. Cut the notch shoulder. I use a bowsaw. Then chisel out the waste (see **photo J**).

4. Cut the notches on the short aprons, making sure that they slip tightly over the long aprons. This way, the short-grain sections are backed up by the long aprons during glue-up.

5. Double-check to make sure that the edges of the dry-fit aprons are flush, or the legs won't sit properly after assembly.

6. Make tick marks on the underside of the shelf to reference the position of all the legs. Each leg sits in 1-in. from the corner of the shelf.

7. Working on a low bench, lay one long apron/leg assembly down flat and insert the shelf fully into the leg notches.

Photo J: After gluing up the long apron and leg assemblies, cut the half-lap notches in all of the aprons.

BASE ASSEMBLY

Because the shelf sits captured between notches in the legs, the base assembly is a bit like a Chinese puzzle. The parts must be assembled in the sequence shown here.

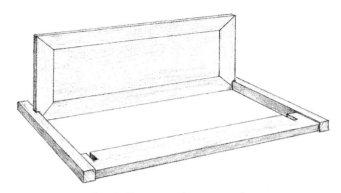

1. Insert the shelf into one long apron/leg assembly; do not use glue.

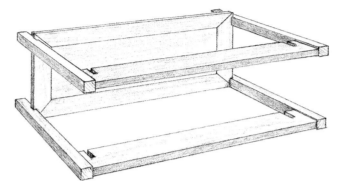

2. Slip the second long apron/leg assembly onto the shelf.

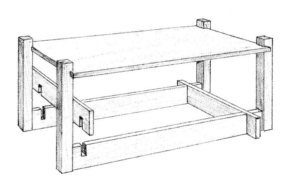

3. Glue the short aprons into the notches on long aprons.

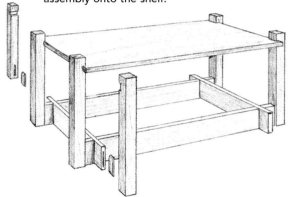

4. Glue the legs to the short aprons. Screw all the legs to the shelf; do not use glue. Finally, plug the screw holes.

8. Slip the opposite apron/leg assembly onto the shelf, as shown in "Base Assembly."

9. Stand the base upside down and align the legs with the tick marks you made earlier.

10. Apply glue to the bottoms of the notches, slip the short aprons into the notches on the long aprons, and clamp them in place. Again, make sure that the top edges of the long and short aprons are flush.

11. Glue the legs to the short aprons, but not to the shelf. Use just enough clamping pressure to pull the joints snug. If your half-lap joints are tight, the short grain should have enough support to prevent breaking, but don't tempt fate by cranking down the clamps. Make sure the tops of the legs are flush to the top edges of the aprons.

12. Align each leg to its tick mark and attach it to the shelf with a 1⅝-in.-long drywall screw. Drilling a pilot hole into the shelf first will prevent it from splitting.

13. Glue wood plugs into the counterbored holes. Lavine used black plugs, which serve as design accents. Alternatively, you could make

a nearly invisible joint by using a plug of the same wood as the leg, orienting the grain of each in the same direction. When the glue is dry, trim the plugs flush.

ATTACHING THE TOP

The top is held in place with S-shaped metal tabletop fasteners, available through many woodworking supply catalogs. One end of the fastener is screwed into the tabletop and the other end fits into a slot cut in the apron.

1. Place the tabletop upside down on the bench and then center the base on it. Position a tabletop fastener on the underside of the top and measure the necessary offset for the apron slots.

2. Stand the base upright and cut the fastener slots in the aprons. I use a biscuit joiner for this (see **photo K**). Three or four slots in each long apron and a couple each in the short aprons are plenty.

3. Place the base upside down on the tabletop again. Insert the fasteners into the biscuit slots.

4. Mark the locations for the screws in the underside of the top, then drill pilot holes and install the screws.

FINISHING UP

Lavine used several coats of lacquer to finish his table. Lacquer imparts a wonderful depth and subtle gloss to the fine woods and inlay work on this table. Unfortunately for many small shops, lacquer must be sprayed. It can also be highly flammable, so it must be applied either outdoors or in a spray booth equipped with explosion-proof lights and venting. If you want a lacquer finish and you're not equipped to spray it, consider taking the table to a professional finisher.

Another good option for bringing out the depth of these woods is to apply several coats of oil. You can use tung oil, Danish oil, or boiled linseed oil. Tung oil darkens wood less than do linseed and Danish oils.

END TABLE

This cherry end table was made by my father-in-law, Arthur Chapin, over 30 years ago. My wife grew up with it and loves it to this day. It's just the right height for a lamp, and the drawer is large enough to accommodate a fair amount of stuff.

Although very unpretentious, this table incorporates some neat little touches. Its solid-wood top sits on nicely tapered legs that are joined to the aprons with simple mortise-and-tenon joints. A dovetailed drawer slips between the two rails in front. The drawer runners—two rabbeted lengths of $1\frac{1}{32}$-in.-square stock—are a marvel of economy. They're easy to make, simple, and strong. The kickers, which keep the drawer from tipping as it's opened, do double-duty as cleats for fastening the top. Slotted screw holes allow the top to expand and contract with changes in humidity.

I have to admit, I'm partially fond of this table because of the hands that made it and what Arthur taught me. I learned more from him than from any other woodworker or any school. He taught me the fine points of the craft: the importance of sharp tools and how to sharpen them. He showed me how to make good joints and how to use different kinds of woods.

His advice on finishing cherry applies to this table. "Don't use stain on cherry," he insists. "Daylight does the darkening, creating a rich, deep color that improves over the years."

End Table

THIS TABLE IS A MODEL of traditional simplicity. The aprons and rails attach to the legs with basic mortise-and-tenon joints. The drawer runners are simply rabbeted lengths of stock. The double-duty kickers attach the top and prevent the drawer from tipping. The false drawer front simplifies fitting the drawer.

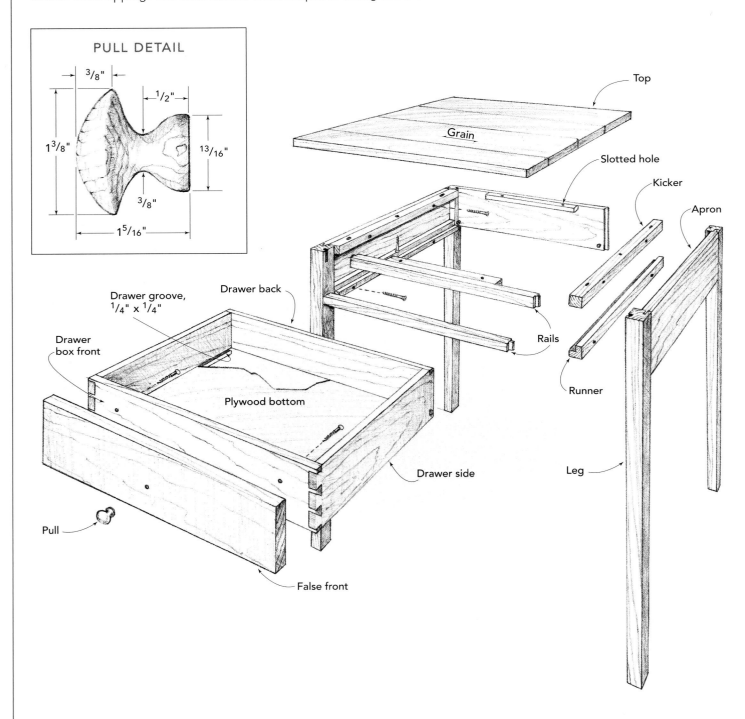

PULL DETAIL

3/8"
1/2"
1 3/8"
13/16"
3/8"
1 5/16"

Top

Grain

Slotted hole

Kicker

Apron

Drawer groove, 1/4" x 1/4"

Drawer back

Rails

Drawer box front

Plywood bottom

Runner

Drawer side

Leg

Pull

False front

TOP VIEW

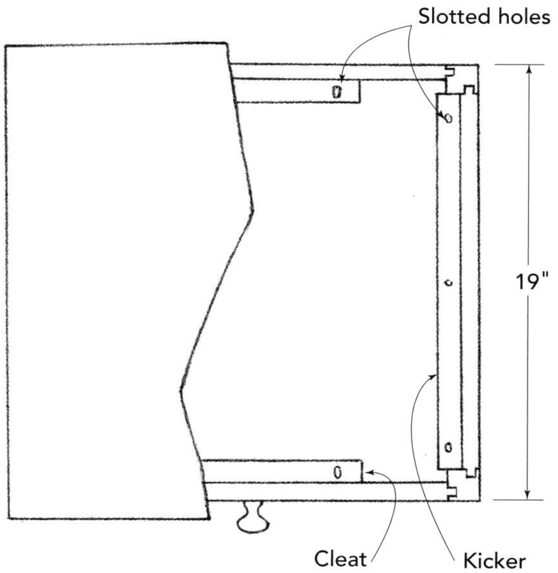

Slotted holes
19"
Cleat
Kicker

CUT LIST FOR END TABLE

Top		
1	Top	¾ in. x 20½ in. x 20½ in.
Carcase		
4	Legs	1⅜ in. x 1⅜ in. x 28½ in.
3	Aprons	¾ in. x 4¾ in. x 17 in.
2	Rails	¾ in. x 1 in. x 17 in.
2	Kickers	1 1/32 in. x 1 1/32 in. x 16¼ in.
2	Runners	1 1/32 in. x 1 1/32 in. x 16¼ in.
2	Cleats	¾ in. x 1 in. x 10 in.
Drawer		
1	Front	½ in. x 2¾ in. x 16¼ in.
1	Back	½ in. x 2¼ in. x 16¼ in.
2	Sides	½ in. x 2¾ in. x 16½ in.
1	Drawer bottom	¼ in. x 15¾ in. x 16¼ in.
1	False front	¾ in. x 2 11/16 in. x 16 3/16 in.

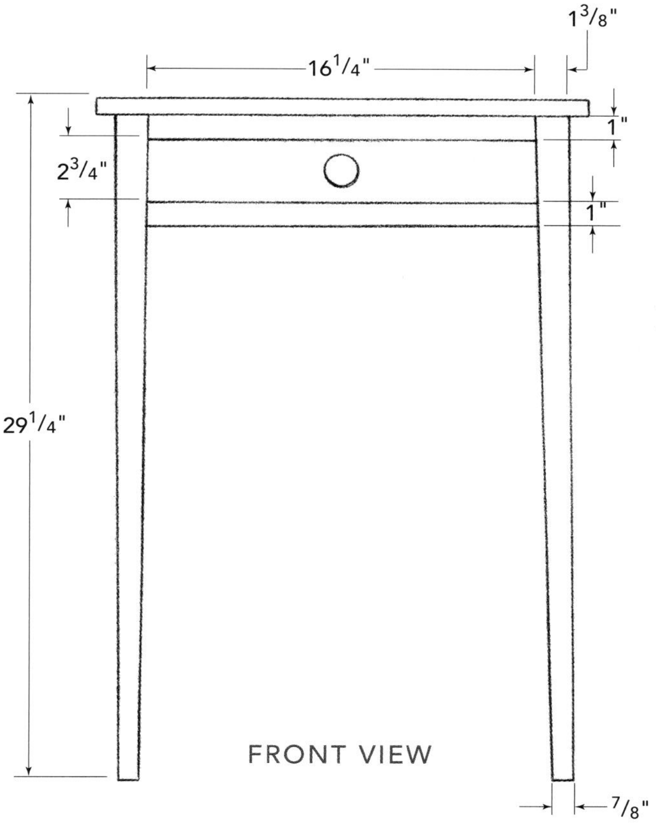

1 3/8"
16 1/4"
1"
2 3/4"
1"
29 1/4"
7/8"

FRONT VIEW

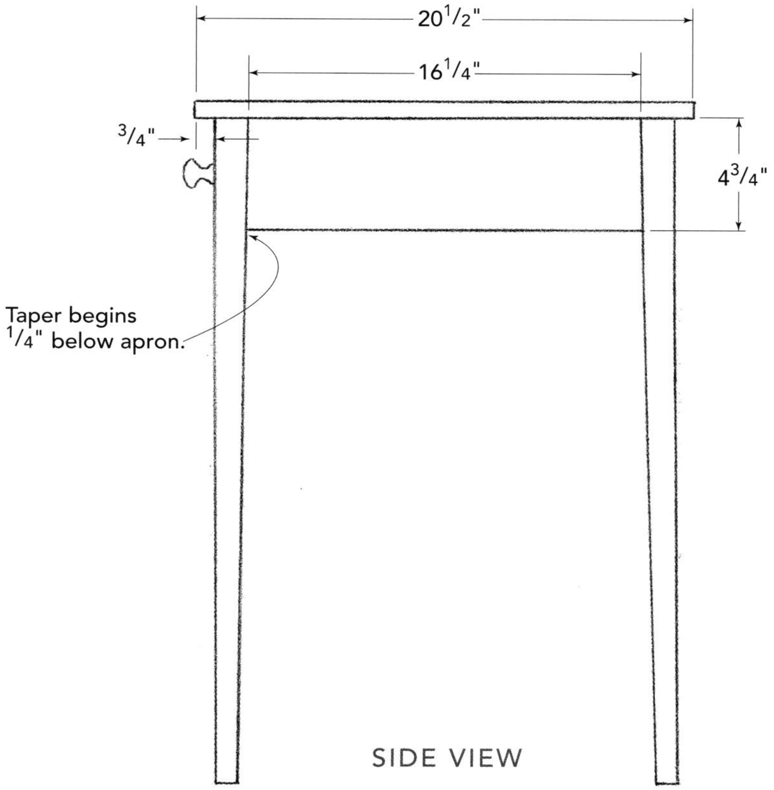

20 1/2"
16 1/4"
3/4"
4 3/4"
Taper begins 1/4" below apron.

SIDE VIEW

BUILDING THE TABLE STEP-BY-STEP

THE TABLE IS BUILT in three stages: the top, the carcase, and the drawer. It's important to make the drawer and runners last, because they are measured directly from the case. The drawer construction provides an excellent opportunity to practice making dovetail joints.

MAKING THE TOP

1. Mill enough ¾-in.-thick stock to make the top panel. Make the pieces slightly oversize in length and width for right now. You'll saw the panel to final length and width after gluing it up.

2. Joint the edges. If you use a handplane for this instead of a jointer, clamp two boards in the vise with mating edges side by side (see **photo A**). This way, any accidental angle will cancel itself out by opposing the angles of the two boards during glue-up.

3. Glue up the top, laying the boards across T-shaped clamping stands, which provide easy access to the clamps (see **photo B**).

4. When the glue dries, scrape any dried excess glue from the panel, then smooth it with a plane or cabinet scraper.

Tip: To keep freshly glued edges from slipping out of alignment under clamp pressure, sprinkle a few grains of coarse sand at the middle and ends of the joint before applying glue.

Photo A: To joint boards by hand, align two adjacent edges in the vise and plane them at the same time.

Photo B: Clamping stands allow easy access to the clamps when edge joining boards. The weight of the clamps on the top also helps pull the panel flat.

Photo C: A shop-made panel-cutting jig helps you squarely crosscut wide stock, such as the tabletop. The body of the jig is guided by a strip of wood that rides in the tablesaw's miter gauge slot.

5. Cut the top to final size. First rip it to width, then crosscut it to length on the table saw using a panel-cutting jig (see **photo C**).
6. Sand the top, rounding over the edges very slightly. Set it aside for now: You'll attach it after the table is completely built.

MAKING THE CARCASE

The carcase consists of three sets of similar components: the legs, the aprons and front rails, and the drawer runners and kickers. You'll need to work on the legs first, so you can fit the apron tenons into their mortises. Wait until the carcase is assembled to make and fit the drawer runners and kickers.

Tapering the legs

1. Dimension the leg stock to 1⅜ in. square, then cut all of the pieces to 28½ in. long. It's wise to cut material for one or two extra legs in case of mistakes. You can also use one of the extras to set up your tapering jig.

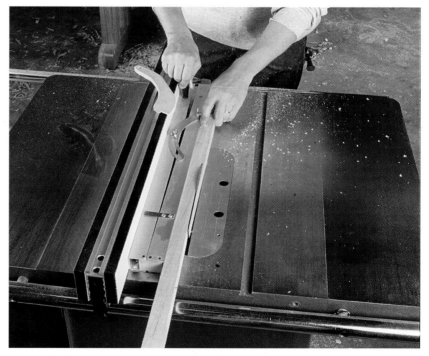

Photo D: Tapering the table legs is easy with a tapering jig. A tab at the operator end of the jig holds the work as you push it forward. As you near the end of the cut, hold the workpiece against the jig with a push stick.

2. Mark out the tapers on the two inside faces of one of the leg pieces, beginning 5 in. from one end. The taper decreases to ⅞ in. at the other end of the leg.

3. Taper the legs on the tablesaw using a jig (see **photo D** on p. 75). You could make your own tapering jig, but the commercial aluminum models cost only about 20 bucks, so why bother?

4. Plan your cutting sequence so that the second taper cut on each leg is made with a flat face of the leg lying on the saw table. Use a push stick and keep your eye on the blade. I like to shut the saw off to set up for each successive cut.

Photo E: **Using a mortising gauge is a fast and accurate way to mark out the leg mortises.**

5. Mount the leg in the jig, adjusting the jig's angle until the marked taper line is parallel to the rip fence. Then set the fence the proper distance from the blade to make your cut.

6. Saw the tapers about ½₂ in. fat, then plane them smooth afterward.

Mortising the legs

You can rout the mortises if you prefer, but the simple ⅜-in.-wide by ⅜-in.-deep mortises in these substantial legs can be easily chopped out by hand without fear of splitting the legs. Cutting mortises by hand isn't difficult, but it requires attention to technique. For a well-fitting, square joint, it's critical that you cut the mortise walls square to the face of the workpiece. But don't worry, that's something you eventually develop a feel for.

1. Lay out the mortises using a mortising gauge (see **photo E**). Adjust the gauge cutters so they're ⅜ in. apart and ³⁄₁₆ in. from the gauge fence. When marking the mortises, register the fence against the outside faces of the legs. Remember that one face of each front leg will get two short mortises for the rails.

2. Begin by selecting a mortising chisel that exactly matches the width of your mortise, which is ⅜ in. here. Place the chisel carefully between the mortise wall lines, orienting the sides of the blade square to the workpiece. If a mortise is near the edge of a workpiece, clamp it near the edge of your bench, to provide a sight reference.

3. Chop a series of V-cuts as deep as the chisel will comfortably go. Work outward from the center of the mortise (see **photo F**).

4. When you reach the end of the mortise, chop it square, staying about ⅛ in. away from your layout line for right now.

5. Clean out the chips using a swan-neck chisel (see **photo G**).

6. Repeat these steps until you've reached the bottom of the mortise.

7. Finish up by cutting the ends of the mortise square at your layout lines.

Making the aprons

1. Mill the ¾-in.-thick stock for the aprons and rails, and cut the pieces to their finished lengths and widths.

2. Use a marking gauge to lay out the tenon shoulders on the apron and rail pieces. Then use a mortising gauge to lay out the ⅜-in.-thick tenons on the ends of the pieces (see **photo H** on p. 78).

3. Saw the apron and rail tenons. You can do this on the tablesaw or with a router, but I prefer to cut them by hand and then plane them to a perfect fit. I use a bowsaw, because I find that it cuts faster and more accurately than many backsaws (see **photo I** on p. 78).

4. Saw the tenon shoulders to remove the waste.

5. Plane the tenons to thickness with a rabbet plane (see **photo J** on p. 79). The correct fit is not so tight that you need to hammer the joint together but snug enough that you need to use some hand pressure.

Photo F: Use a mortising chisel and mallet to cut the leg mortises. Begin by making a series of V-cuts, moving outward from the center of the mortise toward the ends.

Photo G: Even up the depth of the mortise with a swan-neck chisel.

Photo H: Mark out the widths of the apron tenons using a mortising gauge adjusted for a ⅜-in. tenon.

Photo I: Although you could use a back-saw to cut the tenon shoulders, I prefer a bowsaw for its speed and accuracy.

Assembling the carcase

1. Dry-fit the carcase together to make sure everything fits well. This is also a good opportunity to rehearse your clamping procedure before doing the actual glue-up.

2. First glue the side aprons to the legs with yellow glue. Make sure that the legs don't cock out of alignment under clamping pressure, or it will be difficult to attach the back apron and front rails. Check the diagonals to make sure the assemblies are square and then let the glue dry.

3. Glue the back apron and front rails between the two side assemblies. Make sure that the rails are parallel and check the diagonals across the top to make sure the case is square. Angle the clamps slightly if necessary to pull the unit into square. Place the table on a known flat surface such as your tablesaw top to make sure it stands solidly.

Making and fitting the drawer runners and kickers

Now that the case is assembled, you can mark the drawer runners and kickers directly from

Photo J: **Planing the tenon shoulders with a rabbet plane allows fine-tuning of the tenon thickness for a perfect fit in the mortise.**

it. It's important that the runners and kickers project slightly into the drawer opening (see "Drawer Runners and Kickers").

1. Mill up the runners and kickers.

2. Cut the blanks slightly oversize, then hold each one in position against the carcase to mark its final length.

3. Place each piece in the carcase and mark for the final thickness and rabbets, allowing for the 1/32-in. projection into the drawer opening.

4. Make the cleats that attach to the back apron and upper front rail. The dimensions on these aren't critical. Align them with the top edges of the rail and apron and attach them with screws or glue.

5. Attach the kickers, aligning them to the top edge of the aprons, as shown. Use screws, but not glue, in case you have to adjust them later.

6. Drill and counterbore holes in the kickers and cleats for attaching the top. Elongate the front and rear holes by about 3/16 in. with a rat-tail file to allow for movement of the top.

DRAWER RUNNERS AND KICKERS

When fitting the drawer runners and kickers, make sure they project 1/32" into the drawer opening.

Kicker

Leg

Runner

1/32"

1/32"

Drawer opening

7. Attach the runners with only one screw in the front end. Align them parallel to the kickers and clamp their rear ends to the case sides for now. You'll do the final positioning and attachment later when you fit the drawer.

MAKING AND FITTING THE DRAWER

Arthur cut half-blind dovetails for his table drawer, but it's quite acceptable to use through dovetails with an applied front. This makes it easier to center the drawer front in the opening. The drawer sides, box front, and back are made of white pine; the false front is cherry. You'll build the drawer box to fit its opening exactly, then plane it to the final fit after assembly.

Dimensioning the parts

1. Thickness plane enough white pine to ½ in. to make the drawer sides, box front, and back.
2. Thickness plane stock for the false front to ¾ in. Make sure that all of the pieces are wider than the height of the drawer opening.
3. Rip the sides, drawer box front, and false front to width. To eliminate possible errors, mark the width of all of the pieces (which represents the drawer height) directly from the case. Rest one of the drawer sides on the bottom rail and mark where it meets the top of the drawer opening. Set your tablesaw fence to this distance.
4. Mark the length of the box front and back pieces. Cut one end of each piece square, then place it against the leg at one side of the drawer opening. Make a mark on each piece at the other end of the drawer opening and crosscut the pieces to length.
5. Mark the length of the false front directly from the drawer opening, subtract ¹⁄₁₆ in. from the length, and crosscut it to that dimension. Cut the drawer sides squarely to length.
6. Saw or rout a ¼-in. by ¼-in. groove into the drawer sides and front to accept the plywood

bottom. Then rip the drawer back to width, which is the distance from the top of a drawer side to the top of the bottom groove.

Cutting the dovetail joints

Hand-cutting dovetails imparts a look that's impossible to duplicate with a router jig. It's also faster than setting up a jig if you have only one or two drawers to make. The following technique, which I learned from Frank Klausz, is a particularly efficient way to work. The front piece gets three tails; the narrow back needs only one. There's no need to space the tails evenly; just make sure that the

Photo K: Use a marking gauge set to the thickness of the drawer stock to establish the baseline for the pins and tails.

groove in the front piece runs through a tail, not a pin. Cut the pins first, then the tails.

1. Mark the top edges of all of your drawer parts to identify the front, back, and left and right sides. Also be sure to mark the inside face of each piece.

2. Set a cutting gauge to the thickness of your drawer stock plus 1/32 in. That builds in a total of 1/16 in. clearance for the drawer fit after you plane the projecting pins when the drawer assembly is complete.

3. Mark a line completely around the ends of each side piece, registering the gauge fence against the end (see **photo K**).

4. Mark a gauge line across the faces of the front and back pieces, but don't bother to mark across the edges. The gauge lines will serve as baselines when you cut the pins and tails.

5. Clamp the box front in your bench vise with the inside of the drawer facing you. Follow the steps in "Cutting the Pins," sawing down to the gauge line. There's no need to mark the angles, just saw by eye, cutting the angles somewhere between 8 and 12 degrees. It's important to hold the saw vertically for these cuts. When you're done, cut the pins on each end of the drawer back.

6. Chisel out the waste between the pins. Clamp the boards together on the bench with the narrow end of the pins facing up. Standing behind the work, place the chisel—with its back toward you—about 1/32 in. away from the gauge line in the waste area. Holding the chisel vertical and gripping it near the cutting edge, give it a couple of smart smacks with a mallet (see "Removing the Pin Waste" on p. 82). This beginning cut should drive the chisel backward to the gauge line. Make these initial cuts on all of the pin waste shoulders.

7. Angle the chisel away from you, holding it by its handle. Place the cutting edge on the waste area about halfway between the gauge

Cutting the Pins

VIEW FROM ABOVE

1. Cut the half pins at the ends.

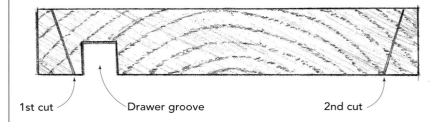

1st cut   Drawer groove   2nd cut

2. Cut the first side of the second pin.

Waste

3rd cut

3. Bisect the second and third cuts.

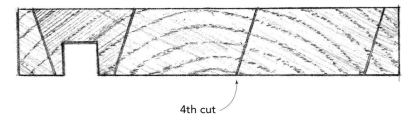

4th cut

4. Complete the pins.

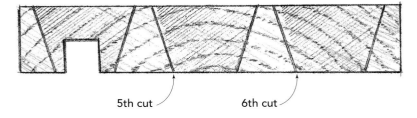

5th cut   6th cut

REMOVING THE PIN WASTE

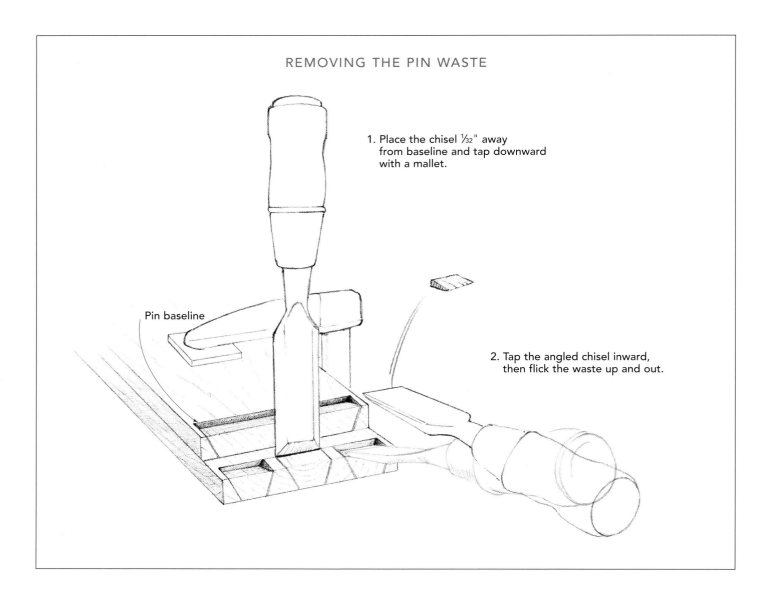

1. Place the chisel ¹⁄₃₂" away from baseline and tap downward with a mallet.

Pin baseline

2. Tap the angled chisel inward, then flick the waste up and out.

line and the end of the workpiece. With one tap of the mallet, slice down at an angle toward the end grain. Complete the motion by flicking the waste away with the chisel. Do this for all the pin waste areas.

8. Deepen the waste cuts by repeating the previous two steps—chopping downward at the gauge line, then making the backward angle cut. When making the gauge line cut, angle the chisel to follow the slope of the pins. When you're about halfway through both workpieces, flip them over, clamp them,

and repeat the process until the waste pieces have totally broken free.

9. Unclamp the work and clean up any fiber residue in the interior corners. Cut the pins on the other ends of the drawer front and back in the same fashion.

10. Lay the drawer sides on your bench with their insides facing up and their bottom edges next to each other. Stand the drawer front on end on top of its corresponding drawer side corner, aligning the edges, as shown in "Marking the Tails."

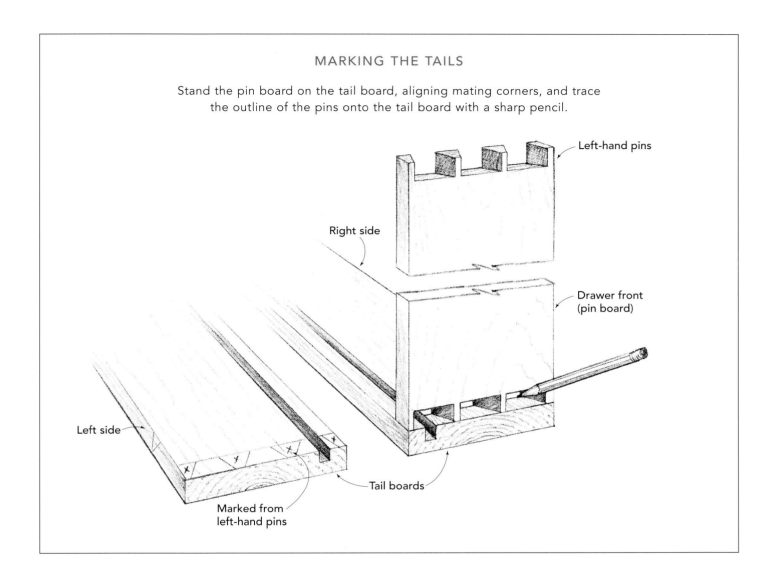

MARKING THE TAILS

Stand the pin board on the tail board, aligning mating corners, and trace the outline of the pins onto the tail board with a sharp pencil.

Left-hand pins

Right side

Drawer front (pin board)

Left side

Marked from left-hand pins

Tail boards

11. With a sharp pencil, transfer the shape of the pins onto the drawer side. Repeat for all corners of the drawer; mark the waste areas.
12. Clamp the drawer side upright in the vice with the pin outlines facing you. You may want to mark square lines across the end of the workpiece until you get the hang of cutting squarely by eye. Using a backsaw or bowsaw, cut down to the gauge line on the waste side of your pencil lines (see **photo L** on p. 84). When you've sawed all the tails, chisel

out the waste just like you did between the pins (see **photo M** on p. 84).

Assembling the drawer

1. Dry-fit the drawer, tapping the joints together, then measure for a snug-fitting drawer bottom. Make the bottom, ensuring that its corners are square; then set it aside.
2. Assemble the drawer box, spreading plenty of glue on all of the mating joint surfaces. A white polyvinyl acetate glue (like Elmer's®) is

Photo L: When cutting the tails, saw to the waste side of the lines you traced from the pins. Keep the sawblade square to the face of the stock.

Photo M: To make the initial baseline cuts on the tails, tap the chisel straight downward.

a better choice than yellow glue for dovetails, because it's slower setting, allowing you more time to work. Tap the tails firmly into their pin sockets. A hardwood wedge placed on top of a tail between the pins makes a great hammer-tapping block. If your dovetails are snug, there's no need to clamp the drawer.

3. Stand the drawer on its front, and slip the drawer bottom into the side grooves, tapping it firmly into the groove in the drawer front. This should square up the drawer, but check the diagonals just to make sure. If the drawer is out of square, it won't fit properly. Nail the drawer bottom into the bottom edge of the drawer back.

4. Plane the pins flush to the drawer sides and the tails flush to the drawer front.

5. Plane the top and bottom edges of the drawer. To avoid tearout, plane around each corner in one smooth motion (see "Planing the Drawer Box Edges Flush").

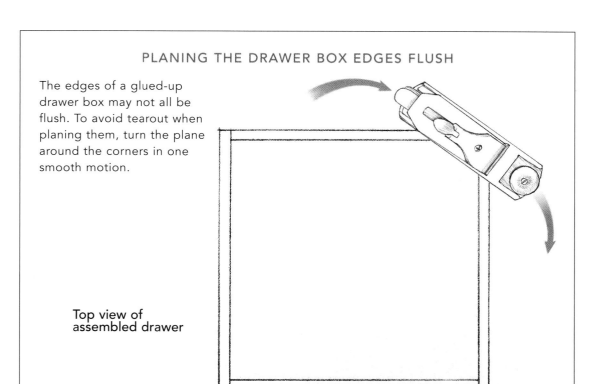

PLANING THE DRAWER BOX EDGES FLUSH

The edges of a glued-up drawer box may not all be flush. To avoid tearout when planing them, turn the plane around the corners in one smooth motion.

Top view of assembled drawer

Fitting the drawer

1. With the rear end of the drawer runners still clamped to the case side, fit the drawer into its opening, planing it a bit if necessary. Ensure that the drawer rides level on both runners, adjusting them up or down, as needed. When the drawer operates smoothly, screw the rear of the runners to the case side.

2. Turn the drawer pull and screw it to the false drawer front from the inside face.

3. Next attach the false drawer front by first pushing the drawer box in ¾ in. from the front of the rails.

4. Center the box between the runners, shimming if necessary, then clamp the drawer sides to the case sides from above, making sure that the drawer is sitting solidly on its runners.

5. Test-fit the false front into the drawer opening. You should have about a ¹⁄₃₂-in. gap on each side. Plane the top and bottom edges to achieve the same gap.

6. Center the false front in its opening using shims and clamp it to the drawer box front. Attach it with screws from inside the drawer.

7. Install the drawer stops, which are simply screws driven into the back apron.

8. Adjust the screws in or out to align the false front flush to the rails.

FINISHING UP

1. Attach the top to the carcase, running screws through the cleats and drawer kickers.

2. Apply your favorite finish. I suggest a couple of coats of linseed oil, waxing it afterward if you want a glossier finish. But under no conditions stain the cherry. You do that and you're gonna have to answer to Arthur.

GLASS-TOP DISPLAY TABLE

John McDonald, a California furniture maker, designed and built this table to display and protect small, fragile art objects. Its glass top showcases the items within.

This piece embodies a number of elegant, thoughtful touches. At first viewing, you notice the lovely wood-framed glass top and the subtle ¼-in. taper on the insides of the legs. Any more of a taper, and the table would look barrel-chested and top heavy. Any less, and the legs would seem boxy.

On closer investigation, you notice that the plate glass, with its slightly rounded top edges, sits ⅟₁₆ in. proud of the tabletop—a nice touch.

Some display tables require removal of the glass top to access the inside, but McDonald's table employs a drawer whose front is cleverly disguised to look like one of the table's aprons. Because a drawer pull would spoil the illusion, the drawer front projects ⅛ in. below the table's front rail for finger access.

A defining characteristic of this table is the drawer bottom, which doubles as a background for the displayed items. Rather than using a single piece of hardwood or plywood for the drawer bottom, McDonald made it using frame-and-panel construction.

McDonald used straight-grained, rift-sawn, red birch for his table, but I used silver maple. Almost any wood, except exotic, showy ones, would be appropriate for this quiet piece.

Glass-Top Display Table

THIS TABLE IS DESIGNED to showcase art objects placed inside. A glass top resting in a rabbet cut into the top frame serves as the tabletop and display window. Art objects are held in a drawer whose front is disguised to look like one of the table's aprons. The frame-and-panel drawer bottom provides a distinctive background for the display objects.

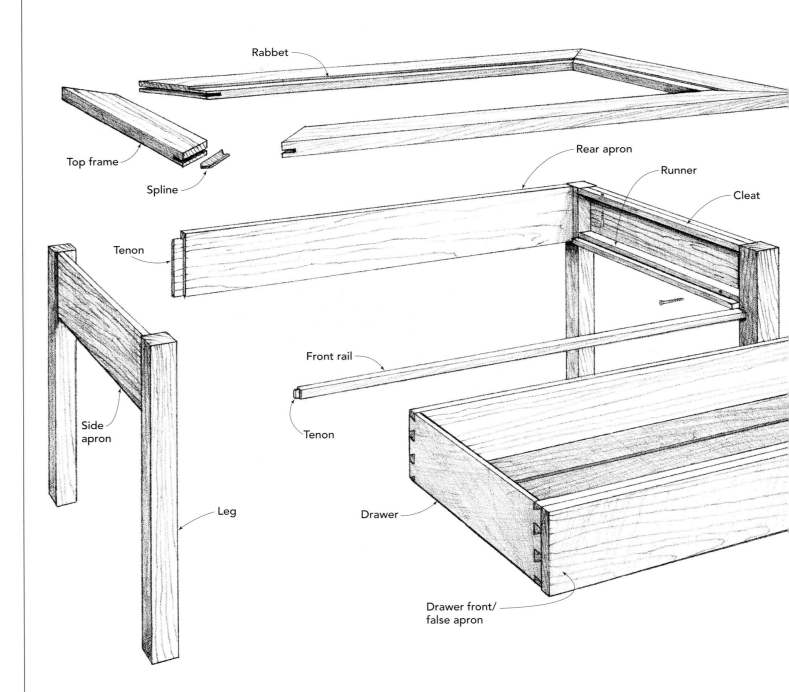

APRON TENON DETAIL

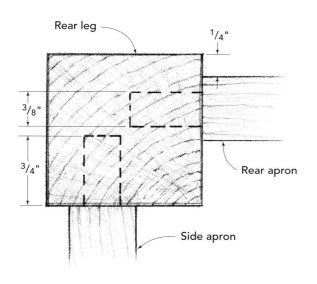

Rear leg

1/4"

3/8"

3/4"

Rear apron

Side apron

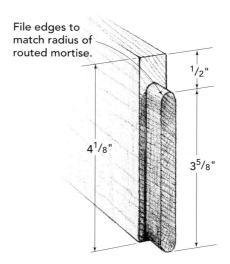

File edges to match radius of routed mortise.

1/2"

4 1/8"

3 5/8"

RAIL TENON DETAIL

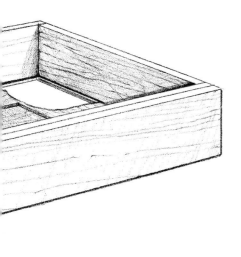

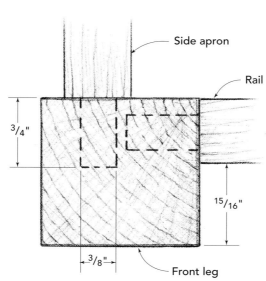

Side apron

Rail

3/4"

15/16"

3/8"

Front leg

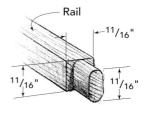

Rail

11/16"

11/16"

11/16"

Building the Table Step-by-Step

Cut List for Glass-Top Display Table

Top		
2	Frame members	11/16 in. x 3 1/8 in. x 21 1/4 in.
2	Frame members	11/16 in. x 3 1/8 in. x 33 1/4 in.
Base		
4	Legs	1 5/8 in. x 1 5/8 in. x 16 5/16 in.
1	Front rail	11/16 in. x 11/16 in. x 30 in. (including tenons)
1	Drawer front/false apron	11/16 in. x 4 1/8 in. x 28 1/2 in. (including tenons)
1	Rear apron	11/16 in. x 4 1/8 in. x 30 in. (including tenons)
2	Side aprons	11/16 in. x 4 1/8 in. x 18 in. (including tenons)
2	Drawer runners	1 in. x 1 in. x 16 1/2 in. (with 11/16-in. x 11/16-in. rabbet)
2	Cleats	11/16 in. x 11/16 in. x 16 1/2 in.
Drawer		
1	Front	1/2 in. x 3 5/16 in. x 28 1/2 in.
1	Back	1/2 in. x 3 5/16 in. x 28 1/2 in.
2	Sides	1/2 in. x 3 5/16 in. x 17 3/4 in.
2	Bottom frame members	1/2 in. x 3 3/8 in. x 28 in.
2	Bottom frame members	1/2 in. x 3 3/8 in. x 10 1/2 in.
1	Bottom frame member	1/2 in. x 3 1/8 in. x 22 1/4 in. (including tenons)
2	Bottom panels	5/16 in. x 4 11/16 in. x 22 1/4 in.

THE TABLE CONSISTS OF three elements: the top, the base, and the drawer. I make the top first. That way I can take it to the glass shop to get the glass cut for it while I build the rest of the table. The base is built next. Then I make the drawer to fit its opening.

Making the Top

The top is simply a mitered frame joined at the corners with splines. For a strong joint, the grain of the spline needs to run perpendicular to the joint line. The inside top edge is rabbeted to accept a piece of 1/4-in.-thick tempered glass.

Making the frame

1. Dimension the stock for the frame members. Leave 1 in. or more excess in length.

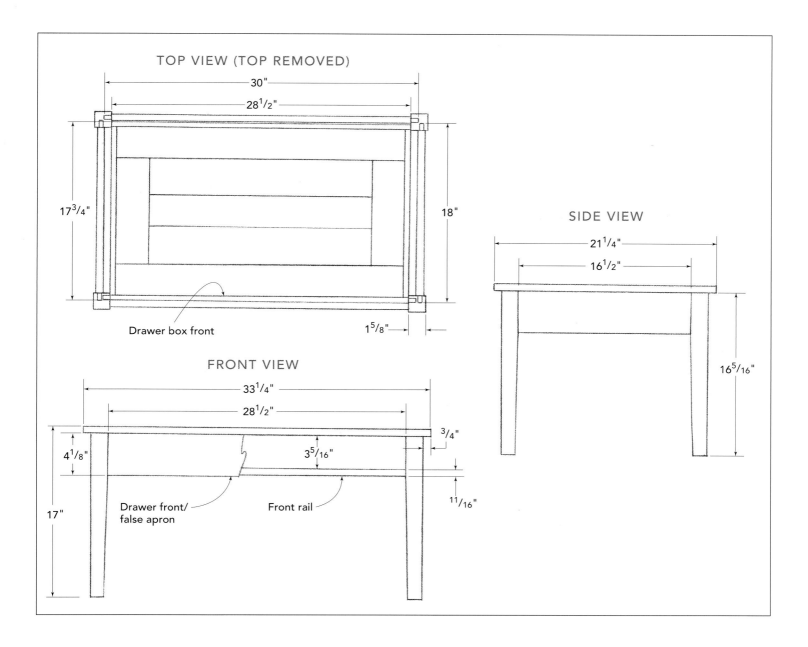

TOP VIEW (TOP REMOVED)

30"

28¹/₂"

17³/₄"

18"

Drawer box front

1⁵/₈"

SIDE VIEW

21¹/₄"

16¹/₂"

16⁵/₁₆"

FRONT VIEW

33¹/₄"

28¹/₂"

³/₄"

4¹/₈"

3⁵/₁₆"

17"

Drawer front/
false apron

Front rail

11/16"

2. Cut the miters on the ends of the frame members. I use a shopmade tablesaw sled for this (see "A Tablesaw Miter Sled" on p. 62). Take care to cut the angles accurately so that the frame lays out square afterward.

3. Cut the ¼-in. by ⅜-in. spline slots in the mitered ends, spacing each one as shown in "Top Frame Corner Detail" on p. 92. I use a dado cutter in the tablesaw, clamping the workpiece to my tenoning jig.

4. Make the spline stock by ripping a short length of material to 5⅛ in. wide and then

planing it to thickness. Aim for a thickness that fits snugly in the slots. You should be able to insert the spline material with finger pressure only.

5. Crosscut the spline stock into ¾-in. lengths to make the individual splines.

6. Dry-clamp the frame with the splines inserted to make sure everything fits well and to rehearse your clamping procedure.

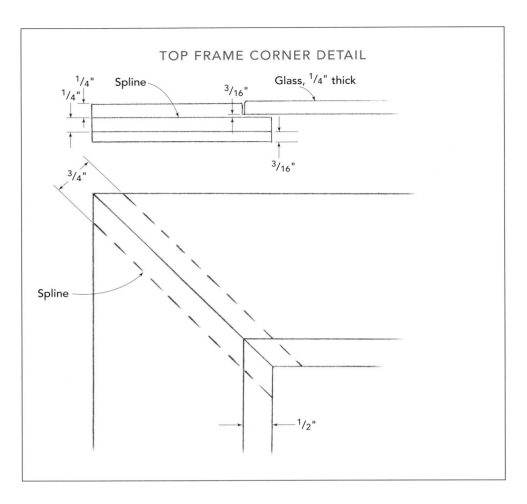

TOP FRAME CORNER DETAIL

1/4"   Spline   3/16"   Glass, 1/4" thick

1/4"

3/4"

Spline

1/2"

Photo A: Rout the rabbet for the glass top, moving the router clockwise inside the frame.

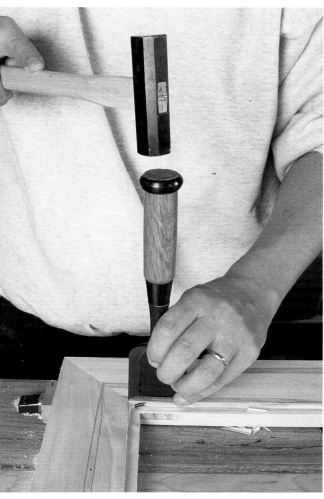

Photo B: **The first step in squaring up the corners of the rabbet is to cut the wall using a wide chisel.**

Photo C: **Clean up the bottom of the rabbet corner with a chisel.**

I use bar clamps—two over and two under—carefully lining up the corners of the rabbets. You could use a band clamp instead, which will line up the outside corners automatically, then apply extra force with bar clamps where needed to tighten the joint or to better line up the corners.

7. Glue up the frame, working quickly. Make sure the assembly is square and that the corners line up well. Let the assembly dry thoroughly.

8. Trim the projecting excess of the splines with a small handsaw. Then pare the remainder flush to the edges of the frame with a chisel. When paring the outside corner, make sure to cut with the grain, working from the corner inward to prevent tearout.

9. Rout the ½-in.-wide by ³⁄₁₆-in.-deep rabbet for the glass (see **photo A**).

10. Square off the rounded corners left by the router with a wide chisel to cut the rabbet walls (see **photo B**). Work carefully to create a crisp 90-degree corner.

11. Chisel out the waste to the bottom of the rabbet (see **photo C**).

12. Take the completed frame to your local glass shop and have them cut a piece of ¼-in.-thick tempered glass to fit snugly within the rabbets. Ask them to "ease" the upper edges of the glass, rounding them over slightly.

MAKING THE BASE

The base is a simple construct: Tenons on the side aprons and the rear apron slip into mortises on the legs. A narrow rail ties the two front legs together and serves as a stop for the drawer front. Two L-shaped drawer runners and two cleats attach to the side aprons.

Making the legs

The legs are made from 1⅜-in.-square stock. Each leg tapers to 1⅛ in. at the foot and is mortised to accept tenons on the ends of the aprons.

1. Saw the stock for the legs to size. McDonald suggests using riftsawn lumber, which displays a straight, sedate figure on all faces, as shown in "Riftsawn Legs."

2. Lay out the tapers on the two inside faces of each leg (see **photo D**). The tapers begin 4⅛ in. from the top of the leg and diminish to 1⅛ in. at the foot.

3. Cut the tapers. You can do this with a tapering jig on the tablesaw, but because the tapers are so slight, I used a smoothing plane.

4. Lay out the ⅜-in.-wide by 3⅜-in.-long mortises to accept the apron tenons. Don't forget to include the ¼-in. setback of the apron from the outside face of the leg (see "Apron Tenon Detail" on p. 89).

5. Lay out the ⅜-in.-wide by ¹¹⁄₁₆-in.-long mortise for the front rail (see "Rail Tenon Detail" on p. 89). The mortise begins 3³⁄₁₆ in. down from the top of the leg. The ¹³⁄₁₆-in. setback from the face of the leg will create a ¼-in. setback for the drawer front/false apron when the drawer is closed.

Photo D: **The tapers on the inside faces of the legs begin 4⅛ in. down from the top and diminish to 1⅛ in. at the foot.**

RIFTSAWN LEGS

Table legs cut from riftsawn stock (identified by its diagonal end grain) will display balanced, straight grain on all faces of the legs. Riftsawn stock is often obtained from the edges of a wide plainsawn board, as shown here.

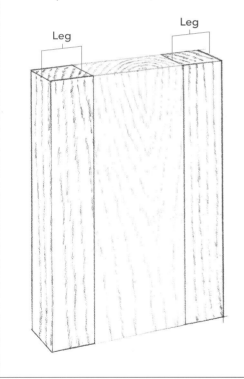

---

6. Rout the ¾-in.-deep apron and rail mortises using a ⅜-in.-diameter straight bit. Use a router fence to guide the cut.

Making the aprons and front rail

1. Plane, rip, and crosscut the aprons and rail to size.

2. Lay out and cut the tenons on the ends of the rear and side aprons. I rip the tenons a bit fat on the tablesaw using a tenoning jig, then cut the haunch with a handsaw and trim the tenons to a snug fit with a rabbet plane.

3. Round over the edges of the tenons with a file to match the round ends of the routed mortises.

4. Lay out and cut the tenons on the ends of the rail.

Assembling the base and fitting the cleats and runners

1. Dry-clamp the base to make sure that all of the joints fit well and to rehearse your clamping procedures.

2. Glue the legs to the side aprons. Keep the clamp screws in line with the aprons to prevent cocking the legs out of line.

3. Glue the rear apron and front rail between the two side assemblies. Don't overtighten the clamp on the rail. You don't want to bend it. Check the diagonal measurements across the top of the table to make sure that it is square while the glue sets up. Otherwise the drawer won't fit well.

4. Make the cleats and drawer runners, fitting them between the front and rear legs. The runners are made by cutting an ¹¹⁄₁₆-in. by ¹¹⁄₁₆-in. rabbet into 1-in.-square stock.

5. Glue the cleats to the side aprons, aligning them flush to the top of the aprons.

6. Attach the drawer runners. For now, use only one screw at the front end of each. You'll make final adjustments and attachments after fitting the drawer.

MAKING THE DRAWER

The drawer consists of a frame-and-panel bottom that sits in grooves cut into the drawer front, back, and sides. Unlike many drawer bottoms that slide into their grooves from the rear of the assembled drawer, this bottom is totally enclosed within the walls of the box. To ensure a good fit, make the drawer sides first, then make the bottom to fit into its grooves.

Making the drawer sides

1. Dimension the stock for the drawer box front, back, and sides.

2. Cut a ¼-in. by ¼-in. groove in all four pieces for the drawer bottom. Cut the groove ⁵⁄₁₆ in. up from the bottom of the pieces, as shown in "Section through Drawer." This raises the drawer bottom so it doesn't scrape on the front rail.

Tip: To easily clean up white or yellow glue squeeze-out, wait an hour or so until the glue has turned rubbery, then pare or slice it off using a sharp chisel.

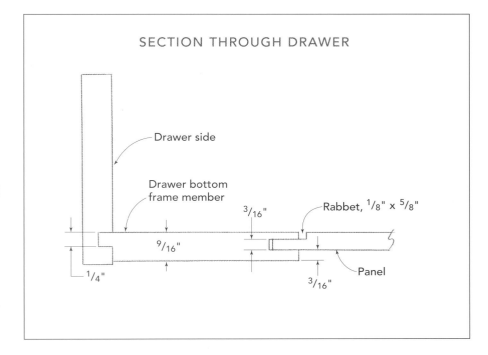

SECTION THROUGH DRAWER

Drawer side

Drawer bottom frame member

Rabbet, ¹/₈" x ⁵/₈"

³/₁₆"

⁹/₁₆"

¼"

³/₁₆"

Panel

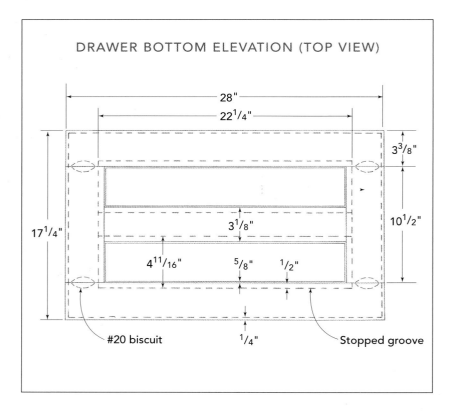

DRAWER BOTTOM JOINERY

Identical front and back frame members join to the side frame members with glue and biscuits.
The two rabbeted floating panels ride unglued in grooves cut into the frame members.

Groove,
$3/16$" x $1/2$"

Center
frame member

Tenon,
$3/16$" x $1/2$",
glued to side.

Floating
panel

Rabbet,
$1/8$" x $5/8$"

Side frame
member

Rabbet,
$1/4$" x $1/4$"

#20 biscuit

Groove,
$3/16$" x $1/2$"

Front/back
frame member

DRAWER BOTTOM ELEVATION (TOP VIEW)

28"

$22^1/4$"

$3^3/8$"

$17^1/4$"

$10^1/2$"

$3^1/8$"

$4^{11}/16$" $5/8$" $1/2$"

#20 biscuit

$1/4$"

Stopped groove

3. Cut the through dovetails for the corner joints of the drawer. Each corner gets three tails and four pins. Make sure the bottom groove runs through the tails, not the pins.
4. Dry-fit the joints. With the tails tapped home, the drawer front and back should be parallel, as should the sides. It's wise to fit the assembly into the base drawer opening at this point to check its width for fit.

Making the drawer bottom

The seven-piece drawer bottom is made of two ⁵⁄₁₆-in.-thick panels set into grooves in the five ½-in.-thick frame members. The top faces of all the pieces are flush to each other to create a level surface for the display objects.

1. Dimension the stock for the frame members. Cut them to the finished sizes—with the following exceptions: Make the front and back frame members 1 in. or so longer. Also make the side frame members about ¹⁄₁₆ in. wider. You'll trim them to final size after assembling the drawer bottom. While you're at it, it's a

Photo E: The first step in cutting the tenon on the drawer bottom's center frame member is to saw the shoulders.

good idea to cut a bit of extra frame and panel stock for test fitting.

2. Dimension the stock for the floating panels. Book-matching the panels by resawing them from the same piece of stock can create a lovely visual balance.

3. Rout the ³⁄₁₆-in. by ½-in. grooves for the floating panels, as shown in "Drawer Bottom Joinery." The 22¼-in.-long grooves in the front and back frame members are stopped, so you'll have to mark their beginning and end locations first, as shown in the "Drawer Bottom Elevation."

4. Because the frame members are oversize in length, mark out the stopped grooves by measuring from the center to the ends of the frame member.

5. Cut the ³⁄₁₆-in. by ½-in. tenons on the ends of the center frame member on the tablesaw, sawing the shoulders first (see **photo E**).

6. Cut the cheeks using a tenoning jig (see **photo F**). I saw the cheeks a bit fat, then trim them with a rabbet plane for an exact fit in the groove.

7. Cut the ⅛-in. by ⅜-in. rabbets on the top edges of the floating panels. These can either be sawn on the tablesaw or routed.

8. Cut the biscuit slots. To lay them out, dry-fit the drawer bottom parts together, then mark for the biscuit locations.

9. Fine-tune the fit of the floating panels, which will ride unglued in their grooves. If you're building during a humid summer day,

Photo F: The second step in cutting the tenon is to cut the cheeks using a tenoning jig.

the panels can fit tightly side to side, because they will shrink later during dry, heated winter days in the house. If you're building during conditions of low humidity, take about ⅟₁₆ in. off each of the panels' long edges so they will have room to expand during more humid weather.

10. Dry-assemble the drawer bottom in preparation for glue-up. Make sure everything fits well and then rehearse your clamping procedures.

11. Glue up the frame, leaving the floating panels unglued to allow them to expand and contract. Make sure that the bottom is flat under clamping pressure. Also check that the assembly is square after clamping by comparing diagonal measurements made across the interior corners of the outer frame.

Fitting and assembling the drawer

1. Crosscut the bottom to its final length (see "Drawer Bottom Elevation" p. 96). Make sure to cut equal amounts off of each side. To ensure that the bottom is cut squarely, crosscut it using a panel-cutting jig.

2. Plane the top surface of the entire bottom with a jointer plane to level the frame and floating panels (see **photo G**).

3. Rabbet the bottom's edges to fit into the grooves in the drawer sides.

If your drawer bottom has remained a fairly consistent thickness even after planing, you can use a rabbeting bit in the router to cut the rabbet. However, if the bottom varies in thickness, the rabbet will too, making a good fit in the grooves difficult. Instead of routing, you can cut the rabbet on the tablesaw, holding the bottom on edge, with its top pressed against the rip fence, to create a tongue of consistent thickness.

4. Dry-assemble the drawer, fitting the bottom into its grooves (see **photo H**). Make sure that all fits well when the drawer box dovetails are tapped home and that the drawer will clamp up squarely. Definitely rehearse your clamping procedures, because you're going to have to work quickly during the glue-up.

5. Glue up the drawer, spreading ample glue on the dovetail joints for one side of the drawer. Tap the joints home.

Photo G: Plane the top surface of the drawer bottom to ensure that the panels and frame members are flush.

6. Then spread glue sparingly into the grooves, insert the panel, and glue up the dovetail joints on the other side of the drawer. If your dovetails fit reasonably well, you won't have to clamp the drawer. But make sure that it is square, and that it's sitting on a flat surface as it dries.

Fitting the drawer to its opening

1. Plane the top and bottom edges of the drawer box with a sharp jack plane or smoothing plane to remove any saw marks.
2. Use spring clamps to temporarily clamp the back end of the drawer runners to the side aprons. Slide the drawer box into its opening and adjust the runners so that they both contact the drawer bottom along their entire length. Remove the drawer and screw the runners in place at the back.
3. Reinsert the drawer and clamp the drawer front/false apron to the drawer box to check its fit. To maintain the illusion of the false apron, its ends should fit against the legs with just a hair's clearance.

4. Glue the drawer front/false apron to the drawer box, carefully aligning its top edge with the tops of the adjoining legs. You could instead screw the false apron on from the inside of the drawer, but you would see the screws through the glass top.

FINISHING UP

1. Attach the top by screwing it on from underneath through the cleats. Make sure to balance the overhang all around the base.
2. Apply your favorite finish to all of the exterior surfaces. McDonald used shellac for the entire table, including the drawer. Whatever finish you use for the outside surfaces, it's wise to use shellac for the drawer, because it won't bleed or leave an odor inside.
3. Clean both sides of the glass and lightly drop in place while wearing cotton gloves.

Part Three
DINING TABLES

KITCHEN TABLE

Many of my childhood memories center around the kitchen table. More than just the scene of family meals, it was the place where my brothers and I did our homework while our mother or our grandmother cooked dinner and where the adults sat to pay bills and drink endless cups of coffee.

This kitchen table, as simple and sturdy as it is elegant, is one where families will want to gather and share the day. In the size shown here, it will comfortably seat four people, and it can easily be scaled to fit six. I've made it in cherry, but maple would work as well if you prefer a lighter color.

This is a good first table project and even a good first woodworking project since it is both basic and challenging. Because it uses the most common type of table construction—four legs, an apron, and a top—it offers an excellent introduction to building with solid wood.

Even if you don't build this kitchen table, you might want to read this chapter. I provide more detail here about basic operations than I will when discussing later projects. The sections on milling rough lumber into dimensioned boards, building a solid-wood top, and mortise-and-tenon joinery are applicable to most of the other tables as well as to this one.

Kitchen Table

THE KITCHEN TABLE offers a good introduction to solid-wood table construction. The four tapered legs join to the apron with mortise-and-tenon joints and are braced with corner blocks for stability. The tabletop, made by gluing up several boards matched for grain and color, attaches to the leg assembly by means of tabletop connectors. The table is sized for informal dining for four adults but an alternate cut list is given for a six-person table.

TOP DIMENSIONS

TOP VIEW

48¹/₂"

42"

56"

34¹/₂"

FRONT VIEW

29¹/₈"

CORNER DETAIL

2³/₈"

7/₈"

1"

1/₂"

3/₁₆"

3/₁₆"

7/₈"

1/₈"

SIDE VIEW

42"

3¹³/₁₆"

30"

7/₈"

1⁷/₁₆"

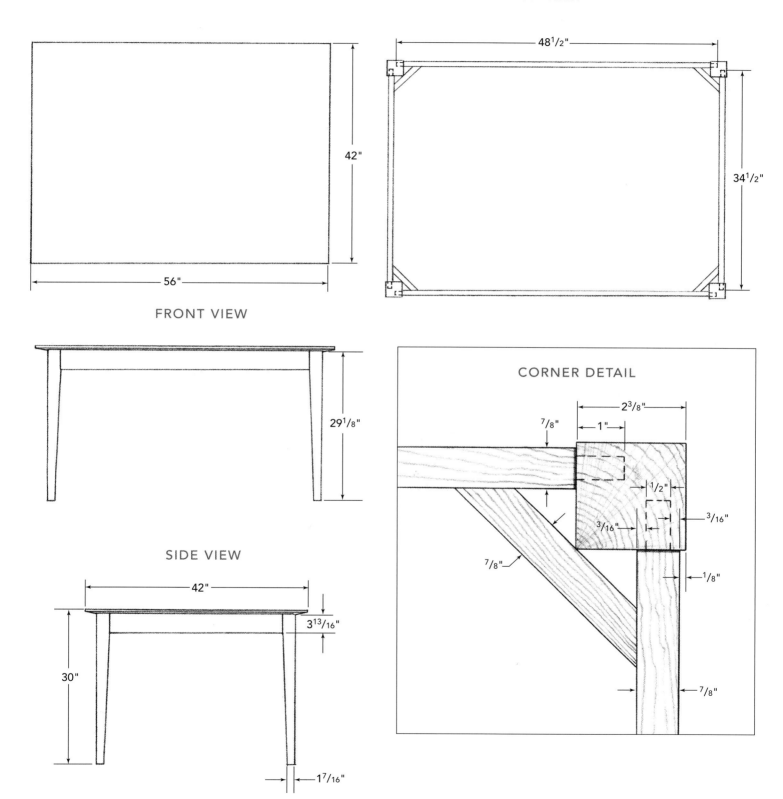

BUILDING THE TABLE STEP-BY-STEP

CUT LIST FOR KITCHEN TABLE

Tabletop and Leg Assembly

1	Tabletop	56 in. x 42 in. x ⅞ in.
2	Short aprons	34½ in. x 3¹³⁄₁₆ in. x ⅞ in.
2	Long aprons	48½ in. x 3¹³⁄₁₆ in. x ⅞ in.
4	Corner blocks	6 in. x 3¹³⁄₁₆ in. x ⅞ in.
4	Legs	29⅛ in. x 2⅜ in. x 2⅜ in.

Hardware

8	Tabletop connectors	
16	Steel wood screws	2 in. by #10
8	Steel wood screws	⅝ in. by #10

ALTERNATE CUT LIST FOR KITCHEN TABLE

Tabletop and Leg Assembly

1	Tabletop	80 in. x 42 in. x ⅞ in.
2	Short aprons	34½ in. x 3¹³⁄₁₆ in. x ⅞ in.
2	Long aprons	66½ in. x 3¹³⁄₁₆ in. x ⅞ in.
4	Corner blocks	6 in. x 3¹³⁄₁₆ in. x ⅞ in.
4	Legs	29⅛ in. x 2⅜ in. x 2⅜ in.

Hardware

8	Tabletop connectors	
16	Steel wood screws	2 in. by #10
8	Steel wood screws	⅝ in. by #10

It's best to mill the lumber for all of the parts of this table at the outset. Milling similar pieces (say, the four legs) one after the other saves you setup time and achieves consistent dimensions. After milling, glue up the tabletop and put it aside overnight to give the glue time to cure. Make the legs first, followed by the aprons and corner blocks, and finally complete the tabletop. After you've sanded all the parts, you'll be ready to assemble and finish the piece.

MAKING THE PARTS

Initial sizing

1. Decide which boards you will use for each part, being sure to pick the best boards for your largest, most visible part—the tabletop. You can cut smaller pieces out from around flaws in the wood. The apron board should include the aprons as well as the corner blocks, which are the same width and thickness as the aprons. Using lumber crayon or chalk, mark each board with the name of the part for which it is intended.

2. Calculate the rough dimensions for each part. Be sure to add at least 1 in. in length and ½ in. in width to the finished dimensions; more is better.

3. Using lumber crayon or chalk, mark divisions on the leg board and on the board for the aprons and corner blocks (see **photo A**).

Milling the lumber

For the table to fit together without gaps at the joints, the boards must be milled so their opposing faces are parallel and their edges meet at right angles. Predimensioned lumber offers little choice of color and grain matching. Milling your own boards gives you more aesthetic control.

Milling requires, at minimum, a jointer, a planer, and a tablesaw or radial-arm saw. A bandsaw allows you to resaw thick boards into thinner ones, giving perfect color and grain matches.

1. Establish a sound end of each board. Even if the board looks sound, it may have cracks, or checks, which must be cut off. Using a slid-

Photo A: **Mark up the boards for the rough cut.**

Photo B: **Knock the cutoff against the saw table to determine whether it is solid.**

Photo C: **Crosscut lumber using a sliding compound miter saw.**

Photo D: **Before you rip boards using a tablesaw, you must face-joint them to minimize the risk of kickback.**

Tip: Use chalk for tentative decisions— it's easier to erase. Lumber crayon is better for final decisions because it won't rub off accidentally.

Tip: If possible, mill the lumber on a dry day. Wood is more stable when the barometric pressure is high.

ing compound miter saw (SCMS) or tablesaw, cut off the board end 1 in. at a time and knock the resulting cutoff hard against the saw table to see whether it is solid. If it cracks or falls apart, continue cutting off 1-in. pieces until you reach sound wood (see **photo B**). Check for staples in the board—they can damage the brittle carbide of your saw's teeth.

2. Crosscut all of the lumber to rough length using a tablesaw, radial-arm saw, or SCMS (see **photo C**).
3. Face-joint all of the boards (see **photo D**).
4. Edge-joint the boards, holding them against the fence of your jointer. This establishes a square corner between one face and one edge.
5. On a tablesaw, rip the boards to rough width.

Photo E: **Use the same setting to plane all of the boards so that you will achieve a uniform thickness.**

Tip: Tabletop boards don't have to be of exactly equal width. It's more important to choose boards that look right together.

6. Rejoint the face and edges of your boards to mill out the deflections. I sometimes mark the face with chalk so I can see exactly where I am in the process.

7. Finally, plane the parts to establish an opposing parallel face and a finished thickness (see **photo E**). To achieve consistent thickness, put all the boards through at one setting, set the planer to the next setting, and put them all through again. Repeat until you achieve your finished thickness.

Gluing up the tabletop

1. Now that you can see the color and grain, decide how to orient the tabletop boards. Flip the boards, turn them around, and rearrange them until you find a visually striking and organic-looking pattern. If you ripped wide boards to fit on your jointer, be sure to match up pieces that were originally part of the same board. Don't rush this step. Matching grain is one of the most important aspects of working with solid wood.

2. Draw a large triangle across the tabletop to help you reassemble the boards later (see **photo F** on p. 109).

3. To make sure your clamps are available and ready for use, do a dry practice clamping.

Tip: Cut two story sticks, one the length and one the width of your finished tabletop. It's easier to use these than to keep measuring the top with a tape measure.

BANDSAW LUMBER TRUING

The order of operations when using a bandsaw is as follows:

1. Edge-joint the parts so you have a flat edge to run against the bandsaw fence.
2. Rip the parts to rough width.
3. Face-joint the parts.
4. Edge-joint the parts again.
5. Plane to thickness.

A bandsaw is preferable to a tablesaw for ripping boards to width. The bandsaw makes rough dimensioning safer and more efficient. Since there is no danger of kickback, you don't need to face-joint before ripping to width, as you would on a tablesaw. Ripping boards releases internal forces, causing them to deflect, so that they must be face-jointed afterwards (this is another reason to leave as much extra width as possible). With a bandsaw, you save a step because you don't have to face-joint before ripping. Even better, you save a problematic step: Face-jointing a wide board wastes material and may leave the edges too thin.

4. Cut a clamp block to protect the wood.

5. Glue up the boards, spreading a thin film of glue on each surface to be glued.

6. Clamp the boards together, alternating the clamps top and bottom to achieve even pressure and keep the boards from bowing (see **photo G**).

Photo G: When you glue up the tabletop, use clamp blocks to protect the edges, clamp cauls to keep the tabletop even, tape to keep the cauls from sticking, and waxed paper to keep the metal clamps from leaving oxidation marks on the boards.

Photo F: Drawing a triangle across the table-top boards helps you line them up the way you want them.

WHAT GLUE TO USE

For the projects in this book, you need only two kinds of glue: yellow glue, or polyvinyl acetate (PVA) for solid-wood and sheet-good joinery, and urea resin glue for veneer work and lamination. If you want to branch out, try hot hide glue, a good choice for solid-wood joints. I confess to a personal preference for hide glue, but in this book I assume you are using PVA and urea resin glue.

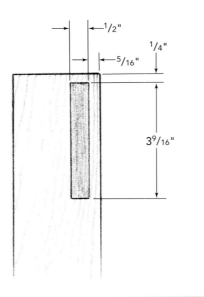

MORTISE MEASUREMENT DETAIL

1/2"

1/4"

5/16"

3⁹/₁₆"

JOINERY AND DETAILS

Making the legs

To construct the legs for this table, lay out and cut the mortises, then cut the tapers. Cutting joinery is easier when the workpieces are square. If you cut the tapers first, you'll have problems cutting the mortises.

Cutting the mortises

1. Start by cutting the legs to final length. Square the end of one leg using your crosscut tool of choice, then set a stop and cut all four legs to the same length. Cut the legs one after the other without changing the stop setting (see "Critical Dimensions" below). It doesn't matter if the legs are 1/16 in. short as long as they're all the same length.

2. Decide which way the grain should run on the legs, and orient the legs so their most

CRITICAL DIMENSIONS

Many woodworkers wonder how precise their measurements need to be. The answer depends on whether you're measuring for a critical or noncritical dimension.

A dimension is critical if a small measurement error will cause the finished piece to function improperly; create extra work for you in building the piece; or make the finished piece "look wrong." The tolerance for critical dimensions should be within a few thousandths of an inch; with noncritical dimensions, you have more slack.

Table leg length is a critical dimension because even the smallest variation will make the table rock. To make the legs equal, set a stop on your saw and cut the legs to length one after the other. Don't take a break and use the saw for something else, or you'll

never get the stop back in the same position and the legs won't match.

The placement of the leg mortise is another example. If it varies, the tenons will have to be individually fit to make the table square—a time-consuming and error-prone operation. To place the mortises consistently, cut them one after the other.

Tools such as tape measures are not accurate enough for critical measurements. Even with high-quality tooling, the human eye doesn't discern gradations of much less than 1/100 in. Critical dimensions should be 10 times more accurate than that. The only way to achieve this level of accuracy is to set up your tooling and mill all the parts that require that dimension at the same time, without changing the setup.

ALTERNATIVES FOR MILLING MORTISES

Although a mortising machine is the fastest way to cut mortises, good alternatives exist. Simplest, cheapest, and most enjoyable is chopping the mortises by hand using a mallet and mortising chisel. First lay out the mortises completely so you'll have lines to chisel to. Be sure to use a mortising chisel, which is thicker than a normal chisel. The thickness acts as a jig to cut square and lever against the wood to remove the waste. With a little practice, this method is very fast.

Another low-tech method is to drill holes using a drill press and clean up using a chisel. I find this method slow and inaccurate, but some people swear by it. With this method you also need to lay out all of the mortises.

You can also use a router, either in a router table with proper fences or with a shopmade jig. This method is very accurate. However, setup time is longer than with a dedicated mortising machine, and the method is more dangerous and error-prone.

Tip: A marking knife makes a finer and more accurate line than a pencil.

attractive faces are outside. Mark the top of each leg with a triangle mark and the inside faces with a witness mark.

3. To lay out the mortises, set a combination square to ¼ in. and use a marking knife to mark the tops of the mortises on the inside and outside of each leg.

4. Reset your combination square to 3¾6 in. and mark the bottoms of the mortises.

5. Mark the sides of the mortises on one leg. First set the knives on your marking gauge to the same width as the mortising bit—½ in. in this instance. Then set the fence on the gauge ⁵⁄₁₆ in. away, making sure it is flush against the outside edge of the leg.

6. Position the fence on the mortising machine so the edge of the hollow chisel is on the layout lines. Make sure the chisel is square to the fence. If you don't have a mortising machine, see "Alternatives for Milling Mortises" above.

7. Next, position the leg against the fence and eyeball the starting position of the cut. Cut the mortise, eyeballing the end of the cut (see **photo H**).

8. Cut the remaining seven mortises. The mortises must be in the same place on every

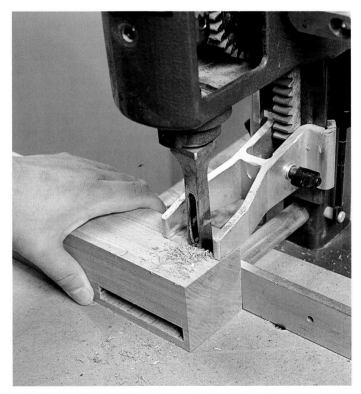

Photo H: **Use the mortising machine to mill the mortises.**

Photo I: Orienting the leg taper so that you turn the piece clockwise after the first cut is safer because it leaves more wood on the saw table during the second cut.

leg. Even if you made a mistake in setting up the machinery for the first leg, cut all four legs with the same mistake.

9. Clean up the bottoms of the mortises using a chisel.

Cutting the taper on the legs

The safest way to cut a taper on a leg is by using a bandsaw. Mark the taper line with a pencil, bandsaw $\frac{1}{16}$ in. off the line, and clean up using a jack plane.

If you don't have a bandsaw, do the following:

1. Make a jig to cut the tapers (see "Simple Taper Jig" below) or use a commercially available taper jig such as the one shown in **photo I**.

2. Using a rip blade on a tablesaw, cut tapers on the inside faces of the leg. The jig holds the workpiece at an angle while it rides against the fence. Because this method is awkward, it's potentially dangerous. It's hard to hold the workpiece against the jig so it won't slip, and

SIMPLE TAPER JIG

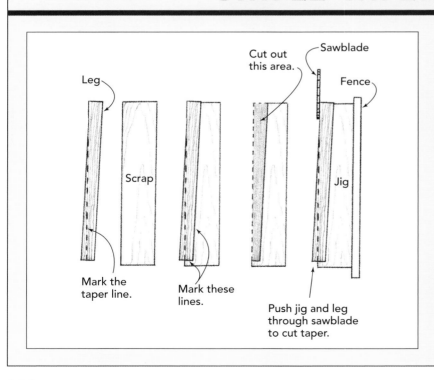

Leg

Scrap

Mark the taper line.

Mark these lines.

Cut out this area.

Sawblade

Fence

Jig

Push jig and leg through sawblade to cut taper.

This jig is so simple that I make a new one each time I need one. Start by marking the taper in pencil on the left side of one leg. Take a piece of scrapwood or sheet stock about 6 in. wide and 2 in. to 3 in. longer than the leg, and lay the leg against it, top facing away from you so the taper follows its left side. With a pencil, trace the right side and bottom of the leg onto the scrap. Following the pencil lines, cut the resulting profile on a bandsaw, cleaning up the edges as necessary. The leg fits into the resulting niche while tapering.

your hand can be too close to the blade for comfort. *Always* use your blade guard and splitter. Orient the leg so you will turn it clockwise to make the second cut. The first taper will face upward as the second cut is being made, leaving a larger surface on the table during the second cut (see **photo I**).

3. Remove the mill marks using a plane, a jointer, or a belt sander.

Laying out the tenons

1. Begin by cutting the apron pieces to length. Square one end of the first short apron piece, then set a stop on your crosscut tool to make the opposing apron piece the same length (apron length is a critical dimension). Repeat for the long apron pieces.

2. Arrange the workpieces in the correct order and draw an orientation triangle on the tops of the pieces.

3. Set your combination square to 1 in. Measuring from the ends of one short apron and one long apron, mark the 1-in. lines.

4. With the marking gauge still set at the width you used to cut the mortises, reset the fence on the gauge to ³⁄₁₆ in. Use the gauge to mark the end grain of one of the short aprons, then reset the combination square to ¼ in. and mark the end grain for the top and bottom of the tenon.

Cutting the shoulders

1. Using a sharp crosscut blade on a tablesaw, place the marked workpiece beside the table-saw blade and adjust the blade to the same height as the knife mark on the end grain. Measuring from the workpiece is much more accurate than measuring the blade height (see **photo J**).

2. Using your miter gauge, position a short apron so the knife mark on its top is split by the blade edge (see **photo K**). Set a stop on the miter gauge fence to mark the length of the tenon. If your miter gauge doesn't have a fence, attach a scrap piece and clamp a stop block at the proper position.

3. Unless you have an overarm blade guard and splitter, remove the guard (this is a good reason to buy an aftermarket blade guard).

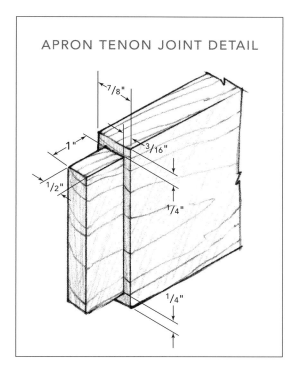

APRON TENON JOINT DETAIL

Tip: If the knife mark is hard to see, rub chalk into it.

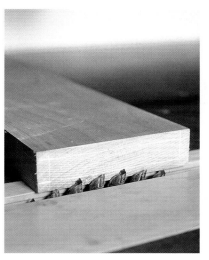

Photo J: **Adjust the blade height to match the knife mark on the end grain of the apron.**

Photo K: **The apron piece is positioned so that the edge of the blade meets the mark you made with the knife.**

Cut the shoulders on all four faces of the
board (see **photo L**). If you cut the first tenon
too short, adjust the stop and recut. However,
if you cut the tenon too long, ignore the mistake. It's only important that the tenons are
all the same length.
4. Flip the board and cut the other four
shoulders.
5. Cut the eight shoulders on the other
short apron.
6. Reset the stop block for the longer aprons
and cut the remaining shoulders.

Photo M: I use a commercial tenon jig to cut
faces, but a shopmade jig will work as well.

Cutting the faces
Although you can make your own jig, the
commercial jig shown in **photo M** is so good
and inexpensive that I consider it a mandatory
accessory.

1. Using a rip blade in your tablesaw, set up
the jig so the first tenon will be a little large,
then test-fit the tenon into the mortise until
it goes in easily but tightly by hand. Sneak
up on the correct width. Remember that
changing the jig setting by, say, $\frac{1}{64}$ in. makes
the tenon $\frac{1}{32}$ in. smaller, since you are cutting
$\frac{1}{64}$ in. from each of two faces.
2. Once the jig is set, cut all of the faces on
all of the aprons.
3. Cut the tops and bottoms of the tenons,
either by hand or by setting the fence and a
stop on the bandsaw. If cut correctly, the mortises and tenons will require no cleanup and
will be interchangeable.

Cutting the beads
on the aprons
If you have a router table, make the bead in
one pass so there is no chance of ruining it
with the second cut. If you don't have a router
table, rout the bead by hand, using a bit with
a bearing and moving the router left to right.

Cutting the grooves for
the tabletop connectors
1. Using a rip blade in your tablesaw, hold the
tabletop connector against the fence and
adjust the fence so the blade's right side is
just to the left of the connector face. When
you screw the connector into the top, the
top will be drawn down tight.
2. Cut the groove onto the top of each
short apron.

Cutting the corner blocks

Corner blocks help distribute lateral forces across the apron structure. They are very effective: I've seen old chairs and tables with loose joinery that remained usable because the corner blocks were intact.

Corner blocks are simply blocks with 45-degree bevels on each end, glued and screwed into the corners. Although you might think you couldn't glue the block's end grain to the apron's long grain, the 45-degree bevel exposes enough of the long fibers for the glue to hold.

1. Set the SCMS or tablesaw blade to 45 degrees and cut off one end of your board.
2. Set a stop at 6 in. It's better to make the block too long than too short—if it's too short, you'll hit the side of the table leg.
3. Flip the board and cut the first corner block. Continue flipping the board until you have four blocks.
4. Drill pilot holes for the screws perpendicular to the face of the corner block. Situate the holes so the screws will enter the apron at the inside edge of the corner block, traveling through the full thickness of the block and as much of the apron as possible.
5. On each end of each block, mark and drill two holes. The screw shank for a #10 screw is $\frac{5}{32}$ in. The holes should be large enough so

that the screw shank can slide in and the threads can draw the corner block into the apron (it's worth getting the correct bit). Finally, countersink holes for the screw heads.

Neatness counts here. Identical blocks will be interchangeable when it comes time to screw them to the table.

DIMENSIONING THE TABLETOP

Flattening

1. Remove the tabletop from the clamps and check for flatness using a long level. If the tabletop is within $\frac{1}{8}$ in. or $\frac{1}{16}$ in. of flat, plane or belt-sand off the high points on the top and bottom surfaces (the tabletop won't sit flat unless its bottom surface is flat).
2. If the tabletop is not close to flat, see "Correcting a Badly Cupped Tabletop" below.

Cutting the tabletop

1. Looking at the rough-cut tabletop, decide where to make the final cuts. There may be knots on the ends of the boards, or the clamps may have left a damaged edge. When you've marked a blemish-free area, rip a reference edge along one edge of the panel using your tablesaw. Place the tabletop right side up so you get a clean cut on the top side.

CORRECTING A BADLY CUPPED TABLETOP

Occasionally a tabletop cups, or warps, after it's glued. A friend of mine made a conference tabletop that cupped so badly that the center of the table was 2 in. below the edges. In this case sanding or planing would result in thin edges or a thin middle. More extreme measures are called for.

The best strategy is to cut the boards apart at the seams, edge-joint them again,

and glue up the tabletop again. This should flatten the top enough so that you can plane or belt-sand it to flat. This solution works only if you have enough material to spare: Each cut will subtract more than $\frac{1}{8}$ in. If your tabletop is made from many narrow boards, you can lose a lot of width. Try to leave enough waste so that you can make this correction if you need to.

Photo N: The tabletop panel faces down when you crosscut it using a circular saw and straightedge.

Photo O: If you use a jack plane to cut the bevel, plane the table ends first so any break-out at the end of the cut will be planed off when you bevel the sides.

2. Reset your fence to the width of the table and rip the opposing edge.

3. As the best way to make the crosscut without specialized equipment, use a circular saw and ride it against a straightedge. Note that the top of the panel should face down to get a clean edge on the top (see **photo N**).

COMPLETING THE TABLE

Finishing the edge

This edge treatment, a simple steep undercut, makes the top seem to float above the undercarriage. Interestingly, a thin tabletop doesn't produce the same effect. It takes the full thickness of the top combined with the undercut to produce that "floating" feeling.

1. If your tablesaw blade tilts to the left and you have headroom, attach a high auxiliary fence to your tablesaw fence and cut the bevel using the tablesaw. Use a featherboard to hold the panel tight and a zero clearance insert to keep it from dropping.

2. Alternatively, use a right-tilting blade if you have enough room to the left of the fence.

3. If you cannot set up the tablesaw safely, make the edge treatment by hand using a jack plane, as shown in **photo O**. (Even if you cut with the tablesaw, you'll need to clean up by hand.) Mark the bevel onto the underside and side of the table.

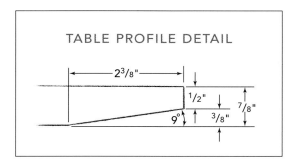

TABLE PROFILE DETAIL

2³/₈"
1/₂"
7/₈"
9°
3/₈"

Sanding the tabletop

Many people find sanding dreary, but I disagree—I love to sand. I find the gradual revelation of grain and color beautiful. Sanding gives you a great deal of information about how the finished piece will look.

1. Starting with the bottom of the tabletop, use a belt sander with a 150-grit belt to remove mill marks, crayon lines, and other marks and to flatten the surface. Keep the belt sander moving! Switch to a random-orbit sander (ROS) with a 180- or 220-grit disk and sand the outside 3 in. to 4 in. of the bottom. You need to sand the outside edge because people will feel under there, but don't sand the center any further.

2. If you're good with the belt sander, use it to sand the bevel. Use a 150-grit belt and then finish with an ROS to 220 grit. If you prefer, use the ROS starting with 80 grit or sand the bevel by hand.

3. Sand the outside edge of the table by hand—a sanding block is easier than a moving machine to hold perpendicular. Start by using a sanding block with 80-grit paper, remove the mill marks, then proceed to the next grit.

4. Turn the tabletop over and belt-sand the top surface with 150 grit to flatten it. Then switch to the ROS and sand to 220 grit.

Sanding the legs and aprons

1. Using the ROS, start with 80 or 100 grit and sand to 220. In machine-sanding, it's easier to reorient the workpiece than to change the paper on the machine. Chalk-mark all of the leg and apron surfaces and sand them with 80 grit, then chalk-mark the surfaces again and sand to 100 grit. This way

if you're interrupted you'll know when you come back that the chalked surfaces still have to be sanded. Continue through the grits. If you prefer, you can sand the leg and apron parts by hand.

2. Sand the insides of the aprons only with the lowest grit to remove construction marks. The tops of the aprons and the tops and bottoms of the legs should not be sanded at all.

3. Next, sand the decorative bead on the aprons by hand. The ROS would flatten the outside edge of the bead and destroy its character.

4. To break the sharp edges and corners, use a sanding block with 220-grit paper and sand each with two or three passes. Softening these edges makes the piece more pleasant to touch without changing its look.

ASSEMBLING AND FINISHING UP

If you're well organized, glue-up and assembly are easy. Have all parts and tools ready and at hand so you don't have to look for anything in the middle of the glue-up.

Practice a dry glue-up before the live run to make sure your clamps are available and preset, your clamp cauls are ready and in place, your glue bottle is filled, and your dead-blow hammer, tape measure, and other tools are at hand. You'll also find out whether you have to prepare a special glue-up area. For example, if the floor in your shop isn't flat, you should prepare a flat surface to glue up the leg and apron assembly.

Finally, the dry glue-up will tell you whether you can do the real glue-up in the time available before the glue grabs. For this table, you have about 10 minutes—less in hot weather—to glue up eight mortise-and-tenon joints and clamp and square the table. If your dry glue-up takes longer, either use glue that stays open longer than PVA (such as bottled hide glue), or build in points where you can stop and gather your wits about you. It's better to find this out during the dry run.

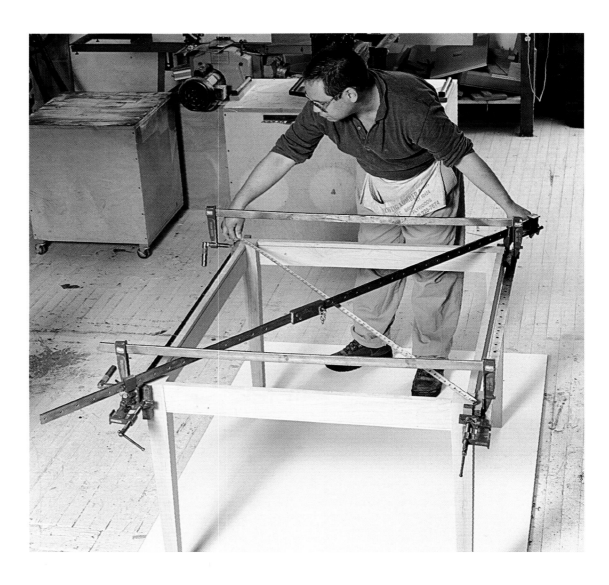

Leg assembly

As I mentioned, it's best to glue up the entire leg and apron structure at once so you can square the whole structure.

1. Glue the shorter aprons to the legs. Using a glue brush, which spreads the glue quickly and easily, spread glue into the two opposing mortises. Since the microclimate in the mortises keeps the glue moist, you have effectively extended your open time.
2. Spread glue onto the tenon faces but not onto the shoulders.
3. Insert the tenons into the mortises, making sure the aprons are oriented correctly.

4. Turn the structure upside down onto a flat surface and knock the bottoms of the legs and the apron next to the legs with a dead-blow hammer. This seats the legs and aprons, making them level.
5. Put clamping cauls in place and clamp between the legs with a single bar clamp. Make sure you hit the spot opposite the middle of the tenon on the outside of the leg so you get even pressure.
6. Measure from the top of one leg to the bottom of the other, then compare that measurement with the opposing measurement. If they're equal, the structure is square. If not, correct the assembly by adjusting the skew of

the clamp to press in on the longer of the two measurements.

7. Glue up the opposite apron and legs and square them.

8. Spread glue into the remaining mortises and on the faces of the remaining tenons. Insert the tenons, and level the tops of the aprons with the tops of the legs. Clamp between the legs and check for square on the two long sides.

9. Check for square across the top and correct it, if necessary, by clamping across the long diagonal (see **photo P** on p. 118).

10. Finally, clean up the glue squeeze-out when it gets rubbery but before it hardens completely.

Installing corner blocks

After the glue dries on the leg assembly—give it a couple of hours to be safe—remove the clamps and install the corner blocks.

1. Make a clamp block with a 45-degree V-groove, fit it outside the corner, and clamp through the corner to hold the corner block in place.

2. Using the predrilled corner block as a jig, drill holes into the aprons using a ⅛-in. drill bit. If the corner blocks are a tad short, knock the inside corners of the legs off with a sharp chisel to fit the blocks snugly into the corners.

3. Spread glue onto the end grain of the corner blocks and onto the apron where the corner blocks abut. Using a 2-in. #10 steel wood screw, screw the corner blocks onto the apron. You don't need to clamp the corner blocks because the screws act as clamps.

Installing tabletop connectors

Now you can attach the top to the legs.

1. Spread a protective blanket over your bench or work surface, then turn the tabletop upside down and put it onto the blanket. Turn the leg structure upside down and put it on the underside of the tabletop. Using a combination gauge, center the leg structure on the tabletop.

2. Insert a tabletop connector into the groove on the apron and mark for the screw holes. You'll need four connectors along the short aprons. Measure ⅜ in. from the tip of a ⅛-in. drill bit, and wrap a piece of masking tape around the drill bit to act as a drill stop. Drill the holes and attach the top.

Checking for flaws

You're not done yet.

1. Taking the tabletop off again, examine every surface and corner. Look for sanding marks that haven't been removed, glue residue that needs cleaning up, and dirt and pencil marks you might have missed. Use a sanding block with 220-grit paper to clean up any errors. I once visited a furniture gallery in New York City to see a $50,000 cabinet made by a famous furniture maker. In the reveal where the leg met the cabinet sides, just at eye level, was a tiny bead of hardened yellow glue. This is your chance not to make that mistake.

2. Put the tabletop back on the table.

3. If you sign your work, now is the time. Construction is done. You're ready for finishing.

Finishing

A kitchen dining table gets a lot of wear and tear. It needs a finish that will look good even after it's taken some abuse. I suggest a combination of tung oil and varnish—you can buy the two already combined. Don't use stain because cherry is already a beautiful color and darkens with age.

Tip: You can remove glue squeeze-out by washing it off immediately with hot water or by letting it dry fully and removing the hardened glue with a sharp chisel or chisel plane. All these methods work; choose whichever is best suited to your operation.

TRESTLE TABLE

Traditionally, trestle tables were knockdown tables, made to be moved in pieces. The Shakers were partial to them because they could carry them easily among their scattered communities. Trestle tables are also useful if your guests are the kind who don't bring their own furniture. These tables can be stored in pieces in the back of a closet and easily reassembled whenever a crowd descends on your household.

This maple table, designed and built by Peter Turner of Portland, Maine, is easy to knock down but much too handsome to be stored out of sight. It's fine for every day if you don't need to seat more than six people on a regular basis. Inspired by an early 17th-century table, it is long and narrow like all traditional trestle tables. Trestles aren't as strong as apron-and-leg assemblies, and if they are made too wide the joints could fail.

You will find this table relatively simple to build—in fact, since the joinery is standard and forgiving, it is nearly as good a choice for a first table project as the kitchen table.

Trestle Table

IN A TRESTLE ASSEMBLY, the stretcher keeps the table from racking while the cleats, or cross braces, distribute load across its width. Keys hold the stretcher securely in place. The cleats are screwed to the table using eight wooden tabletop fasteners that slide in grooves cut into the cleats to permit seasonal wood movement.

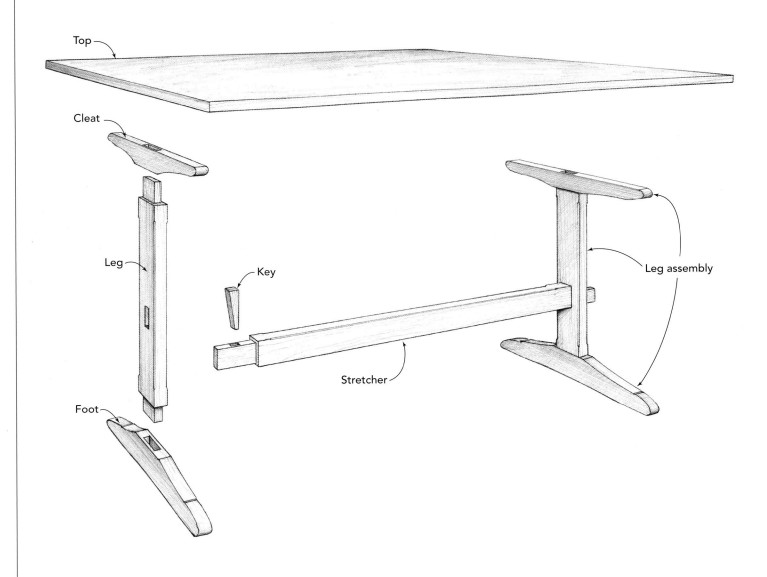

Top

Cleat

Leg

Key

Leg assembly

Foot

Stretcher

TOP VIEW

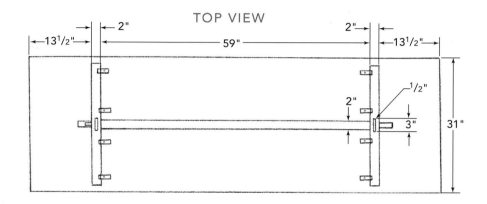

13¹/₂"   2"   59"   2"   13¹/₂"

¹/₂"

2"

3"

31"

SIDE VIEW

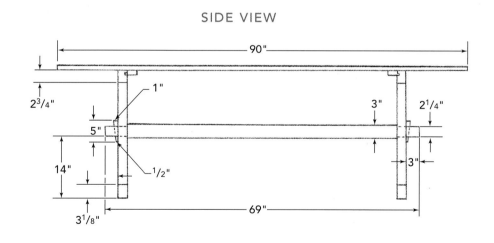

90"

1"

2³/₄"

5"

14"

3¹/₈"

¹/₂"

3"

2¹/₄"

3"

69"

END VIEW

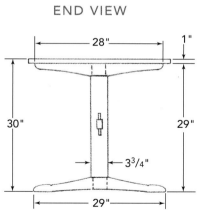

28"

1"

30"

29"

3³/₄"

29"

BUILDING THE TABLE STEP-BY-STEP

CUT LIST FOR TRESTLE TABLE

Tabletop and Trestle Assembly

1	Tabletop	90 in. x 31 in. x 1 in.
1	Stretcher (sometimes called rail)	69 in. x 3 in. x 2 in.
2	Cleats (sometimes called cross braces)	28 in. x 2¾ in. x 2 in.
2	Feet	29 in. x 3⅛ in. x 2 in.
2	Legs	29 in. x 3¾ in. x 2 in.

Connectors

2	Keys	5 in. x 1 in. x ½ in.
8	Tabletop fasteners	2½ in. x 1 in. x ¹⁵⁄₁₆ in.

Hardware

8	Wood screws	#10 x 1½ in.

Peter Turner used curly maple to make this table, but any American hardwood would be suitable. Bird's-eye maple, cherry, curly cherry, walnut, or chestnut would be good choices.

The solid-wood tabletop is like the one on the kitchen table, and the mortise-and-tenon joinery is similar to the joinery used in that table. The only tricky joints are the exposed tenons on the ends of the stretcher and the angled mortises cut into those tenons for the keys.

However, while the kitchen table contained only straight lines, the trestle table has curves on the feet and cleats. The best way to make these curves identical is to use patterns. Patternmaking is a technique that has broad application and will be used in several other projects in this book.

MAKING THE PARTS

Preparing stock

The critical dimensions in this table are the thickness and width of the cleats and feet and the thickness and length of the legs. On the other dimensions, you can be off by a mile and it won't matter.

1. After the wood is jointed, plane all of the tabletop boards at the same time to achieve a consistent thickness. Leave enough extra length in the boards to give yourself plenty of options in matching them.

2. Rip the feet, cleats, legs, and stretcher to rough width on a tablesaw, then stand these pieces on edge and plane them to width using a planer. Using a planer rather than a tablesaw to "rip" boards to final width is unusual, but it gives more accurate and consistent results. Thin, wide boards like the tabletop boards would be too unstable to pass through the planer safely. But the other pieces are thick enough to stand on edge, so you shouldn't have any difficulty running them through the planer.

3. Pass all trestle parts through the planer to establish a final 2-in. thickness.

4. Crosscut the cleats, feet, legs, and stretcher to finished length.

5. Don't cut the tabletop fasteners (which connect the cleats to the tabletop and allow for wood movement) or keys to length yet. Simply mill a board about 25 in. long by 1 in. wide by ¹⁵⁄₁₆ in. thick for the fasteners, and one about 14 in. long by a little more than 1 in. wide by a little less than ½ in. thick for the keys.

6. Rip all of the tabletop boards to width on the tablesaw and joint the sawn edges. Some woodworkers glue up boards with edges directly off the tablesaw. However, I find I'm

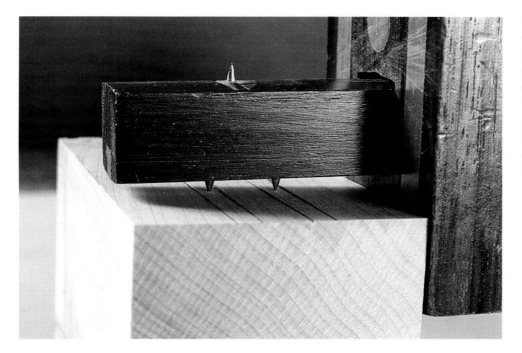

Photo A: It is important to center the mortises on the feet and cleats. Using a piece of scrap the width of the workpieces, mark from both edges, then reset the marking gauge so it splits the resulting lines. Repeat until the lines from the marking gauge overlay when marked from both edges.

less likely to get gaps between boards when they've been edge-jointed.

Building the tabletop

The success of this design, as with all solid-wood tabletops, depends on getting a good grain match. Mix and match your boards to get the best match you can.

1. Start by cutting clamp blocks and setting up your clamps. Do a dry glue-up to make sure everything is in place. Using PVA glue, spread glue on both edges of the board and glue up the tabletop. Alternate your clamps top and bottom. Place waxed paper between the clamps and the tabletop so the iron in the clamps won't discolor the wood.
2. Leave the top in clamps overnight to allow the glue to cure, then remove the clamps and clean up the glue drips with a scraper.
3. Rip the top to width on the tablesaw and crosscut the panel to length. If your tablesaw can't accommodate large panels, use a circular saw run against a straightedge.

Making the joinery

It is always preferable to cut joinery while the workpieces are still square.

1. Mark out and cut the mortises on the cleats and feet, then on the legs (see **photo A**). I use a dedicated mortising machine for these cuts, but you could use a mortising chisel or a plunge router and template as well.
2. Next, mark out and cut the leg tenons using a tenon jig. Either make a jig for this purpose or use a commercially available jig.
3. Mark out and cut the stretcher tenons. Since these tenons are 5 in. long and the maximum depth of cut for a 10-in. tablesaw blade is only about 3⅛ in., you can't cut them out completely using the tenon jig. The approach I use is to cut a shoulder at the 5-in. length, then cut a second shoulder at the 3-in. length and use the tenon jig to cut out the first 3 in. (see **photo B**). This leaves you 2 in. more to the original shoulder, which you can cut either by using a bandsaw and a fence or by using a tablesaw and dado set (see **photo C**). In either case, cut the remaining 2 in. a little fat and then clean up the waste using a sharp chisel

Tip: If you're using figured wood, wet the stock before you put it through the planer to reduce chipout and make the fibers more pliable. Wet a rag, squeeze out the excess, dampen the wood, then plane.

Photo B: Leave the tenon a little tight. As an exposed decorative joint, it will be sanded and finished. The sanding will bring it down to the correct dimension so that it slips in and out of the mortise easily.

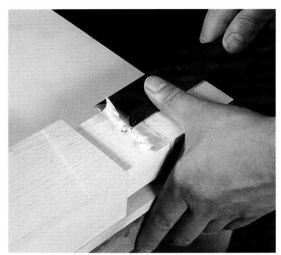

Photo D: Use the 3 in. of the tenon cut with the tenoning jig as a flat surface jigging a sharp chisel. Bring to level the 2 in. of the tenon cut with the dado or bandsaw. Then using a sanding block, hand-sand it to final size.

Photo C: For extra-long tenons, use a bandsaw to reach the area the tablesaw and tenon jig can't get to. Leave the shoulder a bit heavy and clean it up using a chisel.

and a shoulder plane, jigging the tool against the clean faces cut by the tablesaw (see photo D).

4. Once you have cut the tenons for the stretcher, cut mortises in them for the keys. These mortises should be slightly recessed into the leg surface so that when the keys are inserted they will maintain tension in the stretcher. To achieve this recessing, mark the inner edge of the mortise at a distance from the shoulder equal to $\frac{1}{16}$ in. less than the thickness of the leg (see the illustration on the facing page). Final sanding will remove about $\frac{1}{32}$ in. from the surfaces, leaving the mortise edge very slightly recessed. Even if you cut these mortises using a mortising machine, cut the angle by hand with a mortising chisel and mallet. Clamp a piece of scrap to the underside of the tenon so the chisel will go through the tenon cleanly. Make sure the wider parts of both mortises face the top of the stretcher.

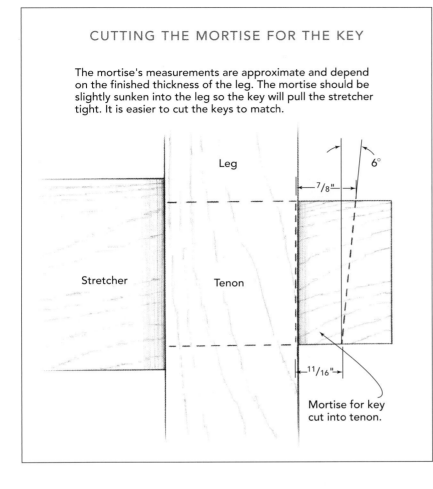

CUTTING THE MORTISE FOR THE KEY

The mortise's measurements are approximate and depend on the finished thickness of the leg. The mortise should be slightly sunken into the leg so the key will pull the stretcher tight. It is easier to cut the keys to match.

Leg

6°

$7/8$"

Stretcher

Tenon

$11/16$"

Mortise for key cut into tenon.

Tip: Tenons that are exposed as decorative joints should be fine-tuned by hand, rather than cut to fit off the machinery like other joints. An exposed tenon must fit easily through its mortise so it can be taken apart, but it can't be too loose. It should be a heavy $1/16$ in. less in thickness and width than the tenon you would make for a glue joint. Size the tenon so it's a little too large, then sand, scrape, or plane it down to the correct size.

Making the cleats and feet

Making the groove for the tabletop fasteners

1. Place a $1/2$-in. straight bit into your router and position a fence $1/2$ in. away from the bit.
2. Cut grooves in the cleats, stopping and starting the cut approximately 2 in. from the beginning and end of each workpiece.

Making the curved surfaces

To make the curved surfaces of the cleats and feet, transfer the illustration shown on p. 128 onto the workpiece, then cut the parts out.

1. Make a full-sized version of the illustration on p. 128, which shows scaled 1-in. squares overlaying the cleats and feet (the two curves are slightly different, so you'll need to copy both of them). You can enlarge the drawings at a copy shop or scan them into a computer drawing program that can enlarge them. You could also transfer the drawings by hand, marking full-size 1-in. squares on a piece of paper and matching up where the drawing lines cross the squares. You only have to do half of each drawing because the cleats and feet are symmetrical.
2. To make the curves, trace the full-size drawings onto the workpieces and use a bandsaw to cut them out. This is the easiest and fastest method since there are only four pieces. If you don't have a bandsaw, you can cut the curves by hand using a coping saw. Clean up the curves with a rasp or spokeshave and sand them smooth. Since these curves are purely decorative and not structural, making exact copies is not critical.

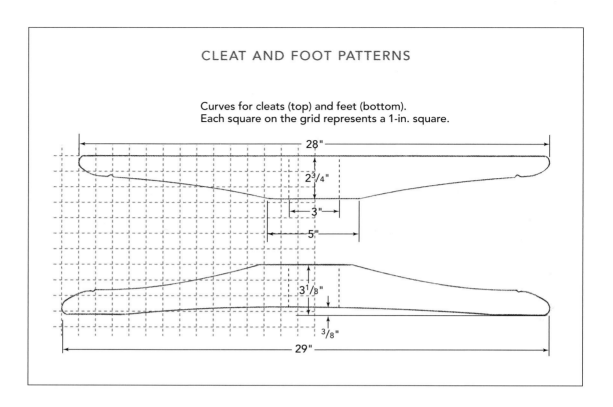

CLEAT AND FOOT PATTERNS

Curves for cleats (top) and feet (bottom).
Each square on the grid represents a 1-in. square.

28"

2³/4"

3"

5"

3¹/8"

³/8"

29"

MODIFYING THE SHAPES OF THE TRESTLE PARTS

Of all the tables in this book, none allows for such easy modification as the trestle table. Because the curves on the cleats and feet are decorative, they can be changed to suit your fancy. Bead details can be changed or removed. The shape of the leg can also be changed, as can the placement of the stretcher—the Shakers preferred to raise it to the top of the leg, where diners' knees wouldn't hit it. The only critical dimensions remain the width of the uncut cleats and feet and the length of the leg. The sum of these three dimensions, plus the thickness of the top, makes up the height of the table. Feel free to experiment with your own designs. The technique for making a trestle table described here remains the same.

The method I used takes longer than simply bandsawing, but it allows you to make any number of identical curved pieces. It requires a bandsaw and a drill press and makes use of a pattern and a cutting tool to follow that pattern (see "Making Patterns" on the facing page). It's a good technique to know and one that's used in one form or another for several projects in this book.

3. Using sprayed contact cement, glue the plan for the foot to a piece of scrap sheet good (I used a ¾-in. piece of MDF).

4. Bandsaw out the waste, leaving just a little over the line of the plan. Don't cut out the bead; just continue the line past it.

5. File, rasp, and sand with a sanding block until you have a perfectly fair curve. Even a little dip in the pattern will show up on the finished part, so take the time to make the pattern exactly as you want the part to look (see **photo E**).

MAKING PATTERNS

Tablesaw fences, miter gauges, and even the flat tops of the tablesaw and router table act as jigs to force the workpiece into a defined configuration with the cutterhead. Normally these jigs force the workpiece into a rectilinear orientation with the cutterhead. But if you want to make identical curved parts or make two halves of a symmetrical curve identical, you must make a curved "fence" that an appropriate cutterhead can follow. This curved fence is called a pattern.

Typically, patterns are made from sheet material. For a pattern that you plan to use many times, ¼-in. or ½-in. clear Plexiglas® is an ideal material. Plexiglas mills easily using standard woodworking tools and stands up well to repeated use. If you're going to use the pattern only a few times, almost any material will do. I use whatever piece of scrap I have available, usually MDF or tempered Masonite®.

Many tools can be used to follow the pattern. Most common is a router bit with a bearing. In this project, I used a bandsaw with a shopmade guide and a sanding drum with a bearing.

Photo E: **Leave the line when cutting out the waste. Then use a sanding block to sand down to the line, fairing the curve as you go.**

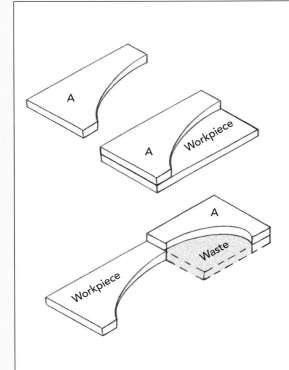

You can duplicate the "A" piece by using it as a pattern to make multiple copies. This is called a full pattern. You can also use "A" to make a workpiece symmetrical by simply turning it upside down. When used in this fashion, "A" is called a half pattern. Making the original pattern is the most time-consuming and difficult part of the duplication process. If you can use a half pattern or even a quarter pattern, you'll work faster and achieve more consistent results.

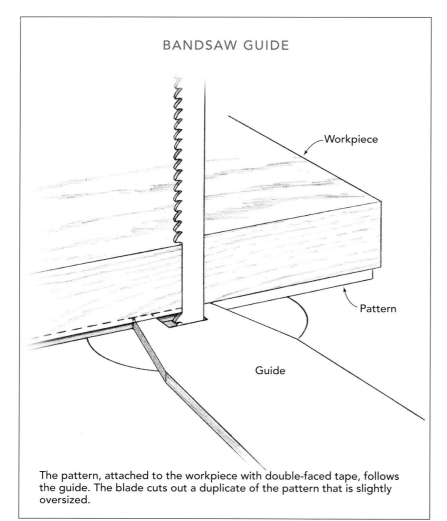

BANDSAW GUIDE

Workpiece

Pattern

Guide

The pattern, attached to the workpiece with double-faced tape, follows the guide. The blade cuts out a duplicate of the pattern that is slightly oversized.

Photo F: The pattern taped to the bottom of the workpiece rubs against the Plexiglas guide, creating identical pieces that can be easily cleaned up using a drum sander.

6. Repeat the process for the cleat pattern.

7. Using double-faced tape, attach the two completed patterns to the workpieces.

8. Set up the pattern-following guide on the bandsaw as shown in the illustration above. Adjust the guide to leave about $\frac{1}{32}$ in. of waste—just enough so you can remove the mill marks during cleanup.

9. Use the bandsaw with the pattern-following guide to rough out the first two parts: half of the first foot and half of the first cleat. Don't remove the patterns yet (see **photo F**).

10. To clean up the bandsaw mill marks, mount a drum sander with a bearing onto the drill press for final shaping. Depending on whether the bearing is on the top or bottom, you may need a secondary table on top of the drill-press table for the drum to fit into. Using a coarse-grit drum, sand the pieces flush with the pattern (see **photo G**).

11. Remove the patterns, flip them, and reattach them to the other halves of the workpieces. Repeat the bandsaw pattern-cutting and sanding-drum work to complete the first foot and first cleat. To make the second foot and second cleat, repeat the entire process.

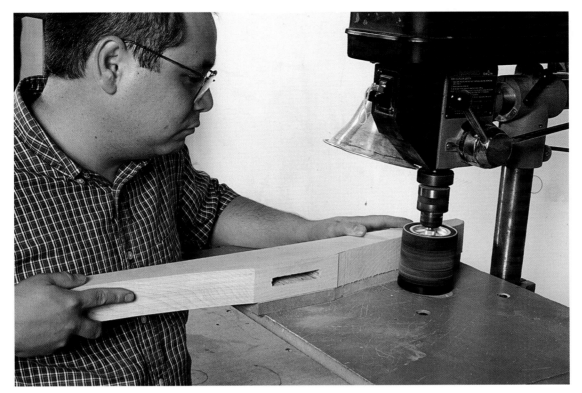

Photo G: The Robo-sander™ has a bottom-mounted bearing that rubs against the pattern, sanding the workpiece to the precise shape.

Tip: Be especially careful when sanding end grain with the Robo-sander—it's possible to get a kickback in this area.

MAKING THE BEADING DETAILS

The beading detail on the stretcher and legs is made using a ¼-in. corebox bit and a V-groove jig.

Making the jig

1. Tilt the tablesaw blade at a 45-degree angle, then put a rip blade onto the saw and make the first cut to full depth.

2. Flip the board and lower the blade so a sliver of material will be left after you make the second cut (see **photo H**). This prevents the cutoff from kicking back. Make the second cut and break off the V-shaped piece of waste, then clean up the groove with a chisel.

3. In the middle of the jig, drill a hole slightly bigger than ¼ in.—the exact size doesn't matter.

Photo H: To make the V-groove jig, set the tablesaw blade to 45 degrees, cut all the way through the board, then glue both halves to a thin substrate.

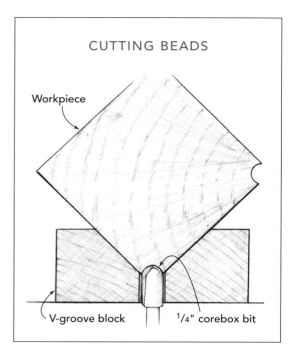

CUTTING BEADS

Workpiece

V-groove block   1/4" corebox bit

Photo I: Using masking tape, mark start and stop lines on the V-groove block using a combination square. You can start and stop when the lines align with the shoulder.

Cutting the beads

1. With a ¼-in. corebox bit in the router on the router table, center the bit in the hole of the V-groove jig and clamp the jig to the router table. Raise the bit to the proper height, and make a few test cuts in scrapwood until you get the results you want.

2. Cut the beads in the stretcher and legs (see **photo I**). To achieve consistent results, make each bead in one pass. Be careful not to burn the treatment at the end of the cut.

3. To make the bead detail on the feet and cleats, clamp a straightedge to each piece and rout the bead. Again, make each bead in one pass.

KEYS AND FASTENERS

Making the tabletop fasteners

1. On your tablesaw, install a dado set that will plow a ⅜-in. dado, and raise the dado set to ¹⁵⁄₃₂ in.

2. Using a miter gauge, cut dadoes into the tabletop fastener board at 18 in., 12¾ in., 7½ in., and 2¼ in.

3. Change the blade in the tablesaw to a crosscut blade, and set a stop on your miter gauge fence for 2½ in. Cut off eight 2½-in. tabletop fasteners.

4. Drill a screw hole on the top of each fastener.

Making the keys

Because you cut the mortises for the keys by hand, you should also cut the keys by hand and fit them individually. The blank you milled for the keys should be slightly narrower than ½ in. so the keys can be inserted and removed easily. Keep the blank a little wide until you fit the keys.

1. Cut the keys long (about 7 in.).

2. Using a bevel gauge, measure the angle in the first mortise. Transfer that angle to the workpiece.

3. Cut out the waste using a bandsaw. Using a block plane, trim and clean up the angle.

4. Test-fit the key into the mortise. When the fit is correct, measure 1 in. from the top and bottom of the tenon onto the key. Cut the key to length at those two points.

5. Repeat for the second key.

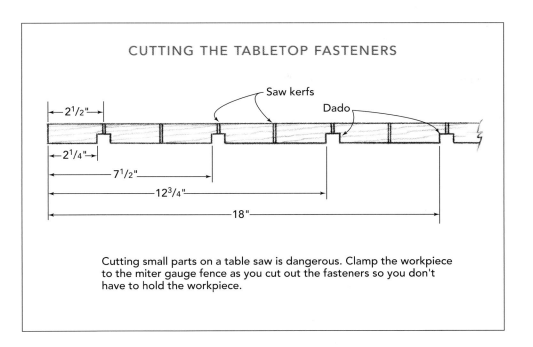

CUTTING THE TABLETOP FASTENERS

Saw kerfs

Dado

2½"

2¼"

7½"

12¾"

18"

Cutting small parts on a table saw is dangerous. Clamp the workpiece to the miter gauge fence as you cut out the fasteners so you don't have to hold the workpiece.

ASSEMBLING AND FINISHING UP

Assembling the leg structures

In most projects, you would sand all of the pieces before assembling them. On this table, however, if a mortise on a foot or cleat is not perfectly centered, the sides of the legs won't be level with the foot and cleat. You want to sand the pieces to level *after* the joints are together so you can see where the discrepancies are.

1. Assemble both leg structures dry to make sure everything fits together properly. Use waxed paper between the leg and glue blocks, as shown in **photo J**, so the blocks don't stick to the leg. Dry-clamp the assembly to make sure you have everything in order.

2. Spread PVA glue into the cleat and foot mortises on one leg structure and then onto the tenons on the leg. Insert the tenons and

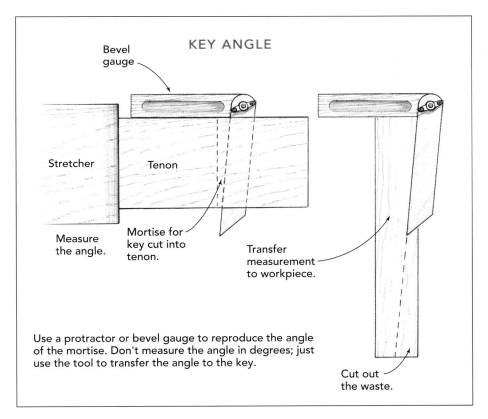

KEY ANGLE

Bevel gauge

Stretcher

Tenon

Measure the angle.

Mortise for key cut into tenon.

Transfer measurement to workpiece.

Cut out the waste.

Use a protractor or bevel gauge to reproduce the angle of the mortise. Don't measure the angle in degrees; just use the tool to transfer the angle to the key.

Photo J: Measuring across the diagonals ensures a square trestle. When the two diagonals are equal, the leg structures will be square.

knock them home with a dead-blow hammer. Clamp the structure, making sure all of the joints are tight. Repeat for the other leg structure.

3. Measure for square across the diagonals and correct any deviation.

Sanding

1. Using a plane or belt sander, flatten the bottom of the tabletop. If you use a belt sander, start with a coarse enough grit to remove material quickly. When the underside is flat, flip the tabletop and flatten the top. Change belts to 150 grit and sand both the top and the

Photo K: Having a variety of shopmade and commercial sanding blocks in different shapes and sizes is useful when hand-sanding.

bottom. Then, using a random-orbit sander, run through the grits, sanding the top to 220.

2. Sand the sides of the table by hand. Using a sanding block, start with 80 grit to remove the mill marks. Run through the grits to 220 grit.

3. With a 220-grit sanding block, break all of the edges of the tabletop.

4. Using a random-orbit sander, start with 80-grit paper to remove the mill marks on the flat faces of the legs and stretcher. Run through the grits to 220 grit. Don't sand the tops or bottoms of the feet or cleats; this would alter the heights of the leg structures.

5. To sand the cleat and foot curves, use a curved, hard rubber sanding tool and sand by hand. Once again, start with 80 grit to remove the mill marks and run through the grits to 220 grit. If you're using a hand-rubbed finish, wet the surfaces after sanding at 220 grit, let them dry, and sand at 320 grit. Don't use the sanding drum without the pattern and bearing to sand these curves—you'll sand dips into the curve. Also, never hand-sand without a tool. You can't level the surfaces properly if you're holding the sandpaper in your bare hand (see **photo K**).

Final assembly

1. Lay a blanket on your workbench, then turn the tabletop upside down on it.

2. Assemble the trestle structure, knocking the keys into place with a light tap from a dead-blow hammer.

3. Turn the trestle upside down and center it on the tabletop. Put the tabletop fasteners in place, and use an awl through the screw holes to mark the screw placement.

4. Remove the tabletop fasteners and drill the screw holes, using a piece of masking tape on the drill bit as a depth gauge. Don't drill through the tabletop! Replace the fasteners and screw them in place.

Final check

Turn the table right side up and, with a sanding block in one hand, inspect every surface with your hand and eye. Remove any glue beads, mill marks, or other blemishes you may have missed. Sign your work if you want to.

Finishing

Peter Turner originally finished this table with wiping varnish.

VINEYARD TABLE

The vineyard table is almost as old a design as the trestle table, dating back 300 years or more. Some sources claim these tables were used by grape pickers in French vineyards for working lunches, while others say they were used in wineries for wine tastings. Both stories may be true, since the tables fold easily for storage and transportation. The central "harp" spins around on one set of dowels and the tabletop flips on a second set of dowels to create a remarkably compact package.

Neal White of San Jose, California, designed and built this table as a second table for family gatherings at his house. He found it too useful to stow away between occasions, and it's taken up permanent residence in his living room.

The vineyard table is similar to the trestle table on p. 120 except that hinges have replaced the joints between the legs and cleats, and the tabletop is held level by a beautiful harp-shaped support.

I love the look of the figured white oak in this table, but the original tables were made by carpenters from whatever woods were available locally.

Like all trestle tables, this one is easily modified to suit the builder's taste and talents. Vineyard tabletops are typically round or elliptical, but you can make the top for this table in almost any size or shape as long as the width clears the feet when the table is flipped.

Vineyard Table

THE VINEYARD TABLE is similar to a trestle table in construction, except that the cleats are hinged instead of joined to the legs, allowing the tabletop to flip down or be removed for storage and transportation. The harp-shaped structure pivots outward to support the tabletop when the tabletop is set up for use.

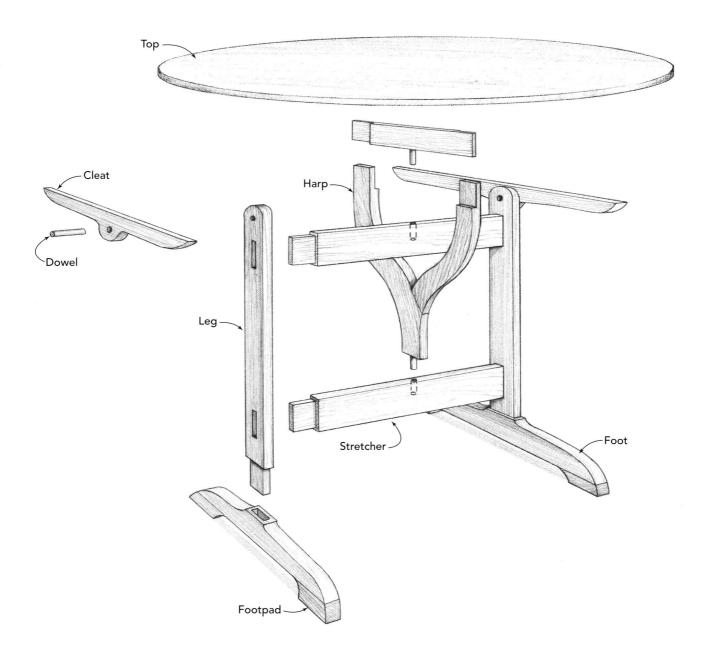

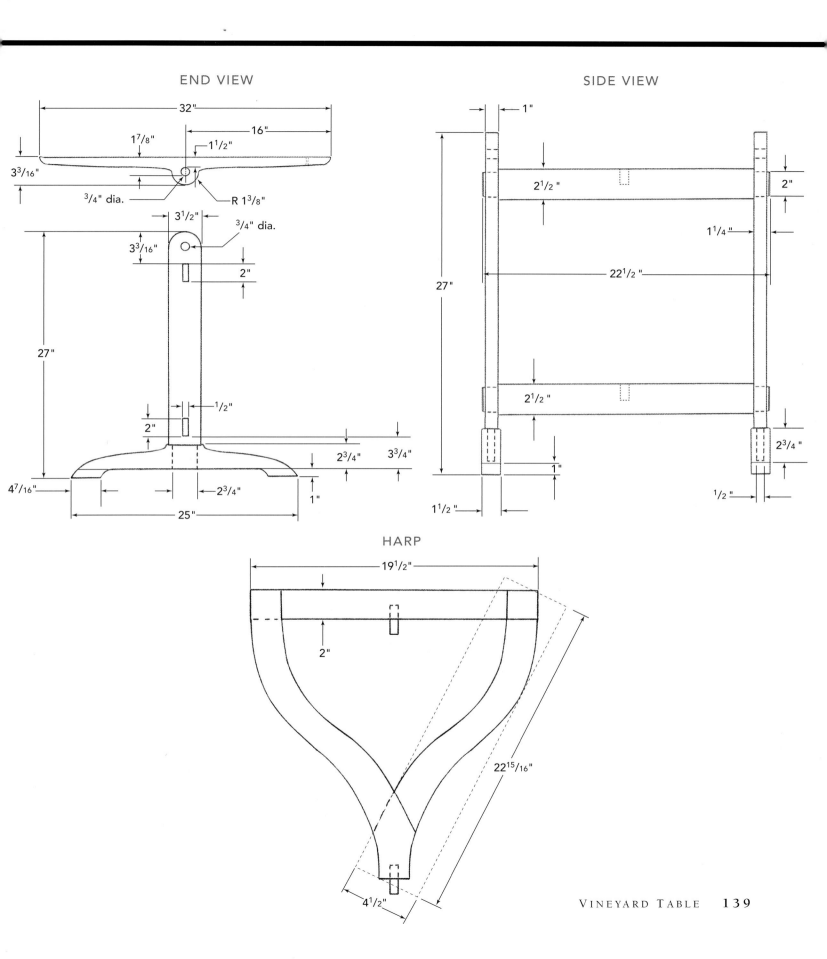

END VIEW

SIDE VIEW

HARP

BUILDING THE TABLE STEP-BY-STEP

CUT LIST FOR VINEYARD TABLE

Tabletop and Leg Assembly

1	Tabletop	60 in. x 46 in. x 1 in.
2	Legs	27 in. x 3½ in. x 1 in.
2	Feet	25 in. x 2¾ in. x 1½ in.
4	Footpads[1]	5 in. x 1 in. x 1½ in.
2	Stretchers	22½ in. x 2½ in. x 1 in.
2	Cleats	32 in. x 3³⁄₁₆ in. x 1 in.
2	Harp legs	22¹⁵⁄₁₆ in. x 4½ in. x 1 in.
1	Harp cross bar	19½ in. x 2 in. x 1 in.
2	Leveling blocks[1]	5 in. x 1⅜ in. x 2 in.

Hardware

2	Hardwood wooden dowels[2]	¾ in. diameter x 3 in.
2	Hardwood wooden dowels[2]	½ in. diameter x 3 in.
4	Steel wood screws	1½ in. by #10

[1]The leveling blocks and footpads can be cut from the foot cutoffs.
[2]See Sources on p. 282.

The elaborate pattern-cutting techniques described for other projects in this book can be used for this table. However, since vineyard tables are traditionally simple, carpenter-made furniture, I've chosen to stick to basic tools and techniques. A jigsaw, coping saw, or bandsaw is all you need to cut out the parts; scrapers, planes, and sandpaper can be used to sculpt them to final shape.

Mortise-and-tenon joints hold the legs and stretchers together, but the lap joint, a very basic joint, is used for the harp pieces, and doweled hinges are used for the moving parts. Another new but simple technique introduced here is drawing the ellipse for the tabletop.

The most challenging task is to fit the pieces together so that the tabletop opens and closes easily and remains level when open. Since every table is slightly different, adjustments to the dowels and leveling blocks should be made dynamically.

MAKING THE PARTS

Preparing the stock

The critical dimensions in this table are the lengths of the legs, the widths of the feet, and the lengths of the stretchers. If these aren't equal, the trestle won't be square. In addition, the width of the tabletop must clear the feet when the table is flipped up for storage. The shape of the tabletop determines how much clearance you have. Rectangular tables have about 45 in. of clearance, while round tables have nearly 49 in. because the curved shape clears the feet.

1. Begin with 8/4 rough stock for the feet and footpads and 6/4 rough stock for all other parts. Although 5/4 might work, you would risk not being able to get all the parts out.
2. Crosscut the trestle parts 2 in. oversize in length. Face-joint and edge-joint the boards and plane them to finished 1-in. thickness, then rip the parts to finished width.
3. Cut all tabletop boards to the same length. When cutting to rough length, leave them several inches oversize. Face-joint and edge the boards, then rip them to width and plane to finished thickness.

Making the tabletop

1. Glue up boards for the tabletop in a rectangular shape, arranging and aligning the boards to get the best match for color and grain. Clamp the tabletop, using plenty of clamps (see "How Many Clamps?" on the facing page), and allow the glue to cure overnight.

HOW MANY CLAMPS?

The object of clamping is to put pressure on all of the surfaces being glued. Imagine clamp pressure as radiating 45 degrees on either side from the point of application. If the clamps are spaced too far apart, as shown in illustration "a" below, there may be little or no pressure at some points on the glueline. Moving the outer clamps toward the center, as shown in "b," solves the problem in the middle but creates new low-pressure areas near the edges. Some woodworkers recommend springing the boards so they meet at the ends but gap slightly in the center. The board acts as a combination spring and caul, closing the gaps. I prefer using enough clamps to provide pressure at all points on the gluelines, as shown in "c." In this example, I needed five clamps to get enough pressure. With a panel the same size and narrower boards, I would have needed even more clamps.

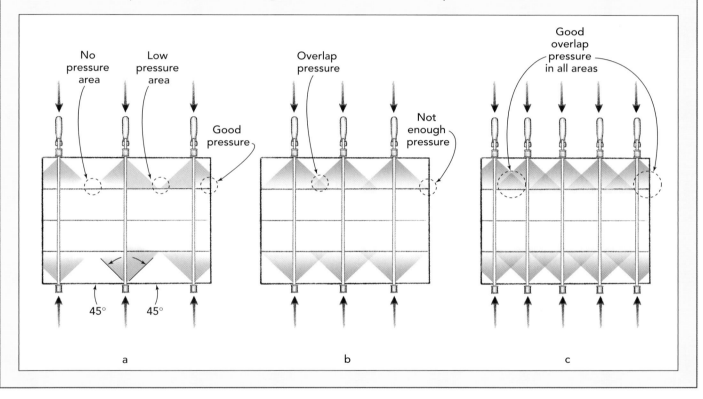

2. After the glue cures, remove the clamps and place the tabletop upside down on your workbench.

3. Draw an ellipse on the underside of the tabletop as described in "Drawing an Ellipse" on p. 142, and cut out the ellipse using a jig-saw or coping saw.

4. Finish shaping the ellipse with a belt sander held against the edge or a sanding block with 80-grit sandpaper.

Making the feet

1. Cut the feet to final length.

2. Mark out the ½-in. mortises with a mortis-ing gauge, making sure the mortise is centered on the foot, and cut them out with a mortising machine or chisel.

3. Glue the footpads to the feet and allow the glue to cure overnight (see **photo A** on p. 143).

DRAWING AN ELLIPSE

Every ellipse has two foci, or focus points. The sum of the distances to the two foci is equal from any point on the ellipse. Following this definition, you can lay out an ellipse with two nails, a pencil, and a piece of string. By varying the position of the nails and the length of the string, you can generate an infinite number of ellipses.

To generate the ellipse for this table, draw a 38½-in. line on the underside of the tabletop, centered along the long axis.

Place a small finishing nail at each end of the line to mark the foci. Next, draw a line crossing the center of the first line at right angles. Mark a point 23 in. along this line—this will be the end of the table's short axis. Take a piece of string about 100 in. long, tie it in a loop, and put the loop around the nails. Adjust the position of the knot so that a pencil held against the taut string will hit the point you've marked. (The loop of string, once adjusted, should measure 98½ in.) Finally, draw the ellipse.

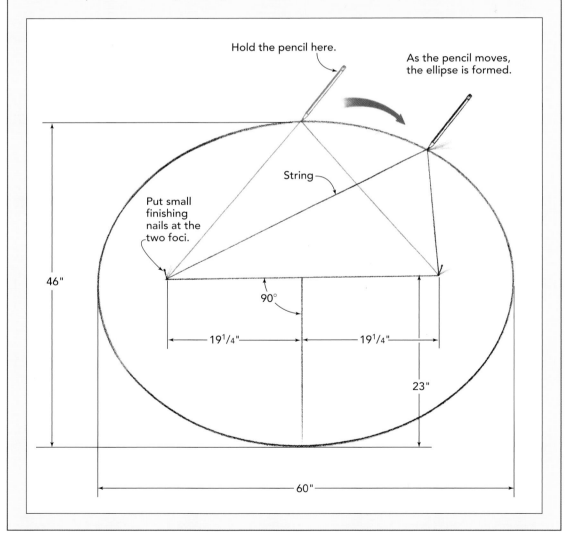

Hold the pencil here.

As the pencil moves, the ellipse is formed.

String

Put small finishing nails at the two foci.

46"

90°

19¹/₄"   19¹/₄"

23"

60"

4. Enlarge the illustration below to full size or create a pattern of your own, then trace it onto the feet.

5. Using a bandsaw or coping saw, cut out the feet, then plane, scrape, or sand the edges smooth.

Making the legs

1. Cut both legs to final length.

2. Mark out the mortises for the top and bottom stretchers, then cut these with a mortising machine or mortising chisel.

3. At the top of each leg, lay out a 3½-in. square. Draw diagonals between the corners to find the center of the square. Use a compass to draw a half-circle at the top of each leg (see **photo B**).

4. Mark the shoulders of the bottom tenons and use a tablesaw to establish the shoulder line.

5. Using a tenon jig and the tablesaw, remove the tenon cheeks. Sneak up on the final width so the tenons will fit snugly into the mortises of the feet without binding.

Photo A: **Clamp across the joints to register the sides of the footpads with the sides of the feet.**

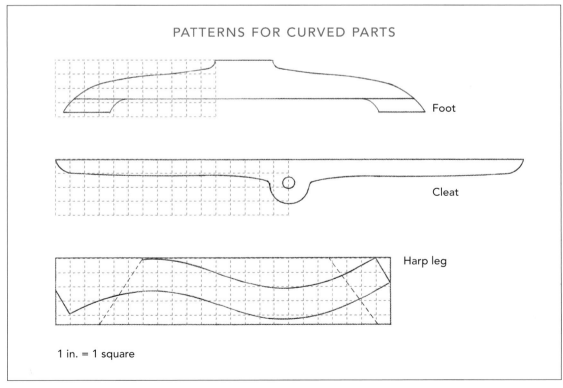

PATTERNS FOR CURVED PARTS

Foot

Cleat

Harp leg

1 in. = 1 square

Photo B: Mark the outside circle before drilling the pivot hole.

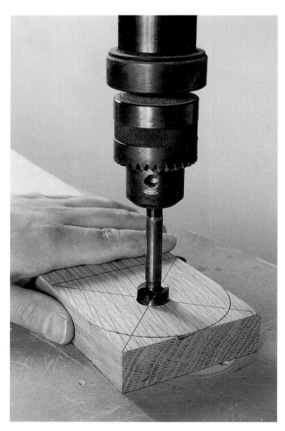

Photo C: Forstner bits leave clean entry holes even in difficult wood. Back up the exit hole with a piece of scrap so the exit is clean.

6. Use a bandsaw or coping saw to cut out the half-circle.

7. Sand the half-circle to shape using a sanding block with 80-grit paper.

8. Drill out a ¾-in. dowel hole at the marked center, using a Forstner bit as shown in **photo C**. Don't use a paddle or high-speed bit for this hole—you won't get clean or accurate results.

Making the stretchers

1. Cut the two stretchers to length.

2. Find the center of the top edge for both stretchers, then drill ½-in. holes 1 in. deep at both spots to accept the pivot dowels on the harp.

3. Mark the shoulders on one end of a stretcher. Set a stop on your miter gauge, and cut the shoulders for all four tenons on your tablesaw.

4. Using a tenon jig, cut the tenons. The tenons should fit snugly into the leg mortises. You don't want a loose fit here, so sneak up on the fit until it's just right.

USING A MORTISING CHISEL

A mortising chisel is thicker than an ordinary chisel; the extra thickness allows the chisel to self-jig once the mortise is started. It also absorbs the stresses of mortising. You can order the chisels, and the wooden mallet used with them, by mail from specialty tool catalogs (see Sources on p. 282).

Body positioning is the trick to successful use of a mortising chisel. Just as you tune woodworking machinery, you must also train your body to use hand tools.

Start by laying out the mortise with a marking gauge, combination square, and marking knife. The knife lines are important because they delineate the top and bottom of the mortise. Clamp the workpiece to your bench so that it's on your right side if you're right-handed or on your left side if you're left-handed. Position the chisel at the far end of the mortise with the bevel facing you, and hold it with your nondominant hand. Align your body with the workpiece (see the top photo). If you do this correctly, the chisel will be vertical.

Holding the wooden mallet in your dominant hand, hit the chisel hard with a single whack. Don't be shy and tap-tap-tap on the chisel. The chisel should cut ⅛ in. or more into the wood with each blow. Next, reposition the chisel ⅛ in. closer to you and whack it again.

Pry the chisel toward you, and the chip between the first and second cut will come out (see the bottom photo). Keep working down the mortise until you get to the near end.

Reverse the chisel so the bevel faces away from you, then cut the other shoulder of the mortise square. Now reverse the chisel to its original position and go back to the far end of the mortise. Continue the mortising operation until the mortise is deep enough. The width of the chisel acts to jig the tool in the mortise that's already cut. If you position your body correctly, and you aren't shy about whacking the chisel, hand-mortising can be very fast and accurate.

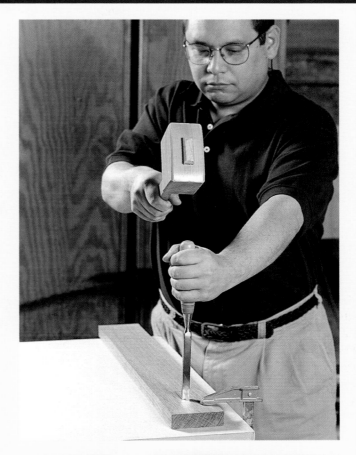

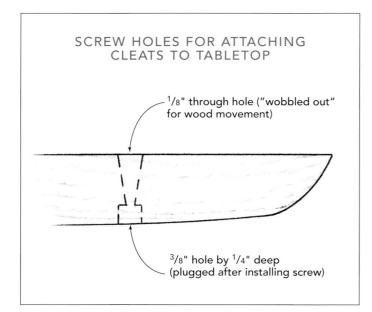

SCREW HOLES FOR ATTACHING
CLEATS TO TABLETOP

1/8" through hole ("wobbled out"
for wood movement)

3/8" hole by 1/4" deep
(plugged after installing screw)

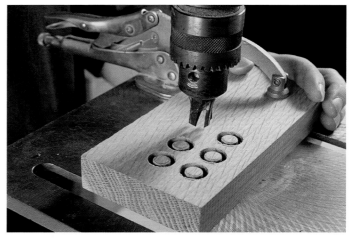

Photo D: **If you cut your own plugs, you can match the
grain direction and make the plugs almost invisible.
Clamp the stock to the drill-press table so the workpiece
doesn't spin.**

*Tip: For the harp
legs, the two lap
joints are on the
same side. The two
halves of the harp
are identical.*

Making the cleats

1. Mark the positions for the pivot holes.
2. Mark the positions for the 1⅜-in. radius circles.
3. Either enlarge the illustration on p. 143 to full size or make up your own shape, then mark the pattern onto the cleats.
4. With a ¾-in. Forstner bit, drill out the pivot holes.
5. Saw out the pattern using a bandsaw or coping saw, getting as close as you dare to the line. Mill up to your lines using planes, scrapers, and sanding blocks with 80-grit sandpaper.
6. Mark for and drill the four tabletop attachment screw holes on the cleat bottoms. First drill the plug recesses ⅜ in. in diameter by ¼ in. deep and 3 in. from each cleat end. Through the center of each recess, drill a hole ⅛ in. in diameter all the way through the cleat, "wobbling out" the bottom slightly to allow for seasonal wood movement (see the illustration above).
7. Using a ⅜-in. plug cutter as shown in **photo D**, make four plugs from scrap.

Making the harp

The harp is assembled with lap joints that are glued but not screwed or pinned together. Cutting them can be complicated because they are angled, but if you follow the sequence you won't have any trouble. As always, cut the joinery while the workpieces are still square, then cut out the shapes.

1. Practice this joint on scrapwood first. Put a dado set on your tablesaw, and using two pieces of scrap the same thickness as the harp pieces, mark half the width on each of them. Raise the dado set so it just meets the half-width line, and make two cuts in the scrap using a miter gauge (see **photo E**). Test the joint, adjusting the height of the dado set until you achieve a perfect fit. Adjusting height dynamically is much more accurate than trying to measure. Now that the scrap joint fits, you're ready to cut your money joints.
2. Cut the two harp legs to length.
3. Rotate your miter gauge counterclockwise, setting it to a heavy 61 degrees. Set a stop block on the miter gauge, and cut the shoulder of the lap joint for the top joint on one leg. Repeat the process for the second leg, then

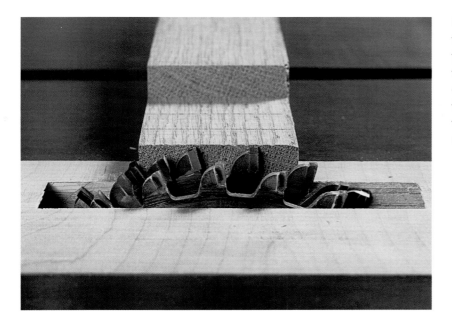

Photo E: **Cut the joint slightly thick, then turn the practice piece over to see the difference between the blade and the remaining work.**

remove the stop block and cut out the waste on both top joints.

4. Rotate your miter gauge clockwise, setting it to a heavy 57 degrees. Set a stop block on the miter gauge, and cut the shoulder of the lap joint for the bottom joint. Repeat for the second harp leg, then remove the stop block and cut out the waste on both joints.

5. Glue the two harp legs together while they're still square.

6. Now that the bottom joint is finished, mark out and cut the harp shape. Enlarge the illustration on p. 143 to full size or make your own design and trace it onto the workpiece. Cut out the design using a bandsaw or coping saw.

7. Make sure the shoulders of the two top laps are perpendicular. Set the fence on your table saw so you just slightly trim the front shoulder, then flip the harp and trim the other leg (see **photo F** on p. 148).

8. Measure across the top of the legs of the harp and cut the cross bar to final length.

9. The measurement for the two laps on the cross bar probably won't be identical, since bandsawing out the harp is not an accurate method of making symmetrical parts, so take a measurement for one of the shoulders from one leg of the harp using a combination

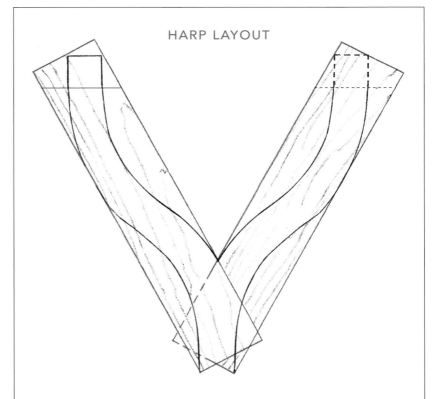

HARP LAYOUT

Glue up the workpieces while they're still square. That way you can glue up across the joint, using the nibs to hold the clamps. The lines of the harp are purely decorative, so don't worry about making them exact. Your only concern is to fit the top bar accurately between the legs. Do this by trial.

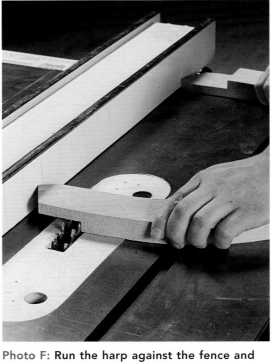
square. Transfer it to one end of the cross bar,
then repeat the procedure and transfer the
measurement to the other end of the cross bar.

10. Set a stop on your miter gauge so that
one shoulder on the cross bar is correctly
positioned. Cut the shoulder using the dado
set (see **photo G**). Reset the stop for the second shoulder, then turn the workpiece around
and upside down so that the cut you just
made faces up, and cut the second shoulder.
Remove the stop and cut out the waste on
the two joints.

11. Mark the center of the bottom edge of the
cross bar and drill a ½-in. hole there. Fit that
hole with a 3-in. by ½-in. hardwood dowel and
glue it in place. Fit the cross bar to the harp
leg assembly with the dowel facing down and
glue and clamp it.

12. When the glue is dry, cut off the two top
nibs using a handsaw. Sand the top flush with
an 80-grit sanding block.

Photo F: **Run the harp against the fence and
cut the top shoulders square.**

Photo H: After you've glued the cross bar to the harp and cut off the nibs, run the cross bar against the fence to cut the harp bottom. This ensures that the bottom is parallel to the cross bar.

Tip: Make sure the pivot holes on the stretchers are facing up.

13. To cut the bottom of the harp, run the top rail of the harp against the tablesaw fence, cutting off the bottom. This ensures that the bottom is parallel with the top (see **photo H**).
14. Turn the harp upside down and find the center of the harp bottom. Drill a ½-in. hole into the bottom and fit that hole with another 3-in. by ½-in. hardwood dowel. Glue the dowel into place.

ASSEMBLING AND FINISHING UP

Sanding

Sand the legs, feet, stretchers, cleats, tabletop, and harp to 220 grit, using a random-orbit sander on the flat surfaces and sanding blocks on the curves. Start with a belt sander on the tabletop, using a 150-grit belt, then finish up with the random-orbit sander. Break all of the edges using a sanding block so the edges are comfortable to touch.

Assembling the trestle

The top stretcher must be inserted through the harp before the trestle assembly is glued up. If you forget, you won't be able to get the harp on. As usual, doing a dry glue-up will prevent problems from arising when you're gluing for real.

1. Assemble both leg structures dry to make sure everything fits together properly. Use waxed paper between the leg and glue blocks so the blocks don't stick to the leg, and dry-clamp the assembly to make sure you have everything in order.
2. Spread PVA glue into the foot mortises on one leg structure and then onto the tenons on the leg. Insert the tenons, then clamp the structure, making sure all the joints are tight. Repeat for the other leg structure.
3. Measure for square across the diagonals and correct any deviation.
4. Spread glue into the four leg mortises and onto the stretcher tenons. Insert the stretcher

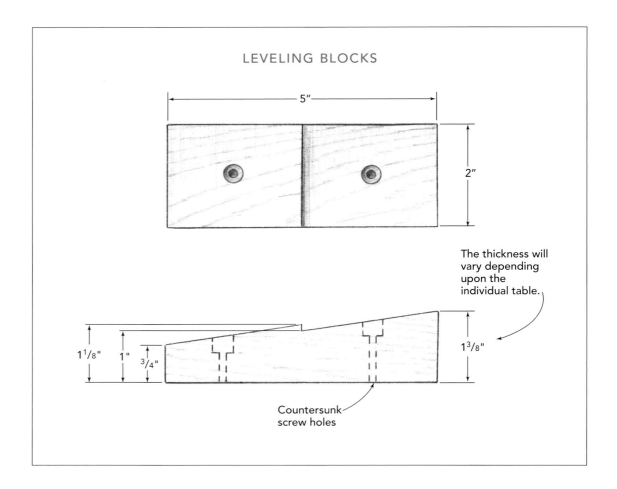

LEVELING BLOCKS

5"

2"

The thickness will vary depending upon the individual table.

$1^1/8$" 1" $3/4$"

$1^3/8$"

Countersunk screw holes

tenons into one of the leg structures and hammer them home using a dead-blow hammer.

5. Place the harp, which is already assembled, through the top stretcher.

6. Insert the tenons into the second leg and clamp the structure, using clamp blocks on both sides of the exposed mortise to get good clamp pressure. Make sure the trestle sits square on a flat surface. If it doesn't, adjust the clamp pressure.

7. Remove excess glue and allow the glue to cure overnight.

8. Remove the clamps and, using a sharp chisel, chamfer the edges of the exposed tenons, which should show about ¼ in. on each side of the legs.

Attaching the cleats to the tabletop

With the trestle complete, you can fit the cleats to the underside of the tabletop. It is easier and faster to do this dynamically than to try to measure them.

1. Set the trestle on the floor, and insert a 3-in. by ¾-in. hardwood dowel through the hole in one of the cleats and into one of the legs. The dowel should stand slightly proud of the surfaces. Cut it to correct length using a handsaw, and chamfer the edges of the dowels slightly using sandpaper or a chisel to make them easy to insert. The dowels should be sized to go in and out of the holes with finger pressure. Sand them to size if needed.

2. Attach the other cleat to the other leg.

3. Turn the tabletop upside down onto your workbench, then put the trestle, with cleats attached, upside down on the overturned tabletop. Prop up the trestle so it doesn't fall over. Center the trestle on the top.

4. Predrill for screws and screw the cleats into the top, using 1½-in. by #10 steel wood screws.

5. Pull out the pivot dowels and remove the trestle. Glue ⅜-in. wooden plugs into the screw holes. When the glue is dry, cut off the plugs, then level using a sharp chisel followed by sanding.

Adjusting the harp

The harp should pivot on the dowels in their holes, rather than resting on the stretchers. You can accomplish this by adjusting the length of the dowels so that when they are seated in their holes they raise the harp slightly above the stretchers.

1. Mount the harp into the holes in the stretchers.

2. Measure the distance between the harp and the stretchers and subtract ⅛ in. The correct dowel length between harp and stretchers is ⅛ in., so you're cutting off the extra dowel length, leaving only the ⅛ in.

3. After taking the harp out of the holes, cut off the amount you calculated from both dowels.

4. Remount the harp. The harp should now be riding ⅛ in. above the stretchers.

5. If the harp doesn't swing freely, sand the dowels with 80-grit sandpaper on a sanding block until it does.

Leveling the table

The final step is to install the leveling blocks and level the tabletop in relation to the trestle. Rough dimensions for the leveling blocks are given in the illustration on the facing page, but the final dimensions should be calculated dynamically from the finished table.

1. Remount the trestle on the tabletop, which should still be upside down.

2. Pivot the harp so it is perpendicular to the legs, and use shims to level the trestle until the two legs of the harp are equidistant from the bottom of the table. Measure that "leveling distance," which corresponds to the 1-in. measurement shown in the illustration on the facing page. If your measured leveling distance is greater than 1 in., add the difference to the thickness of the leveling block. If it is less than 1 in., subtract that difference.

3. Make two leveling blocks at the calculated thickness. Bandsaw out the slopes and sand them smooth with 80-grit paper and a sanding block.

4. To test the fit, flip the tabletop level, pivot the harp open, and put the blocks into place. The blocks will be held in place for the moment by the pressure between the tabletop and harp. If the block is too thin, add a piece of veneer or cardboard between it and the table; if it's too thick, plane off the bottom.

5. Position the blocks and predrill for the two screws, making sure to countersink the heads. Then glue and screw the blocks to the bottom of the table with 1½-in. by #10 steel wood screws.

Finishing

Traditionally, vineyard tables were often unfinished, though some had oilcloth covers held on with a strip of wood tacked to the edge. (If you see nail holes around the edge of an antique vineyard table, you'll know what they were for.) A tung oil finish gives this table a natural look while still protecting it from the elements. If you've made the table from scrap or multiple species of wood, you might want to paint it. Milk paint followed by oil will create a period look.

PART FOUR
BEDS

2. With a ⅜-in. straight bit and a ⅝-in. guide bushing in a plunge router, plunge-cut to a depth no closer than ⅛ in. from the opposite side of the rail, taking very shallow passes. Stop and blow out the sawdust as often as necessary to prevent sawdust from building up in the recess.

3. Chamfer or ease the edges of the recess.

Making and installing the cleats

1. Mill up stock for the two cleats (use scrap from making the side rails if you have it).

2. In one of the 1-in.-wide sides of each cleat, lay out the locations for 5⁄16-in. dowel pins. Space them every 5 in., starting 2⁹⁄16 in. from each end (or farther if the cleats are longer).

3. Drill the 5⁄16-in.-diameter holes centered on the thickness of the cleat, and make them about ¾ in. deep.

4. Drill a series of countersunk pilot holes for screws in each cleat, every 6 in. or so and in a zigzag pattern about ⅜ in. from each edge—the cleats will be more secure this way. Spread a little glue into each of the dowel holes, and pound in 5⁄16-in.- by 1¼-in.-long dowels.

5. Wait until after you apply a finish to the side rails before attaching the cleats. This makes the finishing much easier.

FINAL ASSEMBLY

Making the slats

1. Mill enough wood for 15 slats that are ¾ in. thick, and rip to 4 in. wide.

2. Ease all four edges of each slat by routing with a ¼-in. roundover bit (although anything that breaks the sharp edges is fine).

3. Cut the slats a little bit over finished length for now. To get the exact length, you have to actually set up the bed.

4. Once you've cut each of the slats to length, you can cut the dowel notches in the ends. I do this with a jig (see "A Jig for Notching Bed Slats" on p. 170). However, this jig only works if you're making a small bed or have a fairly high ceiling. If you don't, there is no reason

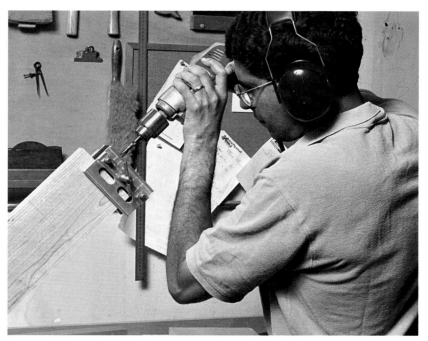

Photo F: Drill the ⅜-in. bolt hole in the side rail with a self-centering doweling jig. It centers the hole well and is simple to use.

Photo G: To cut the 5⁄16-in.-dowel alignment holes in the side rails, use the same drilling guide you used for the posts.

A Template for Routing Nut Recesses

This simple template makes a quick job of cutting the nut recesses on the inside faces of the side rails.

TOP VIEW OF TEMPLATE

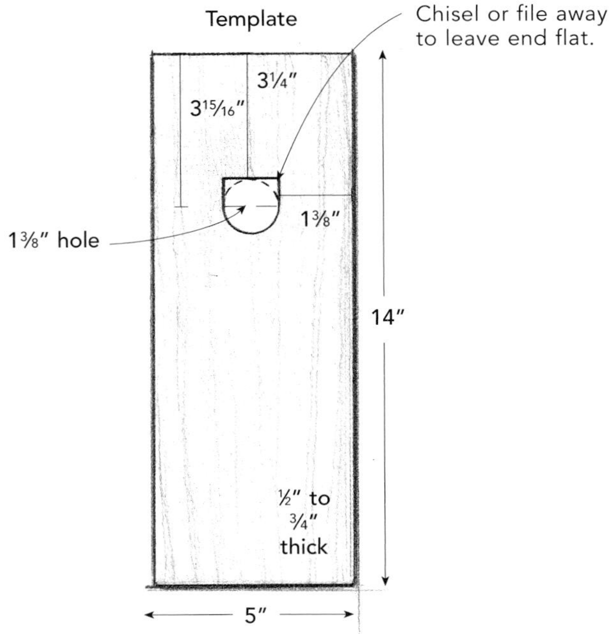
Template
Chisel or file away to leave end flat.
3¼"
3 15/16"
1⅜" hole
1⅜"
14"
½" to ¾" thick
5"

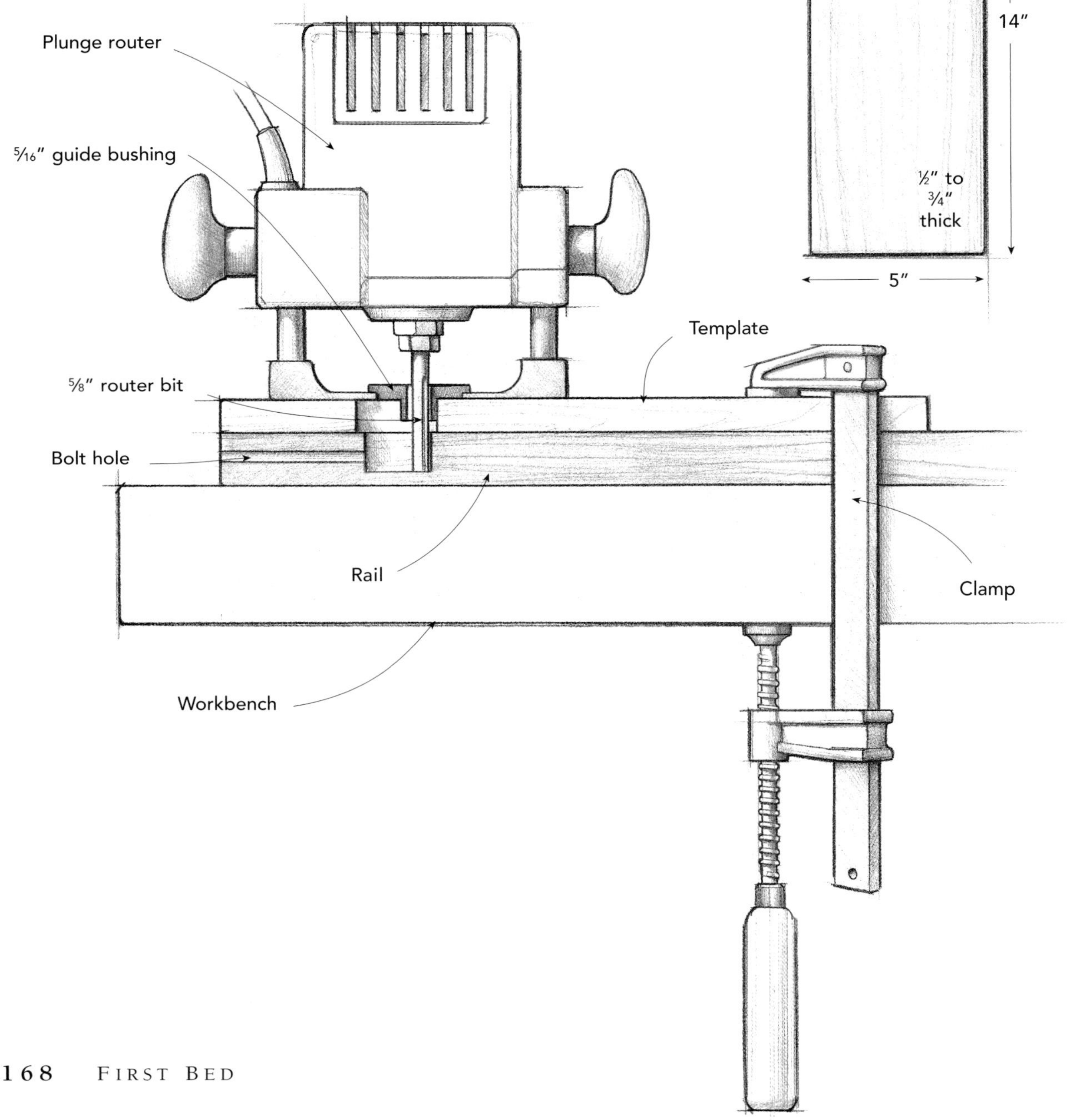
Plunge router
5/16" guide bushing
5/8" router bit
Bolt hole
Template
Rail
Clamp
Workbench

you can't cut the notches on the bandsaw and clean them up with a chisel. To check the fit of the slats, you'll have to assemble the bed.

Assembling the parts

1. Attach the cleats once you've finished and waxed the bed. Line them up flush with the bottom of the side rails, and screw in place.

2. To attach the side rails to the headboard and footboard, lean the headboard upright against a wall or something secure, and place the side rails roughly in position. Place a ⁵⁄₁₆-in. by 5½-in. hex-head bolt with a washer and a second washer and nut at each corner.

3. Insert the dowels on one end of a side rail into the corresponding holes in the headboard post. Insert the bolt and washer from the outside of the headboard, until the end of the bolt is just coming into the nut recess. Now place the other washer on the end of the bolt, and thread on the nut. It helps to rotate the bolt from the outside of the bed when you're doing this (see **photo H**).

4. Use a ½-in. nut driver to tighten up the bolt and a ½-in. open-end wrench to keep the

Tip: Hard maple is the best wood for the slats—it has good stiffness and strength. This is less of a factor with a narrower bed. Any type of wood you can get inexpensively is fine for a twin.

Photo H: To put the bed bolt joints together, insert a bolt with washer from the outside of the bed, until it just reaches into the nut recess. Then place the washer and nut over the end of the bolt, and start turning.

Photo I: To get the second side rail into place, it's easiest to lift the rail in the middle, then work on one end at a time.

A JIG FOR NOTCHING BED SLATS

This jig holds the slats vertically so that perfectly square notches can be cut on the tablesaw with a dado blade. The jig body is composed of two boards joined at right angles. A fence that straddles the tablesaw's rip fence guides the jig through the cut.

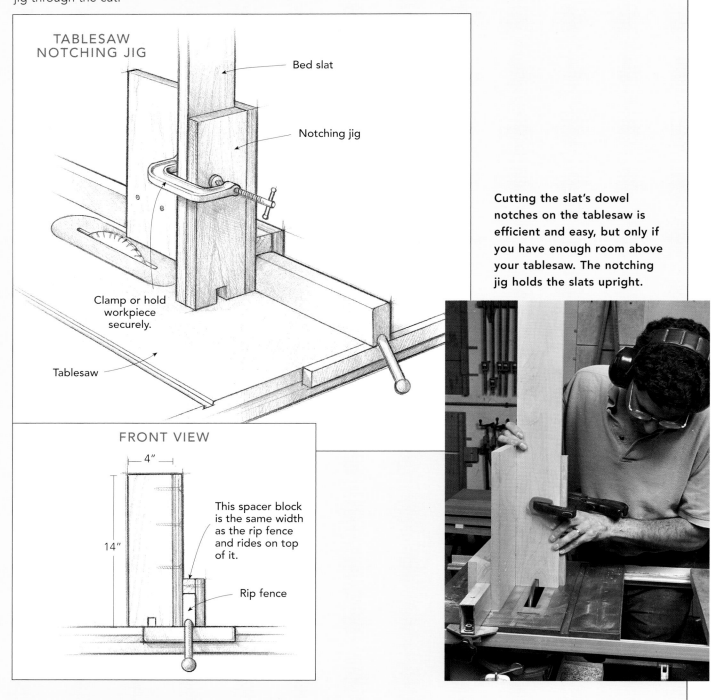

TABLESAW NOTCHING JIG

Bed slat

Notching jig

Clamp or hold workpiece securely.

Tablesaw

FRONT VIEW

4"

14"

This spacer block is the same width as the rip fence and rides on top of it.

Rip fence

Cutting the slat's dowel notches on the tablesaw is efficient and easy, but only if you have enough room above your tablesaw. The notching jig holds the slats upright.

Photo J: Drop the slats into place with the notches around the locating pins in the cleats to complete the bed.

nut from turning. Tighten securely, but don't tighten so hard that you're crushing the wood.
5. Attach the footboard to the other end of the rail the same way you attached the headboard. (Don't try to put the bed together by attaching the second rail before you attach the footboard unless you have help.)
6. Attach the other side rail to the headboard and footboard (see **photo I** on p. 169). Put both of the bolts (with their washers) into the bolt holes in the posts before you pick up the

rail. Pushing both bolts into the rail will guarantee that the locating dowels won't accidentally pop out while you work on getting the washers and nuts on. Check to see that all of the bolts are tight.
7. Drop the slats over the dowel pins on the cleats, hoping they fit, and adjusting them if they don't. Then drop the mattress into place (see **photo J**). Voilà. A bed.

CRAFTSMAN-STYLE BED

The design of the Craftsman-Style Bed should be pretty familiar. There are currently many Craftsman-inspired designs similar to this in furniture stores and catalogs, a reflection of the popularity of the style.

My design does not come from a specific bed of the Craftsman period. In fact, I took most of the details from a Stickley design for a settee. I liked the settee and thought it would work well as a bed. Most of the original Stickley beds had fewer, wider slats and tall legs that extended up past the upper rails of the bed. Interestingly, these beds also had iron side rails that were not meant to be seen—they were normally concealed by the bedspread or covers.

Most Craftsman-style furniture was made of white oak with a rich brown finish created by fuming with ammonia. But this bed looks good in other woods as well. I chose to make the bed in oak, but I stained the wood with a medium-walnut-colored penetrating oil and varnish finish. The dark stain makes the grain patterns prominent.

I like a gentle curve on the bottom edge of the footboard rail. It lightens up the piece a little and, with the curve of the "wings" on the legs, relieves the otherwise overwhelming dominance of straight lines. If there is any chance that the bed will wind up with the headboard end showing, you should curve the bottom edge of the headboard rail as well.

Craftsman-Style Bed

CONTEMPLATING ALL OF THE SLATS may be a little overwhelming, but you don't really have to cut mortises for all of them (unless you want to) The combination of grooves in the rails and dentil strip fillers makes the mortises easily. Note that the bed bolt nuts are hidden by the wings on the outsides of the legs.

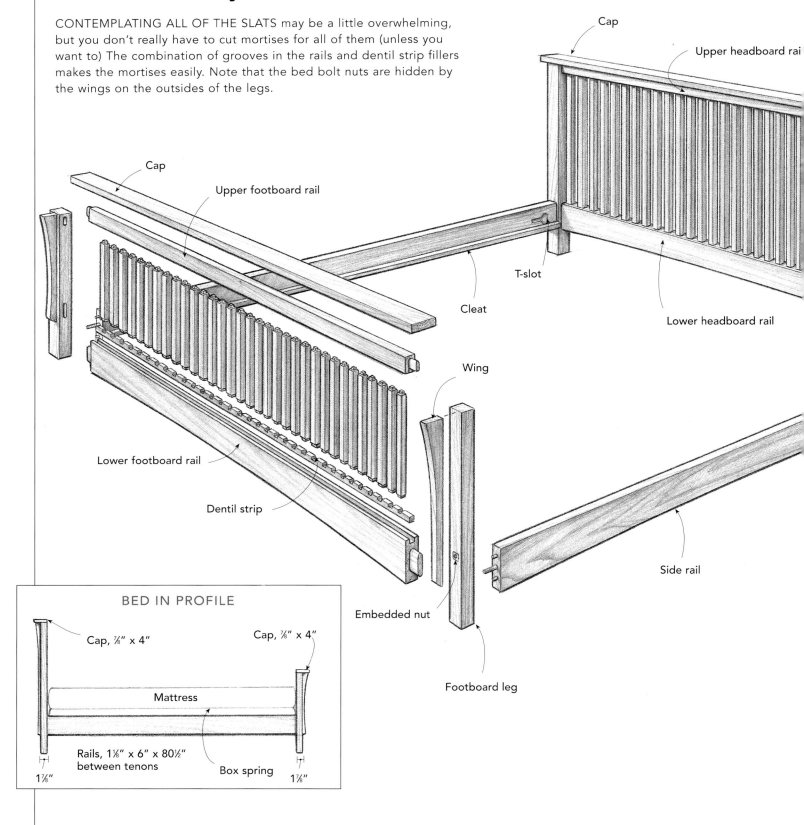

Cap

Upper headboard rai

Cap

Upper footboard rail

T-slot

Cleat

Lower headboard rail

Wing

Lower footboard rail

Dentil strip

Side rail

Embedded nut

Footboard leg

BED IN PROFILE

Cap, ⅞" x 4"

Cap, ⅞" x 4"

Mattress

Rails, 1⅛" x 6" x 80½" between tenons

Box spring

1⅞"

1⅞"

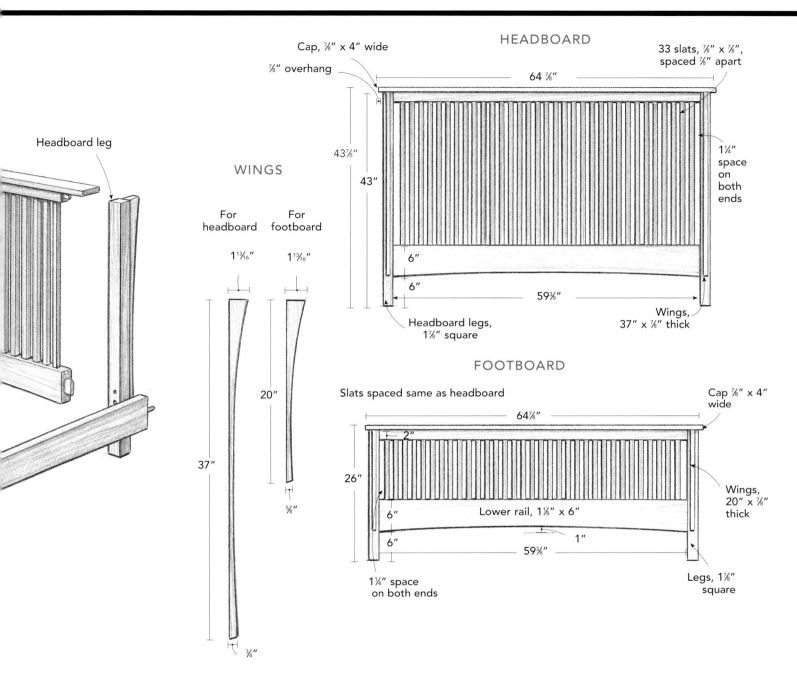

Headboard leg

HEADBOARD

Cap, ⅞" x 4" wide

⅞" overhang

WINGS

For headboard

For footboard

1¹³⁄₁₆"

1¹³⁄₁₆"

33 slats, ⅞" x ⅞", spaced ⅞" apart

64 ⅞"

43⅞"

43"

1¼" space on both ends

6"

6"

59⅜"

Headboard legs, 1⅞" square

Wings, 37" x ⅞" thick

37"

20"

⅝"

FOOTBOARD

Slats spaced same as headboard

Cap ⅞" x 4" wide

64⅞"

2"

26"

Wings, 20" x ⅞" thick

6"

Lower rail, 1⅛" x 6"

6"

1"

59⅜"

Legs, 1⅞" square

1¼" space on both ends

¾"

RAIL LENGTHS FOR OTHER BED SIZES

	Twin	Full	King
For headboard and footboard	38⅜"	53⅜"	75⅜"
For side rail	75½"	75½"	80½"
All measurements are between tenons.			

BUILDING THE BED STEP-BY-STEP

CUT LIST FOR CRAFTSMAN-STYLE BED

Headboard and Footboard

2	Headboard legs	1⅞ in. x 1⅞ in. x 43 in.
2	Footboard legs	1⅞ in. x 1⅞ in. x 26 in.
2	Headboard/footboard rails	1⅛ in. x 6 in. x 62⁹⁄₁₆ in.
2	Upper headboard/ footboard rails	1⅛ in. x 2 in. x 62⁹⁄₁₆ in.
4	Dentil strips	½ in. x ½ in. x 59⅜ in.
33	Headboard slats	⅞ in. x ⅞ in. x 29¹¹⁄₁₆ in.
33	Footboard slats	⅞ in. x ⅞ in. x 12¹¹⁄₁₆ in.
2	Caps	⅞ in. x 4 in. x 64⅞ in.
2	Headboard wings	⅞ in. x 2½ in. x 37 in.
2	Footboard wings	⅞ in. x 2½ in. x 20 in.

Side Rails

2	Side rails	1⅛ in. by 6 in. x 80½ in.
2	Cleats	1 in. x 1¼ in. x 79⅞ in.

Hardware

4	Bed bolts	⁵⁄₁₆ in. x 5½ in.
8	Dowels (for alignment pins)	⁵⁄₁₆ in. x 1¼ in.

#6 x 2½-in. screws, as needed

These dimensions are for a queen-size bed with a box spring and mattress that have a combined thickness of up to 17 in. or 18 in. You may have to adjust your dimensions to suit the bed size, the mattress size, or any differences in wood dimensions.

Tip: Square pieces with end grain running diagonally will usually have straight grain on all four sides. This is sometimes called rift sawn.

THE CRAFTSMAN-STYLE BED takes us into some new but not unfamiliar territory. The most different aspect is the slatted headboard and footboard. This queen-size bed has 66 slats, 33 in both the headboard and the footboard. A less obvious difference is the bed-rail joinery system. The bed is bolted together, even though there are no visible bolt holes on the outside. The bolts go on the inside, with nuts embedded in the outsides of the legs, covered by the wings. The dimensions given are for a queen-size bed.

MILLING PARTS FOR THE HEADBOARD AND FOOTBOARD

Making the legs

1. Choose wood for the four legs that's straight grained on all four sides. This isn't critical, but it looks nice.
2. Mill the four 1⅞-in.-square legs, and cut them to length. Make sure that the legs are square. If they aren't, you'll have problems with the joinery later.
3. Lay out the locations for the mortises (see "Headboard and Footboard Joinery Details"). Use the bottom of the legs as a reference point when cutting the lower rail mortises, and use the tops of the legs when cutting mortises for the upper rails.
4. Cut the mortises however you prefer. I use the jig described in "Mortising Jig for Routing Thin Workpieces" on p. 159.

Making the rails

1. Mill the wood for all of the rails at one time, including the lower and upper headboard and footboard rails and the side rails. Choose the best grain for the footboard rail because it's the one you'll see most.

Headboard and Footboard Joinery Details

The upper and lower rails are the same on the headboard and footboard.

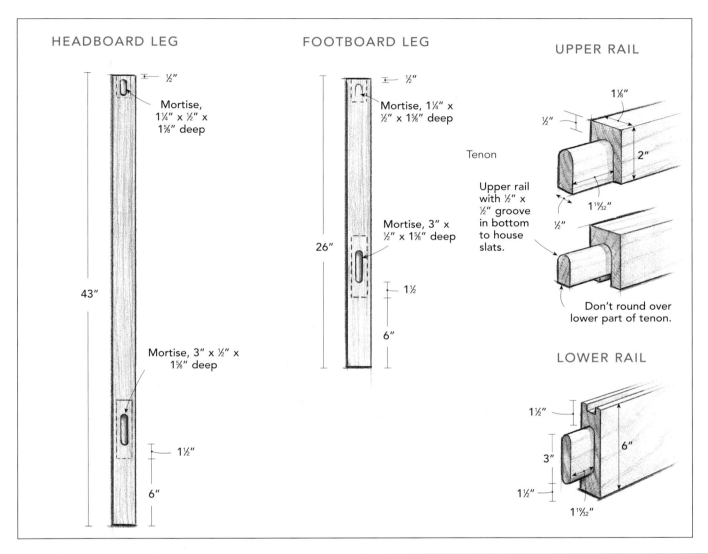

HEADBOARD LEG

½"

Mortise, 1¼" x ½" x 1⅝" deep

43"

Mortise, 3" x ½" x 1⅝" deep

1½"

6"

FOOTBOARD LEG

½"

Mortise, 1¼" x ½" x 1⅝" deep

26"

Mortise, 3" x ½" x 1⅝" deep

1½

6"

UPPER RAIL

1⅛"

½"

2"

1¹⁹⁄₃₂"

½"

Tenon

Upper rail with ½" x ½" groove in bottom to house slats.

Don't round over lower part of tenon.

LOWER RAIL

1½"

3"

6"

1½"

1¹⁹⁄₃₂"

2. Rip the lower headboard and footboard rails and the side rails to 6 in. wide, and rip the upper headboard and footboard rails to 2 in. wide.

Tenoning the rails

1. Cut the tenons with the tenoning jig described in the First Bed, or however else you prefer. For tenon layout, see "Headboard and Footboard Joinery Details."

2. Cut all of the lower rail tenons before moving on to the uppers.

3. Cut the tenon on one side of the upper rail and mark the second shoulder location on the upper rail directly from the lower rail (see "Matching Upper Rail and Lower Rail Length" on p. 178). This technique ensures that the distance between shoulders is the same on both headboard and footboard rails and especially between the upper and lower rails.

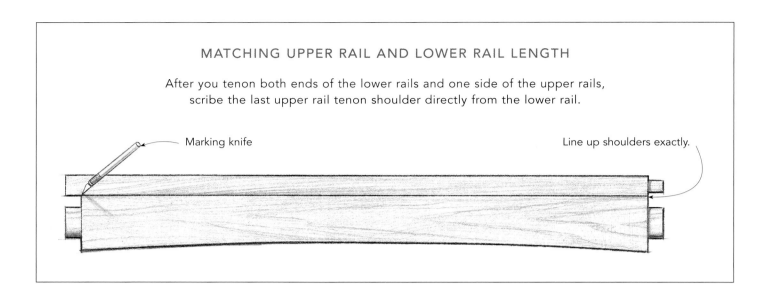

MATCHING UPPER RAIL AND LOWER RAIL LENGTH

After you tenon both ends of the lower rails and one side of the upper rails,
scribe the last upper rail tenon shoulder directly from the lower rail.

Marking knife

Line up shoulders exactly.

LEAVING OUT LAYOUT LINES

When you lay out joinery, it's often tempting to draw every line that describes each joint on every piece. However, you can save a lot of time if you lay out only the lines you really need. And this depends largely on the methods you use to cut the joints.

If you use a chisel to chop a mortise, or a handsaw (or a bandsaw) to cut a tenon by eye, you'll need exact layout lines everywhere. These lines should be made with a marking gauge—or even better, with a mortise gauge that has two scribe points that can be set. This will give you the level of precision you'll need for accurate work.

When you're cutting with a router, the router bit usually defines the size of the mortise. And jigs, fences, stops, or guides determine both the size and the location of the cut, not multiple layout lines. Layout lines are necessary, but only to set up the jigs for the very first cut. Beyond this, layout is wasted effort. I usually make a simple mark to remind me where to cut the joint on a particular part. This is enough to get the part into the jig correctly. And if the jig is well made, repeatable accuracy should be a piece of cake.

4. Round over the ends of the tenons, and fit them into their mortises. Don't bother to round the lower sides of the upper rail tenons. You'll cut a dado through them in a later step.

Making mortises for the slats in the rails

Contemplating the 66 slats for the queen-size bed may be a little overwhelming, but they're really not that difficult or time-consuming to make because you don't have to cut mortises for all of them (unless you want to). The trick is to build what I call "constructed mortises." These mortises aren't cut out of solid stock but are assembled by inserting a dentil strip into a dado (see "Constructed Slat Mortises").

1. Cut a $\frac{1}{2}$-in.-deep by $\frac{1}{2}$-in.-wide dado centered on the top edge of the lower rails and the bottom edge of the top rails. Use a dado blade on the tablesaw to do this.

2. It's best to cut the notches for all four dentil strips in one board, then rip the individual strips out of this board. If you can't do this, you'll have to cut more notches. Start with a piece of wood $\frac{9}{16}$ in. by $2\frac{1}{2}$ in. by $59\frac{3}{8}$ in. long that is a reasonable color match for the rails.

3. Lay out the notch locations on one edge of this board.

Constructed Slat Mortises

Cutting each of these mortises individually would be tremendously difficult. Inserting a dadoed dentil strip into the upper and lower rails makes the joinery easy.

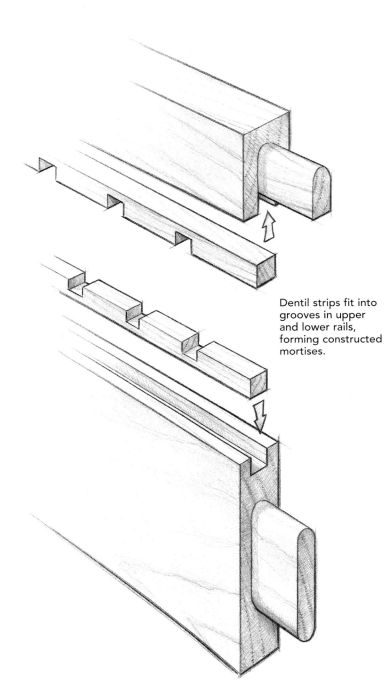

Dentil strips fit into grooves in upper and lower rails, forming constructed mortises.

NOTCH LAYOUT FOR DENTIL STRIP

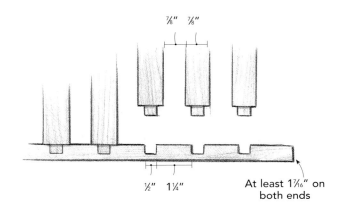

⅞" ⅞"

½" 1¼"

At least 1⁷⁄₁₆" on both ends

GLUING IN THE DENTIL STRIP

Use a slightly curved caul to distribute the clamping pressure.

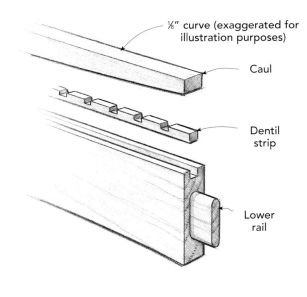

⅛" curve (exaggerated for illustration purposes)

Caul

Dentil strip

Lower rail

Photo A: To cut all of the notches in the dentil strips for the constructed mortises, use a crosscut sled.

Tip: Mark both sides of each joint with a distinguishing letter or number so you don't get them mixed up later.

4. Cut the ½-in.-wide by ⁷⁄₁₆-in.-deep notches on the tablesaw with a ½-in.-wide dado cutter (see **photo A**). I cut the notches using a shop-built crosscut sled. It supports the strip well on both sides of the blade.

5. Make a reference mark across one end of the notched board. This will help you keep track of which way they go—and eliminate any problems if the notches are not perfectly symmetrical. Then rip each strip just slightly wider than the grooves (see **photo B**). Try to plan your rips so you get rid of any tearout from cutting the notches.

6. Carefully plane or sand the strips to fit the grooves in the rails. You'll have to support the fragile strips on both sides and take very light cuts to keep them from breaking as you plane (see **photo C**). You want the strip tight, but you should still be able to insert it into the groove with hand pressure.

Gluing the dentil strips in the rail grooves

1. Make some ¾-in. by 3-in. by 60-in. cauls to press the strips evenly and firmly into the grooves.

2. Plane a slight bow into the edge of the caul so that the ends are slightly narrower than the center (see "Constructed Slat Mortises" on p. 179). This helps apply pressure evenly without using every clamp in the shop.

3. Apply the glue sparingly and only to the bottom of the groove.

4. Line up the ends of the strip so that they are flush with the tenon shoulders on both ends of the rail, and press the strip down into the groove (see **photo D**).

5. Place the caul curved-side down on top of the strip, and clamp into place using as many clamps as needed to seat the strip.

6. Once the glue has dried, plane or sand off any protruding dentils flush with the rest of the rail. Be careful to keep the top of the rail flat, so the slat tenon shoulders will fit tightly.

Tip: If you spread the glue on the walls of the rail groove, you risk getting glue into the dentil strip mortises, which are a pain to clean out (remember there are 132 of them).

Photo B: Use a push stick to guide the thin and fragile strips past the blade, and use an outfeed roller (not shown in photo) if you don't have a helper.

Photo C: The notched strip is too flexible to plane without support. Two plywood strips clamped to the bench keep the strip from bending or breaking.

Cutting the curve on the bottom of the headboard and footboard rails

1. Spring a ³⁄₈-in.- or ¹⁄₂-in.-thick by 1-in. scrap strip between the tenon shoulders to lay out the curve. Adjust the strip so that it just touches the bottom edge of the rail at both ends and is 1 in. up from the bottom edge at the center of the rail.

2. Cut the curve on a bandsaw or with a sabersaw. In either case, stay to the outside of the line, and be careful cutting near the ends.

3. Smooth the curve with a flat-soled hand-plane skewed 45 degrees in the cut. This is fast and works well on gentle inside curves such as these (see **photo E** on p. 182). A belt sander and hand-sanding using a curved block also do a good job.

Photo D: Slowly and carefully push the fragile dentil strip into the rail groove.

Making the slats

1. Calculate how many of each slat length you'll need based on the size of the bed. You'll get a slat for each 1 in. of width of board (assuming a ⅛-in. kerf). It's important to include enough wood for five or six extra slats; you'll want them to replace ones that warp or have loose tenons.

2. Rip the slats from ⅞-in.-thick flatsawn boards that have been handplaned and scraped or sanded on both faces first. This saves smoothing these two faces on the individual slats, which would be much more time-consuming. Rejoint the edge whenever you find that the wood is no longer straight enough.

3. To figure the exact lengths for the slats, dry-assemble the headboard and footboard frames. Measure the distance between the upper and lower rails, then add the tenon

Tip: Arrange the slats so that the quartersawn faces show. This makes it easier to have all of the slats match, and straight grain in the slats looks good with the straight lines of the bed.

lengths. This should be ¹¹⁄₁₆ in. (¹¹⁄₃₂ in. for each of the two tenons).

4. Cut all of the slats for the headboard or footboard to exactly the same length on the tablesaw. Square up one end on each slat, then cut to length with the squared-up end against a stop.

Tenoning the slats

The slat tenons are easy to cut on the tablesaw, especially with a ⁵⁄₁₆-in.-wide dado cutter.

1. Make a wooden auxiliary fence for your tablesaw miter guide or crosscut sled that extends 4 in. to 5 in. across the blade, and screw it into place.

2. Make a stop block for controlling the length of the tenon on the auxiliary fence. It's important that the face of the block be absolutely square, so check this carefully.

3. Clamp the stop block to the auxiliary fence on the far side of the blade, exactly the length of the tenon away from that side of the blade

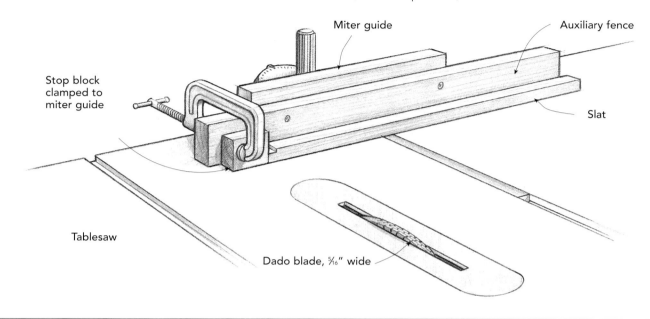

TABLESAW SETUP TO TENON THE SLATS

The tenon is shaped by cutting on all four sides of the slat. This setup works on both a miter guide (shown here) and on a crosscut sled (shown in photo F).

Miter guide

Auxiliary fence

Stop block clamped to miter guide

Slat

Tablesaw

Dado blade, ⁵⁄₁₆" wide

(see "Tablesaw Setup to Tenon the Slats" and **photo F**).

4. Cut a slightly oversize test tenon on a cut-off piece of slat stock.

5. Check the fit of the test tenon in one of the mortises. Adjust the blade height if necessary so that you'll wind up with a snug-fitting tenon. Take your time to get it right. You don't want to have to trim too many of these tenons individually.

6. Cut shoulders on all four sides of each slat end.

Making the caps and drilling for attachment

These boards will be glued and screwed to the upper rails from underneath after the glue-up.

1. Mill the cap boards to size.

2. Lay out and drill six countersunk pilot holes in the upper rails centered between slat locations. Drill from the underside and angle the holes about 5 or 6 degrees toward the out-

Photo F: For cutting the tenons on the slats, the crosscut sled works well, though a miter gauge will work, too. The stop clamped on the far side of the sawblade registers the slat so the shoulder on each side of every slat will be cut the same.

Photo G: An angled cradle helps drill the angled pilot holes in the upper rail for the screws to attach the cap.

Tip: If you cut all of the wings out of rectangular boards, 2½ in. wide, the waste piece can function as a caul when gluing the wings to the legs.

side of the bed. This will leave room for you to drive the screws without too much interference from the slats.

3. To drill the angled holes, use a strip of wood rabbeted on an angle to hold the upper rails in position on the drill press (see **photo G**).

Making the wings

The wings are both a decorative and a structural feature. They add another set of curved lines to the bed and give depth to the headboard and footboard. They also support the cap, making it sturdier.

1. Make patterns for the headboard and footboard wings on ¼-in. plywood or any comparable thin material. Just enlarge the drawings of the wings on p. 175.

2. Trace the pattern onto a piece of stock with some consideration to the grain. It should match the grain on the legs as well as possible so that the wing looks like an integral part of the leg and not an afterthought.

3. Smooth out the curves with planes, spokeshaves, scrapers, and/or sandpaper. The four wings don't have to match precisely because they'll never be seen right next to one another.

ASSEMBLING THE HEADBOARD AND FOOTBOARD

Smoothing and checking the parts before assembly

Even with all of the parts cut and the joints fit, there's just a little more preparation necessary before you begin the glue-up.

1. Smooth all of the parts. If you presanded the slat stock before ripping, this is where you reap the benefits. There's still a lot of work to sand the other two faces on each slat, but it's half the time it would have been.

2. Ease all of the edges, either with a few swipes of a handplane, or by sanding with 220-grit sandpaper.

3. Check to be sure that each of the slats fits into the appropriate mortise in the lower and upper rails. It's worth checking every one. Trying to trim 33 of them during the glue-up with time running out could be a harrowing experience.

Assembling the slats and rails

Glue up the bed in stages. It does not work well to try to glue up everything all at once. Start with the headboard.

Photo H: Work quickly to get all of the slats in place before the glue sets. Organization is important here— a big hammer shouldn't be.

Tip: Don't try scraping around mortises when smoothing parts. The scraper will cut a noticeable dip on either side of a mortise. Careful sanding with a block that is no wider than the mortised part works best.

Photo I: Work on one tenon at a time. A clamp across one end lets you work across to the other side without any tenons coming loose.

Tip: Put all of the parts of the footboard to one side when you glue up the headboard so that you don't confuse them in the glue-up rush.

1. Get together all of the clamps, clamp pads or cauls, glue, glue spreaders, and the appropriate parts you'll need in one convenient place.

2. The slats and the rails go together first. There are a lot of parts to glue and get together, and not all that much time to do it in. Work steadily and methodically, but try to avoid frenzy. It also helps to use a slow-setting glue.

3. Smear a little glue into each of the mortises in a lower rail. Then insert the slats one at a time, until they are all in place. Try to get each slat to seat all the way. A tap or two with a non-marring mallet should help persuade those slats that don't want to go in easily (see **photo H** on p. 185).

4. Once all of the slats are set, spread glue into each of the upper rail mortises. Check the orientation of this rail to be sure the appropriate tenon will line up with its corresponding mortise in the leg.

5. Insert the first slat tenon into the first mortise on the rail. You'll have to hold up the other end of the rail a little. The goal is to work on getting one slat into place at a time.

6. Place a clamp loosely across the end where some of the tenons have started in. This way these slats won't start popping out as you try to work farther along (see **photo I**).

7. Work steadily across to the other side, then tighten slowly and evenly. You'll have to add a few clamps to get even pressure all the way across the rails. You may want to shift some of the clamps around to clamp any open slat joints tighter.

8. Once everything is tight, check to be sure the assembly is reasonably square by measur-

A Flush-Cutting Jig

HOW THE JIG WORKS

Set the router bit depth to cut the thickness of the jig. Clamp the jig to the rail with the proud leg top protruding into the hole, and rout the leg flush.

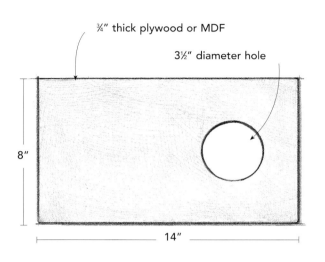

¾" thick plywood or MDF

3½" diameter hole

8"

14"

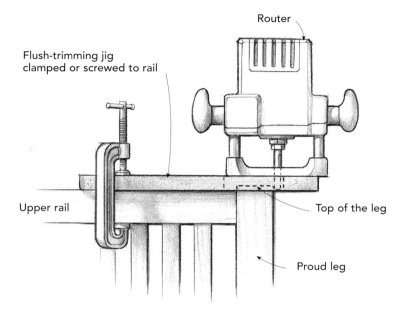

Router

Flush-trimming jig clamped or screwed to rail

Upper rail

Top of the leg

Proud leg

---

ing the two diagonals. Adjust if necessary by loosening, then retightening the clamps at a slight angle in the direction of the long diagonal.

9. Let the assembly sit until the glue is cured.

Adding the legs

The legs go on after the rail and slat assemblies have dried.

1. Check to see if the rail tenons actually line up with the mortises. You can easily correct for minor misalignment by paring or rasping a little bit off the appropriate shoulder of the tenon.

2. Spread glue in the mortises and very lightly on the tenons, put the legs onto the rail assembly, and clamp tight.

3. Check again for square and adjust if necessary.

Cutting the legs and upper rails flush

For the cap to fit well, the rail and legs must be almost perfectly flush.

1. If the rail is slightly higher than the leg, it's easy to handplane away the difference. Be careful not to plane across the leg, or you might split a chunk of wood off on the outside.

2. If the leg is higher than the rail, the quickest way to trim it down is to rout it off. Use the jig described in "A Flush-Cutting Jig."

3. Clamp or screw the jig to the upper rail so the leg is roughly centered in the hole.

4. Set the depth of cut on the router so the bit just barely touches the top of the rail.

5. If you use a plunge router, raise up the bit to start the machine, then plunge down to the set depth.

Photo J: With the cap clamped into position, screw it into place. The scrap of wood I'm holding against the slats is important to prevent the drill chuck from marring the slats.

Tip: If you use a regular router to trim the leg tops, install a guide bushing so you can keep the router bit away from the jig and leg when you start.

6. Rout clockwise slowly around the top of the leg to score the wood, then work your way in toward the center to complete the trim.

Adding the caps

1. Place the cap in position on the upper rail so it overhangs the legs by ⅛ in. toward the inside of the bed and overhangs the sides equally.
2. Mark its location by lightly tracing the top of the leg on the underside with a sharp pencil.
3. Remove the cap, spread a very thin film of glue on the top of the rail, and clamp the cap back in place without marring it.

4. When you're sure the location is correct, drive in the screws from the underside of the rail using a long drill-mounted screwdriver bit. Slip a thin piece of wood between the drill chuck and the spindles to avoid marring the slats with the spinning chuck (see **photo J**).
5. Plug the pilot holes, and carefully cut them flush with a chisel.

Adding the leg hardware

As usual, I chose bed bolts for attaching the side rails to the headboard and the footboard. For visual reasons, the wings look much better if they end even with the bottoms of the rails. However, wings that low get in the way of a typical bed bolt hole. You can use this to your advantage: They make it possible to create a hidden joint. Just embed a nut in the outside of the leg and hide it with the wing. The bed bolts can be inserted from the inside of the rails using a special recess.

1. Mark both the outside and the inside of each leg 9 in. up from the bottom. (This should line up with the center of the rail.)
2. Measure from side to side on the leg to find the center, and mark with an awl.
3. Drill a ³⁄₈-in. hole about halfway through from both sides of the leg. This will help keep the holes centered on both sides (it really needs to be on center on both sides of the leg).
4. When the holes meet up in the middle of the leg, drill through to clean up any misalignment.
5. Drill the two ⁵⁄₁₆-in. alignment pin holes ⁵⁄₈ in. deep on the inside of the leg. See "A Bolt Hole Drilling Guide" on p. 164 for a simple jig that helps with this. These holes should be 1¹⁄₂ in., center to center, both above and below the bolt hole and centered on the leg.

Embedding the square nuts in the legs

1. Use a nut to mark out the shape of the recess, first centering it over the ³⁄₈-in. hole.
2. Chop with a chisel across the grain first, then with the grain, cutting down about ¹⁄₃₂ in. at a time until you reach the full depth needed to recess the nut just below the surface (see **photo K**).

Adding the wings

1. Hold each wing in place, centered on the leg to check that the top of the wing and the underside of the cap fit together well. Adjust the angle on top of the wing if necessary.
2. Hold each wing roughly in place again, but off to one side so you can mark the location of the bolt hole on the back of the wing.
3. Drill a shallow ¹⁄₂-in. recess in the back of the wing for room in case a bolt comes all the

Photo K: Chisel the recess for the nut around the ³⁄₈-in. bolt hole on the outside of the leg. Chop across the grain first.

Photo M: Using the cutoff from bandsawing the wing as a caul makes it easy to clamp the wing in place and ensures even pressure.

Photo L: A recess in the back of the wing allows room for the bolt to come through the leg. Without it, the bolt will break the wing right off when you tighten it during assembly.

way through the leg and nut (see **photo L**). Use the wing cutoff (the caul) to hold the wing in position for drilling.

4. Insert the nuts into the recesses in the legs.

5. Spread glue lightly on the flat side of the wing, staying away from the edges to minimize squeeze-out.

6. Center each wing in place. It should be 7/16 in. from either edge all the way down.

7. Place the caul over the wing, put a scrap strip of wood on the opposite face of the leg as a clamp pad, and clamp the wing into place using at least four or five clamps (see photo M).

MAKING THE SIDE RAILS

Sizing the side rails

The side rails are refreshingly simple after the complicated headboard and footboard.

1. Mill the rail stock to 1⅛ in. thick if you haven't done so already, and rip the rails to 6 in. wide.
2. To figure the length when using a box spring, add about ¼ in. to the length of the box spring. If you're using slats, leave more room—usually between ½ in. and 1 in. over the mattress length.
3. Cut the rails to length.

Cutting the joinery in the side rail ends

The end rails have alignment dowels, like the First Bed. For the reversed bed bolt, you need to cut a T-shaped recess on the inside face of the rail. The T-slot has space to insert the bolt into the hole in the long part of the T and room to tighten the bolt with a wrench at the top of the T (see "Side Rail and Leg Joinery Details").

1. Make a routing template to cut the T-shaped slot (see "T-Slot Routing Template" on p. 192).
2. Align the jig at the end of the rails on the inside face.
3. Cut the T-slots with a plunge router fitted with a ⅜-in. guide bushing and ½-in. straight bit (see **photo N** on p. 192).

SIDE RAIL AND LEG JOINERY DETAILS

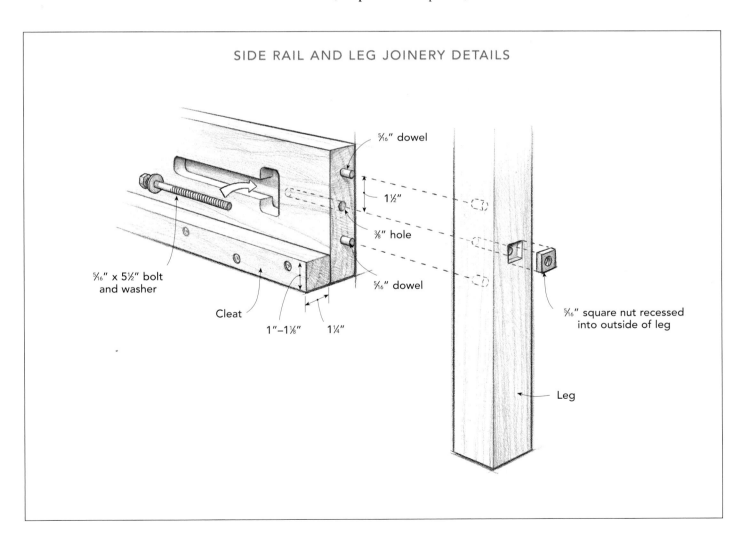

⁵⁄₁₆" dowel

1½"

⅜" hole

⁵⁄₁₆" dowel

⁵⁄₁₆" x 5½" bolt and washer

Cleat

1"–1⅛"   1¼"

⁵⁄₁₆" square nut recessed into outside of leg

Leg

Photo N: Rout the T-slot with a plywood jig as a guide. A cleat at the end of the jig aligns it on the rail.

> *Tip: It's important to apply the finish to the bed at a comfortable height. Place the parts on a low table or a pair of low sawhorses so you won't have to bend over so much to reach all of the slats.*

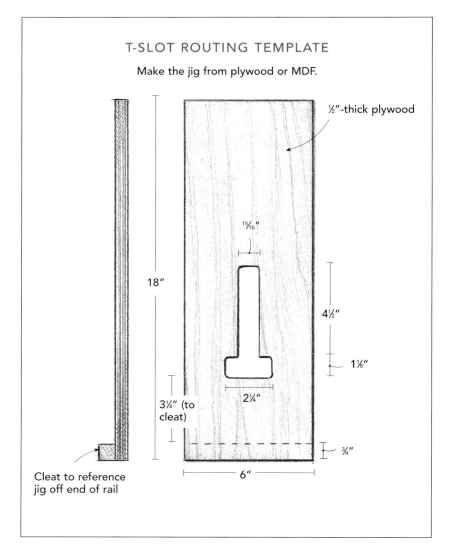

T-SLOT ROUTING TEMPLATE

Make the jig from plywood or MDF.

½"-thick plywood

18"

$\frac{15}{16}$"

4½"

1⅛"

2¼"

3¼" (to cleat)

¾"

6"

Cleat to reference jig off end of rail

4. Drill the bolt and alignment holes in the ends of the rails using the jig described in "A Bolt Hole Drilling Guide" on p. 164.
5. Squeeze a little glue into the alignment pin holes, and insert the ⁵⁄₁₆-in. by 1¼-in. dowels.

Adding cleats or slats

1. Mill up two cleats 1 in. to 1⅛ in. thick, 1¼ in. wide, and ¹⁄₁₆ in. less than the length of the side rails. You can use some of the rippings from milling up the bed rails for this purpose, but any strong hardwood will work.
2. On the wider face of each cleat, drill a series of countersunk pilot holes for screws roughly 6 in. apart. I usually lay out these holes in a zigzag pattern, a little closer to one edge and then to the other.
3. Screw the cleats in place.
4. Mill up slats if you want to make this bed to support a mattress alone. Refer to the First Bed on p. 167–171 for details about making notched slats and adding dowel pins to the cleats.

FINISHING UP

Choosing a finish

Whatever finish you choose, you're in for a bit of work with all the surfaces. Here are some simple strategies for wet-sanding an oil finish or rubbing out a film finish.

1. To finish the slats, work from one side of the bed and sand the face and one edge, whichever is the most comfortable. If you're right-handed, it's usually the right face, and vice versa.

2. Work your way across the great expanse of slats, then go around to the other side (or flip the bed around), and do the same thing with the opposite faces and edges. This is a good way not to miss any.

3. Don't bother finishing the cleats.

Final assembly

There are only minor differences in assembly on this bed. Because the nut is captured, each bolt needs only one washer. Assembly requires the same basic approach, but you are tightening from the inside.

Insert the bolt, and then use a ½-in. open-end wrench to tighten it (see **photos O** and **P**). Remember to install one rail to the headboard and footboard before moving on to the second rail.

Photo O: **To assemble the bed with T-slots, first insert the bolt and washer into the hole and push them forward.**

Photo P: **Then tighten the bolt with an open-end wrench. The space at the top of the T leaves room to rotate the wrench.**

PART FIVE
DESKS

LAPTOP DESK

Stephen Lauziere, who designed this desk, faced an interesting problem. His customer, a writer, wanted a piece of furniture that could serve as a laptop computer desk by day and a living room table by night. Lauziere's problem stemmed from the fact that normal table height is 29 in. to 30 in., whereas the ideal height for a computer keyboard is much lower, at about 26 in.

The obvious solution was to place the computer in a drawer below the desktop so it could be pulled out when needed and tucked away out of sight when not being used. But putting the computer in a drawer would mean that the user's hands would have to hang over the drawer front to type on the keyboard. This would be awkward, uncomfortable, and stressful on the wrists. Lauziere solved the problem by building a slide-out tray that hides behind a drawer front. When the tray is closed, it looks like a regular drawer. But when opened, the drawer front folds down flush with the tray, creating a flat, easily accessible work area.

This desk is practical and sturdy, yet light and elegant in design. The curved, tapered legs and slide-out tray may make the desk appear complicated, but it is actually a relatively easy project to build. The desk is assembled with basic mortise-and-tenon joinery and with a few dadoes and rabbets.

Laptop Desk

TO GIVE SUPPORT TO THE SLIDE-OUT TRAY, an upper and lower inner frame hold vertical support pieces. The tray slides in grooves cut in the vertical supports. The four skirts are glued to the four legs and then the lower inner frame is glued to grooves cut in the bottom of the back and side skirts. After the vertical supports are slid into place and glued, the upper inner frame is glued to the grooves in the top of the three skirts.

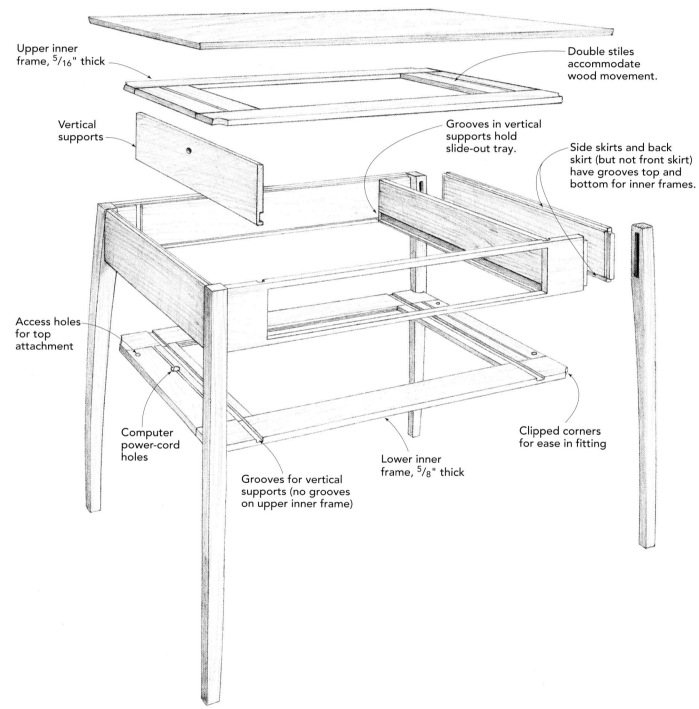

Upper inner frame, $^5/_{16}$" thick

Double stiles accommodate wood movement.

Vertical supports

Grooves in vertical supports hold slide-out tray.

Side skirts and back skirt (but not front skirt) have grooves top and bottom for inner frames.

Access holes for top attachment

Computer power-cord holes

Grooves for vertical supports (no grooves on upper inner frame)

Lower inner frame, $^5/_8$" thick

Clipped corners for ease in fitting

SIDE VIEW

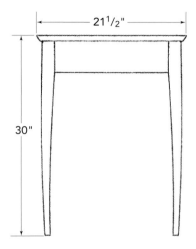

21¹/₂"

30"

FRONT VIEW

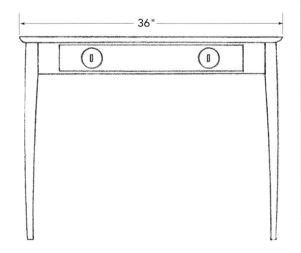

36"

CUT LIST FOR LAPTOP DESK

1	Top	¾ in. x 21½ in. x 36 in.

Base

4	Legs	1⅜ in. x 1⅜ in. x 29¼ in.
2	Side skirts	¾ in. x 4⅝ in. x 18¾ in. (including a ¼-in. x ⅝-in. x 3⅞-in. tenon on both ends)
1	Front skirt	¾ in. x 4⅝ in. x 32¾ in. (including a ¼-in. x ⅝-in. x 3⅞-in. tenon on both ends)
1	Back skirt	¾ in. x 4⅝ in. x 32¾ in. (including a ¼-in. x ⅝-in. x 3⅞-in. tenon on both ends)

Inner Framework

2	Vertical supports	¾ in. x 3¹⁵⁄₁₆ in. x 19 in.
2	Lower frame rails	⅝ in. x 2¼ in. x 33 in.
4	Lower frame stiles	⅝ in. x 2¼ in. x 15¼ in. (including a ¼-in. x ½-in. x 2¼-in. tenon on both ends)
2	Upper frame rails	⁵⁄₁₆ in. x 2¼ in. x 33 in.
4	Upper frame stiles	⁵⁄₁₆ in. x 2¼ in. x 15¼ in. (including a ⅛-in. x ½-in. x 2¼-in. tenon on both ends)

Slide-Out Tray

1	Back rail	1 in. x 2¼ in. x 25 in.
3	Stiles	1 in. x 2¼ in. x 17⅛ in. (including a ¼-in. x 1-in. x 1⅜-in. tenon on one end and a ³⁄₁₆-in. x 3½-in. tongue on other end)
2	Front rails	1 in. x 2¼ in. x 11⅛ in. (including a ¼-in. x 1-in. x 1⅜-in. tenon on both ends)
1	Subrail	⅜ in. x 3½ in. x 25 in.
2	Panels	½ in. x 9⅝ in. x 10⅞ in. (including a ¼-in. x ¼-in. tongue on all sides)
1	Drawer front	¾ in. x 3⅜ in. x 25⅝ in.

Miscellaneous

2	Drawer runners	³⁄₁₆ in. x 1¹⁄₁₆ in. x 18⅝ in.
1	Back stop strip	¼ in. x 1⁵⁄₁₆ in. x 24⅞ in.
2	Stop blocks	¼ in. x ½ in. x 2 in.

Slide-Out Tray

THE DRAWER FRONT FOLDS DOWN FLUSH with the slide-out panel to become part of the computer work surface. The drawer front rests on stiles that extend past the rails of the frame-and-panel slide-out tray. A thin subrail is half-lapped on top of the extended rails. A strip, attached to the back of the tray, stops against blocks screwed to the vertical supports.

SLIDE-OUT TRAY CONSTRUCTION

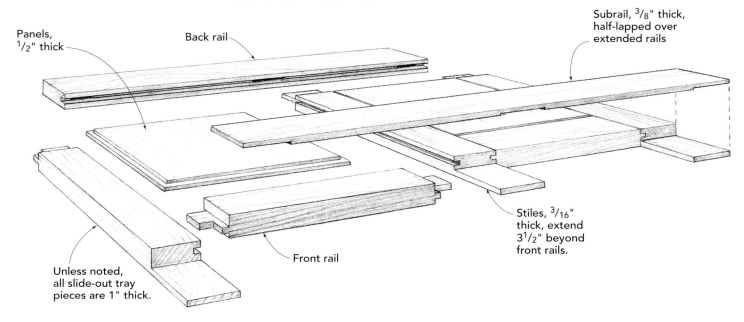

Panels, $1/2$" thick

Back rail

Subrail, $3/8$" thick, half-lapped over extended rails

Stiles, $3/16$" thick, extend $3 1/2$" beyond front rails.

Front rail

Unless noted, all slide-out tray pieces are 1" thick.

SLIDE-OUT TRAY INSTALLED

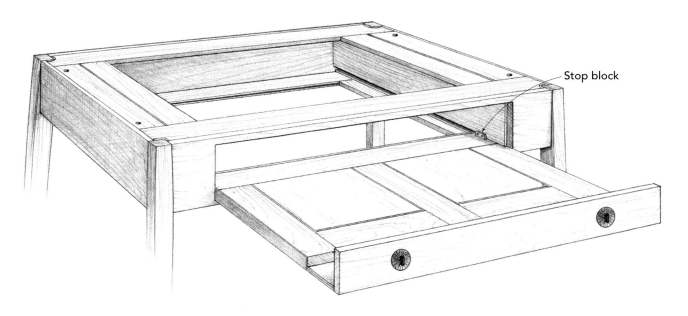

Stop block

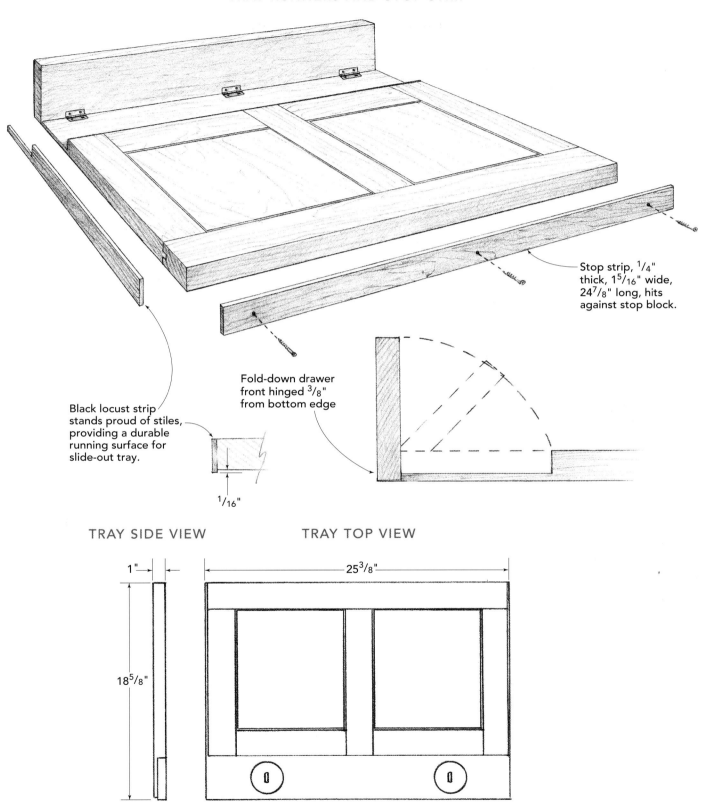

Stop strip, $^1/_4$"
thick, $1^5/_{16}$" wide,
$24^7/_8$" long, hits
against stop block.

Fold-down drawer
front hinged $^3/_8$"
from bottom edge

Black locust strip
stands proud of stiles,
providing a durable
running surface for
slide-out tray.

$^1/_{16}$"

TRAY SIDE VIEW   TRAY TOP VIEW

1"

$18^5/_8$"

$25^3/_8$"

BUILDING THE DESK STEP-BY-STEP

THE LAPTOP DESK can be broken down into four basic components: the top, the base, the inner framework, and the slide-out tray. Begin by making the top, then make the parts for the base. Next, make the inner framework, then assemble it along with the base. Last, make the sliding tray and fit it into its opening.

MAKING THE TOP

The top is the most visible part of the desk, so select your straightest, best-looking stock for it, laying out the boards for good color and grain match.

1. Mill enough stock for the top to make it 2 in. oversize in length and 1 in. oversize in width.

2. Edge glue the boards, making sure the resulting plank is flat under clamp pressure (see **photo A**).

Photo B: After sawing the bevels on the edges of the top, smooth the cut and round the edges using a block plane.

Photo A: Edge glue the boards for the top, alternating the clamps over and under to help prevent the panel from springing under clamp pressure.

3. Surface both sides of the top smooth and flat with a belt sander, plane, scraper, or a combination of the three.

4. Cut the top to size by ripping it to width and crosscutting it to length.

5. Saw or plane a 30-degree bevel on the edges of the top to give it a lighter and more delicate look. Then round over the edges slightly with a plane and some sandpaper (see **photo B**).

6. Finish-sand the entire top.

MAKING THE BASE

The base consists primarily of the legs and skirts, which connect with mortise-and-tenon joinery. When making the skirts, you must also cut the joints for attaching the inner framework. Note that the drawer front is cut from the center of the front skirt to maintain grain continuity across the front of the desk.

Shaping the legs

Each leg is tapered and curved on all four faces. On the two outside faces, the curve begins at the top of the leg, and on the two inside faces, the curve starts 5 in. down from the top.

1. Mill the stock for the legs. Although the finished dimension at the top of the legs is only 1⅛ in. by 1⅛ in., you will need to start with 2-in.-square blanks to leave enough thickness to cut the curves.

2. Determine how each leg will be positioned and clearly mark the ends. This will prevent possible confusion later when laying out the curves.

3. Lay out and cut the mortises on the two inside faces of each leg. Inset each mortise ⅜ in. from the inside corner of the leg (see "Laptop Desk" on p. 198).

4. Make a heavy cardboard or thin wood pattern for laying out the curves on the legs (see "Leg Pattern").

5. Use the pattern to lay out the curves on all of the faces of each leg.

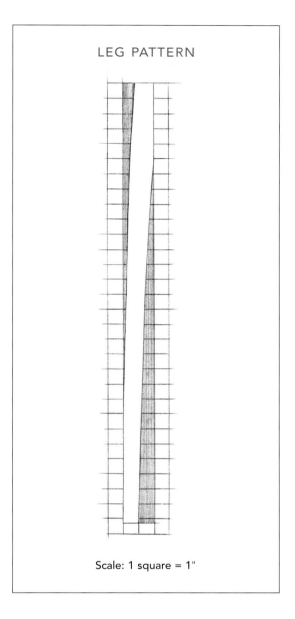

LEG PATTERN

Scale: 1 square = 1"

6. To shape each leg, begin by sawing one outside curve (see **photo C** on p. 204). Next, position the other outside face of the leg facing upward, and use your template to retrace the section of the curve that you just sawed away. Then make that cut.

7. Plane, scrape, or sand the outside faces to create a smooth surface for the workpiece to ride on when making the inside face cuts.

8. Saw the inside faces of the legs, again retracing the curves as necessary after cutting away part of an adjacent face (see **photo D** on p. 204).

Photo C: When cutting the leg curves, saw a bit shy of the cut line, leaving the remaining waste to be cleaned up with hand tools.

9. Clean up the inside faces using a compass plane, spokeshave, scraper, or belt sander (see photo E).

Making the skirt

1. Dimension the side and back skirts, remembering to include the necessary length for the tenon on each end.

2. Mill one board that will be used for both the front skirt and the drawer front. Make the workpiece ¼ in. wider than given to allow for the saw kerf waste created when ripping the skirt into three pieces, as described next.

3. Rip a ⅜-in.-wide strip off the bottom edge of the board and a ⁵⁄₁₆-in.-wide strip off the top edge.

4. Crosscut 3 in. off of each end of the center ripping. These will be reglued onto the skirt. Set the remainder of the center ripping aside; it will later be used for the drawer front.

5. Make the front skirt by gluing the 3-in.-long ends between the top and bottom rippings. Carefully align the pieces in their original positions at the outermost ends of the skirt. Let the glue dry thoroughly.

Photo D: After cutting each face of the leg, align the template with the remaining portion of the original line on the adjacent face and retrace the shape.

Photo E: **I use a scraper to smooth the saw marks from the bandsawn leg.**

6. Lay out and cut the tenons on the ends of the skirts, mitering their ends to meet inside the legs. Make sure the tenons fit snugly in their mortises.

7. Cut the rabbets in the top and bottom edges of the back and side skirts. The front skirt does not get rabbets.

8. Cut the ¾-in.-wide by ¼-in.-deep dadoes in the front and back skirts that hold the vertical supports.

9. Finish-sand the skirts.

BUILDING THE INNER FRAMEWORK

The inner framework consists of an upper and lower frame and two vertical supports. Both frames provide strength and stability to the base, while the upper frame serves double-duty as an attachment for the desktop.

Grooves in the vertical supports provide the bearing surface for the sliding tray.

1. Dimension the two vertical supports, the four long rails, and the eight short stiles. Double stiles are used instead of a single wide stile to minimize wood movement problems (see **photo F** on p. 206).

2. Rip the ¼-in.-wide by ½-in.-deep grooves in the inside edges of the rails, then cut tenons on the stiles to fit.

3. Glue up the frames, making sure they are absolutely square (see **photo G** on p. 206).

4. Sand the frames flat and smooth. Because you won't see them, you don't have to go overboard, but I generally ease all sharp edges and remove any rough spots.

5. Saw the 1-in.-wide by ¼-in.-deep grooves in the vertical supports that will hold the slide-out tray. Space the grooves ¼ in. up from the bottom edge of the supports. Also, cut the

Photo F: **Doubled-up stiles on the inner frames prevent the wood movement problems you might experience with a single wide stile.**

¾-in.-wide by ¼-in.-deep grooves in the lower frame that house the vertical supports.

6. Sand the grooves in the vertical supports to ensure smooth movement of the slide-out tray.

7. Drill four screw holes in the upper frame for attaching the top (see "Laptop Desk" on p. 198). Elongate the holes with a round file to allow for cross-grain expansion and contraction of the solid-wood top.

8. Drill four large holes in the lower frame, aligning them with the screw holes in the top frame. These large holes are for screwdriver access when attaching the top. I made mine ¾ in. in diameter to give myself a little "wiggle room."

9. Drill a 1½-in.-diameter hole in the vertical support and one in the lower frame for passage of electrical plugs.

Photo G: **To pull a freshly glued assembly into square, squeeze a clamp across opposite corners until opposing diagonal measurements match.**

ASSEMBLING THE DESK

I assembled the base and top before making the slide-out tray so I could be sure the tray fit perfectly.

1. Glue the legs and skirts together. Be sure the base assembly is square, or you will run into problems fitting the inner framework.

2. After the leg-and-skirt assembly has been unclamped, glue the lower frame into the rabbets in the back and side skirts. (You will have to notch the corners of the frames to fit around the legs.) Be sure the grooves for the vertical supports line up with the dadoes in the front and back skirts.

3. Apply glue to the dadoes in the skirts and lower frame, then slide the vertical supports into place. Make sure the bottom edges of the grooves in the vertical supports are slightly higher than the opening in the front skirt, otherwise the slide-out tray won't operate properly.

4. Glue the upper frame into its rabbets in the top edges of the back and side skirts.

5. Clean up any glue squeeze-out and give everything a light sanding. Then set the assembly aside while you build the slide-out tray.

BUILDING THE SLIDE-OUT TRAY

The slide-out tray is a frame-and-panel assembly that's actually built more like a door than a drawer. It consists of stiles, rails, and floating panels. The frame members connect with mortise-and-tenon joints, and the panels float unglued in grooves in the frame. The drawer front is hinged to the front edge of the tray.

1. Make the two floating panels, gluing up several boards if necessary to get the width that you need. The dimensions for the panels given are somewhat tight, so expect to trim them to fit after making the frame.

2. Dimension the back and front rails, the subrail, and the three stiles, making sure to include the length of the tenons on one end of each stile.

3. Cut the mortises in the back rail and all of the stiles. Then rip a ¼-in.-wide by ⅜-in.-deep groove in the inside edges of rails and stiles. The bottom edge of the groove should sit ½ in. down from the upper faces of the frame members to align the top face of the ½-in.-thick panels flush with the top face of the frame.

4. Cut the tenons on the back end of each stile and both ends of the two rails. Make sure they fit snugly in their mortises.

5. Use a dado head to cut down the front end of the three stiles to 3⁄16 in. thick. The cut should end 3½ in. from the end of each stile.

6. Cut the three 3⁄16-in.-deep half laps in the subrail.

7. Dry-fit the frames and measure for the two panels.

8. Cut the panels to width and length, allowing for wood movement. After squaring the panels, cut the ¼-in.-deep by ⅜-in.-wide rabbets on the top side to create the ¼-in.-thick tongues that fit in the frame grooves.

9. Glue up the entire tray, making sure the assembly remains square and flat under clamp pressure.

10. After the glue dries, attach the subrail and then sand the entire assembly smooth and flat.

11. Hinge the drawer front to the front of the tray. Begin by mortising the hinges into the subrail. Then align the bottom edge of the drawer front with the bottom face of the subrail and mark out the mortises in the back of the drawer front. After cutting the mortises, attach the drawer front, making sure it folds down flush with the top face of the sliding tray (see **photo H** on p. 208).

12. Attach two hard-wearing wood strips to the sides of the tray to minimize sliding friction and to protect the tray sides from wear.

Photo H: **The drawer front folds down flush with the tray to create a flat working surface. The recessed pulls won't interfere with your hands or the computer.**

Locust, hickory, and white oak are all good choices. Make the pieces ⅟₁₆ in. wider than the thickness of the tray and attach them with the overhang projecting off the bottom of the tray.

13. Screw a ¼-in.-thick by 1⅗₁₆-in.-wide strip to the back edge of the tray to serve as a stop strip. The strip will bump against stop blocks on the vertical supports to prevent the tray from falling out.

14. To install the stop blocks, first insert the tray a few inches into its grooves. Then place the stop block against the rear stop strip and against each vertical support, then drill for the stop block screws. You'll fasten the stop blocks after finishing the desk and installing the tray.

Making the pulls

The pulls are T-shaped pieces of walnut mortised into a carved recess (see "Pull" on p. 211). The recess is easy to make, even for someone with little or no carving experience.

1. Draw two 2¾-in.-diameter circles on the drawer front to establish the perimeter of each finished recess.

2. To provide a depth reference and to remove the bulk of the waste, drill a ⅗₁₆-in.-deep hole in the center of the pull area using a ⅞-in.-diameter Forstner bit (see **photo I**).

3. Begin shaping the recess with a large gouge, cutting inward from the perimeter (see **photo J**).

4. Once the recess is roughed out to its approximate shape, finish off the carving with a narrow veining tool (see **photo K**).

Photo I: **To establish the perimeter and depth of the pull recess, draw its outer diameter, then drill a flat-bottomed hole in the center.**

Photo J: **Rough out the recess with a gouge, carving from the perimeter inward.**

Photo K: **Use a veining tool to texture the recess, spacing the cuts evenly around the circle.**

GLUING UP LARGE PANELS

To minimize chances of a desktop or other large panel warping, I generally don't make the panel from boards wider than about 6 in. Whenever possible, I also reverse the growth rings on adjacent boards (see "Minimizing Panel Warpage"). However, the color and figure of the boards ultimately dictate how they will be arranged. For example, if I have an attractive board that is wide and flat, I may use it as one piece rather than ripping it up and ruining the figure. Or if the back of a board contains sapwood, I won't flip the board over simply to reverse the growth rings. After arranging boards for a panel, I draw a continuous, light pencil line across their faces for placement reference during glue-up.

I generally straighten and square up the edges of a board on a jointer. I find that a well-tuned jointer squares edges better than a handplane in a fraction of the time. If your jointer fence isn't perfectly square to the table, you can cancel out the resulting angles by alternating opposite faces of adjacent boards against the jointer fence.

It's wise to dry-clamp a panel to check for a tight edge joint before applying glue. If you have to really crank the clamps to pull the boards together, then the edges need to be reworked so they don't pull apart over time from the built-in stress. Remove the boards in question and joint them again until they meet without gaps. For bowed or very long boards, I sometimes use biscuits, dowels, or a machined glue joint to help align the edges.

When clamping, alternate the clamps over and under the panel to ensure even pressure and to keep the panel from springing. If the edges of the boards don't quite line up, loosen the clamps a bit, and rap the boards with a rubber mallet (see photo A on p. 202). Once the boards are aligned, tighten the clamps firmly, but not so hard that you crush the wood. The joints should be tight along their entire length and a small bead of glue should squeeze out from each side. It's best to remove glue squeeze-out before it cures, because scraping off hardened glue tends to tear out bits of wood. You can wipe off fresh glue with a wet rag or wait for the glue to skim over, then scrape it off with a knife or chisel.

Although you can often unclamp a glued-up panel in as little as a half an hour, I like to leave boards clamped up at least two or three hours and preferably overnight. If you won't be working the panel right away, lay it across a couple of stickers on a flat bench. Air circulating around it helps maintain a balanced moisture content, minimizing potential warping.

MINIMIZING PANEL WARPAGE

Reversing the growth rings on boards that make up a large panel will result in the panel remaining relatively flat, even if the individual boards cup.

The recesses are roughed out with a gouge and mallet and then finished with a small veining tool. The carved black walnut pulls are glued into stepped through mortises that maximize the gluing surface area.

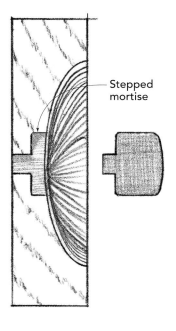

Stepped mortise

Photo L: **To make the tenon on the pull, cut two opposing notches in the pull stock, then crosscut the pull free.**

of the walnut pull. About ⅜ in. of the pull should project from the bottom of the recess (see "Pull"). The pull should fit snugly enough that you need to seat it with taps from a mallet.

7. Glue the pull into its mortise.

FINISHING UP

I like the look of natural unstained cherry so I use a Danish oil finish topped off with a coat of wax for a piece like this. However, if your desk is going to sit in a high-traffic area or be subject to a lot of abuse, I would recommend a more durable finish like a solvent-based polyurethane or water-based lacquer.

5. Make the T-shaped pulls. First, rip a piece of material ¼ in. thick by 1 in. wide. Then use a ¼-in.-wide dado head to cut two opposing ⅜-in.-deep notches, set ½ in. from the end of the piece (see **photo L**). Crosscut the resulting T-shaped section from the piece, then round over the top edges of the pull with sandpaper.
6. Chisel out a stepped mortise at the bottom of the pull recess to accept the bottom section

PEDESTAL DESK

Paul and Michael Wilson, owners of Wilson Woodworking in Windsor, Vermont, have built a number of variations of the pedestal desk pictured here. The design can be easily modified to suit a variety of styles, shapes, and sizes. Sometimes the Wilsons replace one of the pedestals with a simple, standing panel. If the desk will hold a computer they often incorporate a keyboard tray instead of a center drawer. At times, they have even eliminated the feet by bringing the base all the way down to the floor. When building your own version, you can easily alter the size, number, and placement of the drawers to create a desk that suits your own needs (see "Design Options" on p. 218).

The desk draws on elements of Shaker design, yet the clean lines and bright, figured hard maple give it a modern look. The desk is constructed of a series of framed book-matched floating panels that are joined together to form the two pedestals.

Two pull-out boards, commercial drawer slides, and deep drawers make it practical and highly functional for a busy home or professional office. The pull-out boards above the top drawers expand the working area of the desk by more than 3 square ft. but slide out of the way when not in use. The entire assembly is strengthened and stiffened by the top, which is screwed to the pedestals. Although this desk is made of hard maple, cherry or walnut would be good choices as well.

Pedestal Desk

THIS DESK IS CONSTRUCTED OF A SERIES of frame-and-panel assemblies that incorporate the legs as frame members. Six of the eight legs are tapered at the foot and are complemented by the curved lower rails on the front and outermost case sides. The pull-out board runners do double-duty as cleats for attaching the top.

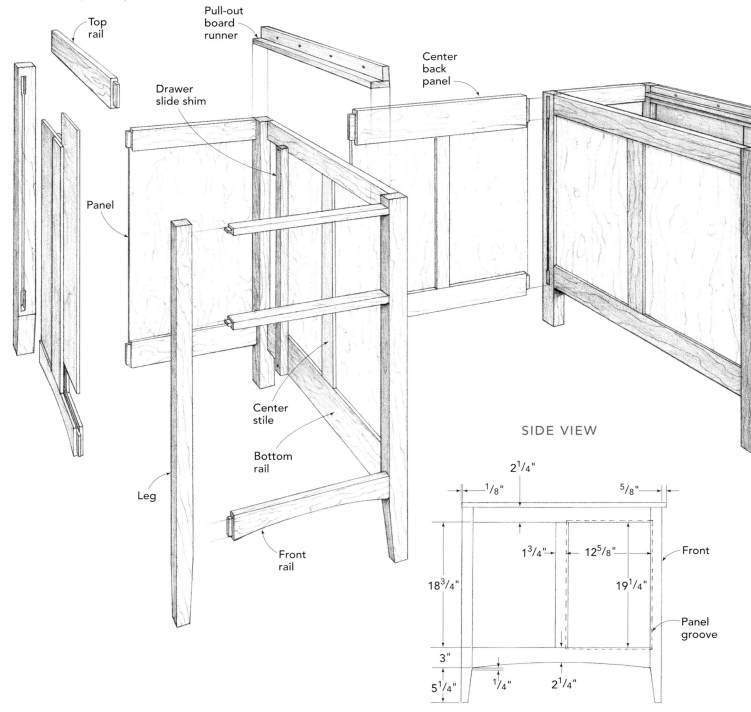

Top rail

Pull-out board runner

Drawer slide shim

Center back panel

Panel

Center stile

Bottom rail

Leg

Front rail

SIDE VIEW

$2^{1}/_{4}$"

$^{1}/_{8}$"

$^{5}/_{8}$"

$1^{3}/_{4}$"

$12^{5}/_{8}$"

Front

$18^{3}/_{4}$"

$19^{1}/_{4}$"

Panel groove

3"

$5^{1}/_{4}$"

$^{1}/_{4}$"

$2^{1}/_{4}$"

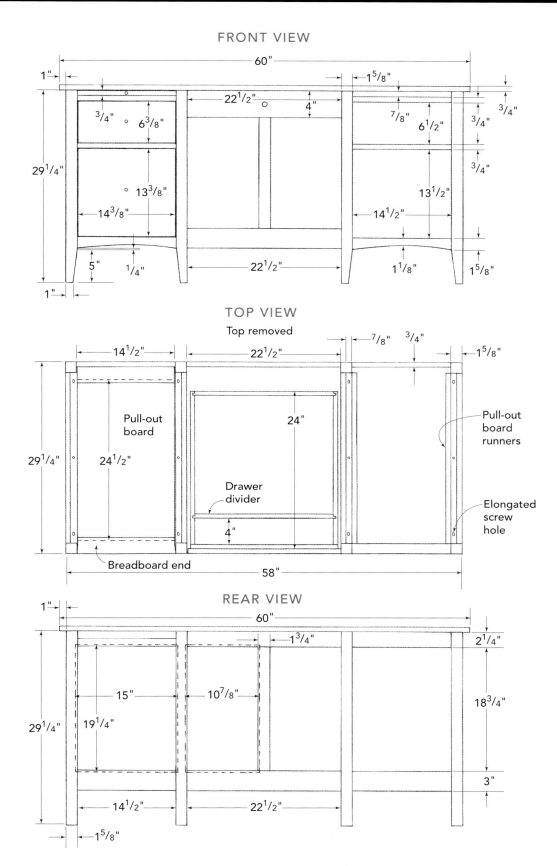

FRONT VIEW

60"

1"

1⁵/₈"

³/₄"

22¹/₂"

4"

³/₄"

6³/₈"

7/₈"

6¹/₂"

³/₄"

³/₄"

29¹/₄"

³/₄"

13³/₈"

13¹/₂"

14³/₈"

14¹/₂"

5"

¹/₄"

22¹/₂"

1¹/₈"

1⁵/₈"

1"

TOP VIEW

Top removed

14¹/₂"

22¹/₂"

7/₈"

³/₄"

1⁵/₈"

Pull-out
board

Pull-out
board
runners

24"

29¹/₄"

24¹/₂"

Drawer
divider

Elongated
screw
hole

4"

Breadboard end

58"

REAR VIEW

1"

60"

2¹/₄"

1³/₄"

15"

10⁷/₈"

18³/₄"

19¹/₄"

29¹/₄"

14¹/₂"

22¹/₂"

3"

1⁵/₈"

Building the Desk Step-by-Step

CUT LIST FOR PEDESTAL DESK

1	Top	¾ in. x 30 in. x 60 in.
8	Legs	1⅝ in. x 1⅝ in. x 29¼ in.

Side Panels

4	Top rails	¾ in. x 2¼ in. x 27½ in. (including a ⅜-in. x 1¾-in. x ¾-in. tenon on both ends)
4	Bottom rails	¾ in. x 3 in. x 27½ in. (including a ⅜-in. x 2½-in. x ¾-in. tenon on both ends)
4	Center stiles	¾ in. x 1¾ in. x 19¼ in. (including a ⁵⁄₁₆-in. x 1¼-in. x ¼-in. tenon on both ends)
8	Panels	⁵⁄₁₆ in. x 12⅝ in. x 19¼ in.

Back Panels

2	Outer top rails	¾ in. x 2¼ in. x 16 in. (including a ⅜-in. x 1¾-in. x ¾-in. tenon on both ends)
1	Center top rail	¾ in. x 2¼ in. x 24 in. (including a ⅜-in. x 1¾-in. x ¾-in. tenon on both ends)
2	Outer bottom rails	¾ in. x 3 in. x 16 in. (including a ⅜-in. x 2½-in. x ¾-in. tenon on both ends)
1	Center bottom rail	¾ in. x 3 in. x 24 in. (including a ⅜-in. x 2½-in. x ¾-in. tenon on both ends)
1	Center stile	¾ in. x 1¾ in. x 19¼ in. (including a ⁵⁄₁₆-in. x 1¼-in. x ¼-in. tenon on both ends)
2	Outer panels	⁵⁄₁₆ in. x 15 in. x 19¼ in.
2	Center panels	⁵⁄₁₆ in. x 10⅞ in. x 19¼ in.

Front Rails

4	Upper rails	¾ in. x 1⅝ in. x 16 in. (including a ⅜-in. x 1⅛-in. x ¾-in. tenon on both ends)
2	Bottom rails	¾ in. x 1⅝ in. x 16 in. (including a ⅜-in. x 1⅛-in. x ¾-in. tenon on both ends)

ORMALLY I LIKE to start with the top when making a desk because it is usually the most visible part. With this desk, however, the floating side panels are the focal point, so I start with them, after which I glue up the top. Next, I make the legs, the frame-and-panel assemblies, and the front rails. Then I assemble the pedestals and connect them with the back center panel. Last, I make the drawers and pull-out boards, and attach the top.

MAKING THE FLOATING PANELS AND THE TOP

Each of the 12 floating panels is made from a wide board that is resawn and book-matched (see "Book-Matching" on p. 219). The desktop need not be book-matched, but should be laid out for a good grain match at the joints. Depending on the quality of your lumber, you will need a minimum of 25 to 30 board ft. of 4/4 material to make the floating panels and the top.

Making the panels and top

1. Select your best 4/4 stock for the panels. As you lay out the stock for each panel, carefully consider its position on the desk to achieve an overall visual balance.

2. Cut each panel blank to rough length and width, leaving each piece a few inches oversize in length and a bit wider than half the dimension of the finished panel.

3. Joint the long-grain edges of the stock, then draw a line across the edge of each piece for future reference when orienting the pieces for book-matching.

4. Resaw each panel blank in half on the bandsaw. Use a wide blade and a high fence. Set the angle of the fence to compensate for "drift" (see "Resawing on the Bandsaw" on p. 220).

CUT LIST FOR PEDESTAL DESK

Pull-Out Boards

2	Pull-out boards	¾ in. x 14¼ in. x 23⅝ in. (including a ⅜-in. x 14⅜-in. x ½-in. tenon on both ends)
1	Breadboard end	¾ in. x 2½ in. x 14⅜ in.
1	Breadboard end	¾ in. x 2½ in. x 14¼ in.
4	Runner side pieces	⅞ in. x ⅞ in. x 26 in.
4	Runner bottom pieces	¾ in. x 1⅝ in. x 26 in.

Top Left and Right Drawers

2	Drawer fronts	¾ in. x 6⅜ in. x 14⅜ in.
2	Box fronts	⅝ in. x 5½ in. x 13½ in.
4	Sides	⅝ in. x 5½ in. x 24 in.
2	Backs	⅝ in. x 4½ in. x 12⅞ in.
2	Bottoms	½ in. x 12⅞ in. x 23¹¹⁄₁₆ in.

Top Center Drawer

1	Drawer front	¾ in. x 4 in. x 22⅜ in.
1	Box front	⅝ in. x 3 in. x 21½ in.
2	Sides	⅝ in. x 3 in. x 24 in.
1	Back	⅝ in. x 2½ in. x 20⅞ in.
1	Drawer divider	⅝ in. x 2½ in. x 20⅞ in.
1	Bottom	¼ in. x 20⅞ in. x 23¹¹⁄₁₆ in.

Bottom Left and Right Drawers

2	Drawer fronts	¾ in. x 13⅜ in. x 14⅜ in.
2	Box fronts	⅝ in. x 12½ in. x 13½ in.
4	Sides	⅝ in. x 12½ in. x 24 in.
2	Backs	⅝ in. x 11½ in. x 12⅞ in.
2	Bottoms	½ in. x 12⅞ in. x 23¹¹⁄₁₆ in.

Hardware

5 pr.	Drawer slides	24 in. long

Design Options

STYLE CHANGES IN THE SIZE, position, and number of drawers greatly change the form of the base.

SINGLE-PEDESTAL DESK

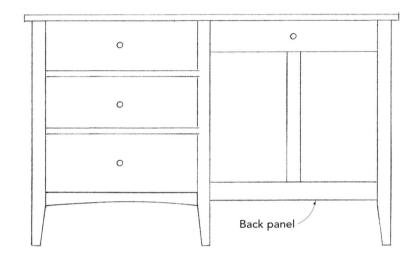

Back panel

DOUBLE-PEDESTAL DESK WITH BASE MOLDING

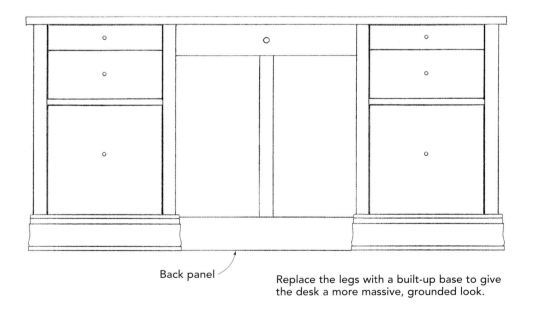

Back panel

Replace the legs with a built-up base to give the desk a more massive, grounded look.

BOOK-MATCHING

Book-matching is the practice of resawing a board into thinner pieces, then gluing the pieces edge to edge to create a mirrored effect with the grain.

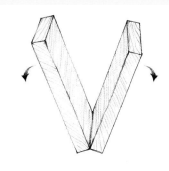

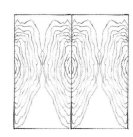

Board cut into two pieces and opened like a book

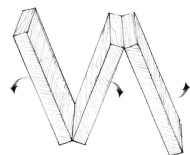

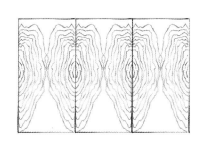

Board cut into multiple pieces

5. If the faces of the boards end up wavy or dished out in areas because of flawed resawing, surface them to a relatively uniform thickness.

6. Edge glue the halves of each panel together, being sure to align them so the grain pattern matches fairly well at the center. After removing the panels from the clamps, stack them on a flat bench with stickers between each one and a few heavy weights on top of the stack. This will minimize warpage as the panels wait to be fitted in their frames.

7. Lay out stock for the desktop, leaving the boards slightly oversize in length and width. Then surface them to approximate thickness and joint the edges.

8. Edge glue the boards to make the top.

MAKING THE LEGS

This desk has eight legs, six of which have a tapered "foot" at the bottom. The legs are connected by the frame-and-panel assemblies that make up the desk sides and back.

1. Lay out enough 8/4 stock to make the legs. Crosscut and rip the pieces slightly oversize.

2. Mill the pieces to 1⅝ in. square. I joint two adjacent faces of each piece, then I run the pieces through a thickness planer to square up the remaining two faces.

3. Crosscut the legs to length, then mark the end of each to indicate the leg's position on the desk.

RESAWING ON THE BANDSAW

To make the book-matched panels for this desk, you'll need to resaw wide boards. The best way to do this is on a bandsaw equipped with the proper blade and a high fence.

Use the widest blade your bandsaw will handle. A wide blade won't flex as much as a narrow one and will cut easier and straighter. However, the width of blade you can use depends somewhat on your saw's power. For example, my saw will accommodate a ¾-in.-wide blade, but I find when using it that the motor bogs down during heavy cuts. So I generally use a ⅜-in.- or ½-in.-wide blade for resawing. I use a hooked-tooth blade with 3 tpi. The blade cuts aggressively and clears out the dust quickly. A blade with more teeth per inch will cut smoother but much more slowly.

When resawing relatively narrow boards, I often make the cut freehand. But when working with wide stock, I use a high fence as a guide. My fence is simply screwed together from scrap plywood. The important things are that it is sturdy; square to the table; and high enough to support a wide, heavy board.

Last, you will need to account for *blade drift*—the tendency of a bandsaw blade to pull to one side of the workpiece when cutting. The trick to cutting straight is to determine the angle of the drift, then set the fence to that angle. To do this, first gauge a line down the center of a piece of scrap that's about 18 in. long. Carefully cut to the line freehand to establish the angle of feed. When you're about halfway through, turn off the saw while keeping a firm grip on the workpiece to maintain its angle of feed. Trace the edge of the workpiece onto your saw table, then set your fence parallel to that line.

A high fence helps guide the workpiece when resawing wood on the bandsaw.

JOINERY DETAILS

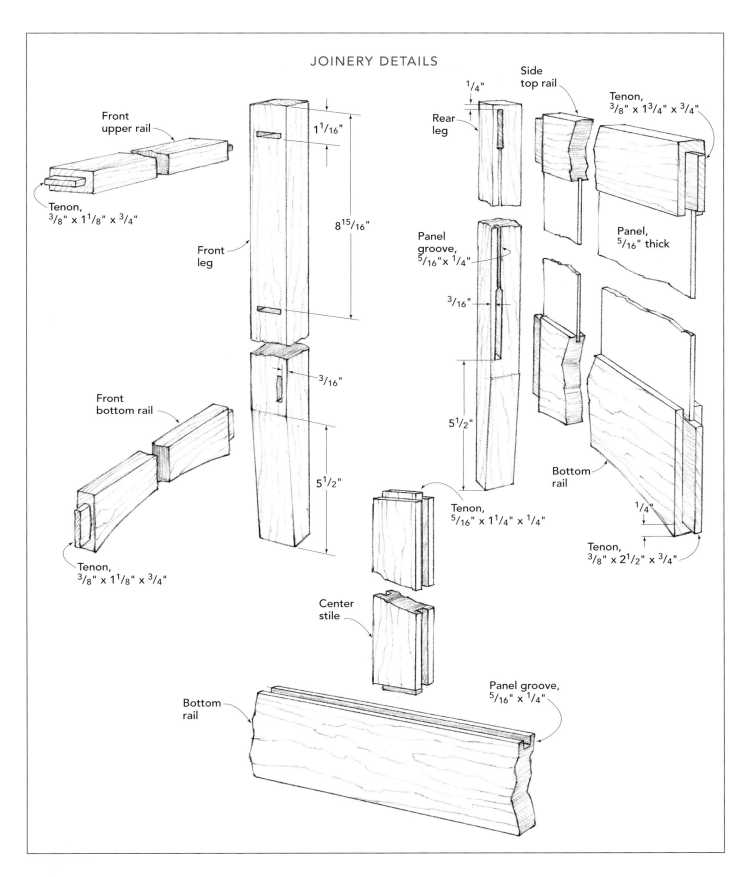

Front upper rail

Tenon, $3/8" \times 1^1/8" \times 3/4"$

Front leg

$1^1/16"$

$8^{15}/16"$

$3/16"$

$5^1/2"$

Front bottom rail

Tenon, $3/8" \times 1^1/8" \times 3/4"$

Center stile

Bottom rail

Rear leg

$1/4"$

Side top rail

Tenon, $3/8" \times 1^3/4" \times 3/4"$

Panel, $5/16"$ thick

Panel groove, $5/16" \times 1/4"$

$3/16"$

$5^1/2"$

Bottom rail

Tenon, $5/16" \times 1^1/4" \times 1/4"$

$1/4"$

Tenon, $3/8" \times 2^1/2" \times 3/4"$

Panel groove, $5/16" \times 1/4"$

Photo A: **A stiff pattern ensures that the taper on each leg will be uniform.**

4. Lay out the mortises to accept the tenons on the rails (see "Joinery Details" on p. 221). Pay close attention to where and how each leg is positioned on the desk.

5. Cut the mortises. You can drill and chop them by hand, use a mortiser, or rout them using a plunge router guided by a router fence.

6. Rout the 5/16-in.-wide by 3/16-in.-deep panel grooves, centering them on the tenon mortises. I cut the grooves on a router table, but you could use a handheld router guided by a router fence.

7. Mark the tapers at the bottoms of the front legs and the outermost rear legs (see **photo A**). The two outermost front legs get a double taper, but the others are tapered on only one face (see "Pedestal Desk" on p. 214). The inner rear legs are not tapered.

8. Cut the tapers on a bandsaw, then smooth the cuts with a belt sander or handplane.

9. Sand only the mortised and grooved faces of the legs for right now, stopping just a bit short of the area where the ends of the rails will butt against the leg.

MAKING THE FRAME-AND-PANEL ASSEMBLIES

At this point, the only pieces needed to complete the pedestal assemblies are the stiles and rails that connect the sides, back, and front of the pedestals. They all get tenons on each end, so it makes sense to machine them all at once.

Cutting and fitting the rails and stiles

1. Mill stock for the rails and stiles. Rip and crosscut the pieces to size, being sure to include the length for the tenons on each end.

2. Cut the tenons, centering them on the ends of the stock (see "Joinery Details" on p. 221). I cut them on the tablesaw, using a dado head (see **photo B**).

3. Saw the ⁵⁄₁₆-in.-wide by ⁵⁄₁₆-in.-deep panel grooves, centering them across the edges of the stock. Although you could rout them, it's much quicker and cleaner to cut them on the tablesaw using a dado head.

4. Lay out the curves on the bottom front rails and the bottom rails of the outermost side panels (see "Pedestal Desk" on p. 214). To lay them out, run a pencil line against a thin strip of straight-grained stock that is held to the bottom corners of each rail and sprung upward the proper amount (see "Side View" on p. 214 and "Front View" on p. 215).

5. Use a bandsaw or jigsaw to cut the curves, and then sand the cut edges smooth (see **photo C**).

6. Sand the grooved edges of the rails, stopping a bit short of the areas where the center stiles meet the horizontal rails. Don't sand the faces of the rails yet.

Photo C: **A spindle sander does a great job of smoothing curves.**

Photo B: **When cutting tenons on a tablesaw, use a stop block to prevent having to bury the dado head in an auxiliary fence.**

Photo D: A tablesaw crosscut sled allows you to crosscut wide panels squarely.

Fitting the panels

To fit the panels, you'll need to dry-clamp each leg-rail-stile assembly in turn, then measure for each panel and saw it to fit.

1. Dry-clamp each of the leg-rail-stile assemblies together to check the fit of the joinery and to measure for the panels. Make sure the assembly is square under clamp pressure, then measure between the panel grooves to determine the sizes of the panels.

2. Mark out the length and width of each panel. It should fit snugly between its top and bottom grooves, but should be sized in width to accommodate future expansion and contraction of the panel. If you're working during the dry, winter season, allow more room. If it's hot and humid, fit the panel more tightly. Lay out the width equally from the center of the panel to ensure symmetry of the book-match.

3. Trim each panel to size on the tablesaw (see **photo D**).

4. After all of the panels have been fit, sand them and apply a couple coats of finish to both sides of each one. If you wait to finish them until after the desk is assembled, the unfinished panel edges concealed in the grooves could shrink away from the frame later, exposing bare wood.

ASSEMBLING THE PEDESTALS

The best way to put the desk together is to assemble the pedestal sides first, then attach the pedestal backs and front rails between the sides.

1. Glue up each of the four side assemblies, being careful to keep glue out of the panel grooves. Make sure that each assembly is flat and square under clamp pressure.

2. After the glue is dry, sand the faces of the assemblies to level and smooth the joints.

Take care not to scratch the panels. Don't sand the outer edges of the legs yet.

3. After the side assemblies are dry, glue the back and the front rails between the sides. Again, avoid getting glue on the back panels. Make sure the pedestals are square under clamp pressure. Otherwise, they may sit unevenly, making the drawers difficult to fit.

4. Sand the rails flush to the legs, avoiding the edge of the inner rear legs where the center back panel will be attached.

5. Glue the center frame-and-panel assembly between the pedestals, then square up the entire base and hold it square by screwing lengths of scrapwood across the top and bottom of the pedestals near the front. This will also allow you to move the desk around the shop if necessary.

6. After the glue is dry, sand the center panel joints flat and smooth.

MAKING THE DRAWERS

The drawer boxes are constructed with dovetails in the front and rabbet-and-dado joints in the back. The drawers will ride on commercially made drawer slides that require ½ in. clearance on each side of the drawer (see **photo E**). The solid maple drawer fronts are screwed to the drawer boxes and conceal the slides that are attached to the sides of the box.

1. Mill and cut the drawer parts to size. Make the drawer fronts from solid maple. You can use a secondary wood for the drawer box; the Wilsons used pine. The side drawers have ½-in.-thick plywood bottoms, but the bottom of the shallow center drawer is made from ¼-in.-thick plywood.

2. Lay out the dovetails, remembering that the drawer bottom groove should pass through a tail, not a pin (see "Drawer Construction"). You can use any spacing you

Photo E: The drawers are installed with commercially made, side-mounted drawer slides.

Drawer Construction

THE DRAWERS ARE CONSTRUCTED with through dovetails at the front and a rabbet-and-dado joint at the back. Lay out the dovetail spacing to your liking, making sure that the bottom groove passes through a tail, not a pin. The bottom of the top center drawer is ¼" thick. All of the other bottoms are ½" thick.

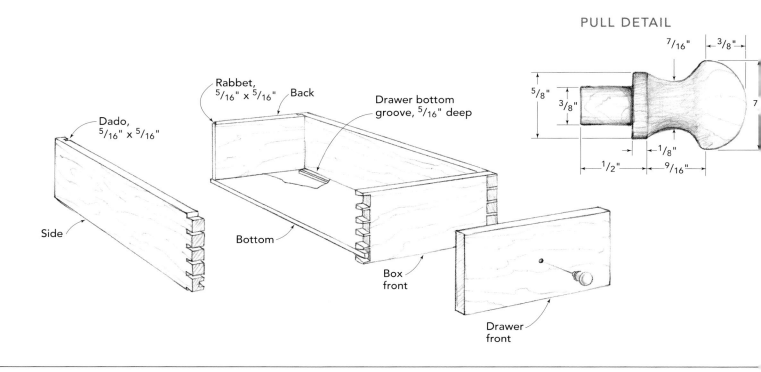

PULL DETAIL

Rabbet, 5/16" x 5/16" Back

Dado, 5/16" x 5/16"

Drawer bottom groove, 5/16" deep

Side

Bottom

Box front

Drawer front

7/16" 3/8"

5/8" 3/8" 7

1/2" 1/8" 9/16"

like, but keep the dovetail angle somewhere between 12 and 14 degrees.

3. Cut the dovetails.

4. Using a dado head in a tablesaw, cut the rabbet-and-dado joints for the rear of the boxes and the pencil divider joint in the center drawer (see "Top View" on p. 215).

5. Cut the grooves for the bottoms, aligning them just under the bottom edge of the drawer back.

6. Glue the boxes together, then slide the bottoms into their grooves. Make sure the drawers are square, then attach the bottoms to the drawer backs with a few screws.

7. After the glue has dried, sand the drawer boxes so the joints are all flush and the sharp edges are slightly eased. You should also sand the drawer fronts now.

8. Screw the drawer slides to the drawer boxes and to the insides of the cabinet, following the manufacturer's instructions. You can attach the front of the slides to the inside face of the front legs, but you'll need to shim out the slides at their centers and rear ends to bring them flush to the front end. The easiest approach is to screw a long piece of ⅞-in.-thick stock to the case rails at the midpoint and rear of the drawer slides. (see "Pedestal Desk" on p. 214).

9. After installing the drawer boxes, attach the fronts. The Wilsons apply a couple of dabs of hot-melt glue to the drawer front, then stick it on the box, quickly aligning it for a

DRAWER FRONT ADJUSTERS

Properly attaching drawer fronts to their drawer boxes can be a fight. Even if you manage to get a consistent gap between a drawer front and its opening, things can still change. Drawer front adjusters are a slick solution. They are basically thick plastic washers with a movable threaded insert at the center that allows for slight shifting of a drawer front.

To install the adjusters, begin by drilling two 20-mm-diameter by $7/16$-in.-deep holes in the backside of the drawer front. Then place 20-mm-diameter dowel centers in the holes. Position the drawer front in its opening and press it firmly against the drawer box to transfer the hole centers to the front of the drawer box. Next, drill holes at those loca-

tions to accept the machine screws that thread into the adjusters. Replace each dowel center with a drawer adjuster, pounding it in with a hammer.

Attach the drawer fronts by inserting machine screws through the box front into the drawer adjusters. Snug up the screws, but not too tightly, then position the front exactly where you want it; the metal inserts in the drawer adjusters allow for as much as $3/16$ in. movement in any direction. When you're happy, tighten the screws. On large drawers, I reinforce the attachment with a screw in each corner of the drawer front.

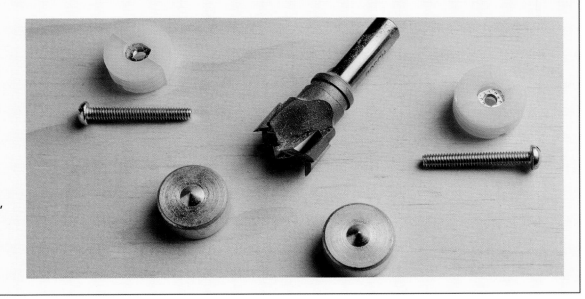

Drawer adjusters, a 20-mm bit, dowel centers, and machine screws.

consistent gap between the drawer front and its opening. Then they anchor the front in place with several screws. You could also use double-sided tape or short nails to align the front before anchoring it with screws. Personally, I prefer to use drawer front adjusters (see "Drawer Front Adjusters").

10. Drill the holes for the pulls, then turn the pulls, but don't install them yet. It is easier to finish the drawer fronts with them off. (Instead of making your own pulls, you can buy them from many mail-order woodworking supply companies.)

MAKING THE PULL-OUT BOARDS

The breadboard ends on the pull-out boards help keep the boards flat. Dowels that ride in slotted holes in the tongue allow the boards to expand and contract with seasonal changes. The front breadboard end is a bit wider than the main body of the board to maintain a close gap in its opening, while allowing the board to expand and contract (see **photo F**).

Building the pull-out boards

1. Glue up the main body of the pull-out boards. To minimize potential warpage, use several narrow pieces rather than one or two wide ones, and edge join the pieces so that the annular rings are reversed on adjacent pieces (see "Breadboard End Construction").

2. Plane or sand the blanks to a thickness of slightly more than ¾ in., but don't bother finish-sanding them at this point. Do try to maintain a consistent thickness on each board, because the thickness of the tongue—thus the breadboard end joint—will be affected by it.

3. Cut the breadboard ends to width and length. Notice that the front piece is ⅛ in. longer than the back.

4. Cut the groove in the edge of each bread-board end. You could rout them, but it's much quicker to cut them on the tablesaw (see **photo G**).

Photo F: The front edge of the pull-out board is feathered back with a sander to maintain a tight fit at the front while allowing for cross-grain expansion and contraction of the board inside the case.

BREADBOARD END CONSTRUCTION

Breadboard end construction is a great way to keep a panel flat. Because the grain of the breadboard ends is perpendicular to the grain of the board, the ends prevent movement of the board. Elongated holes in the tongue allow the board to expand and contract naturally with the seasons.

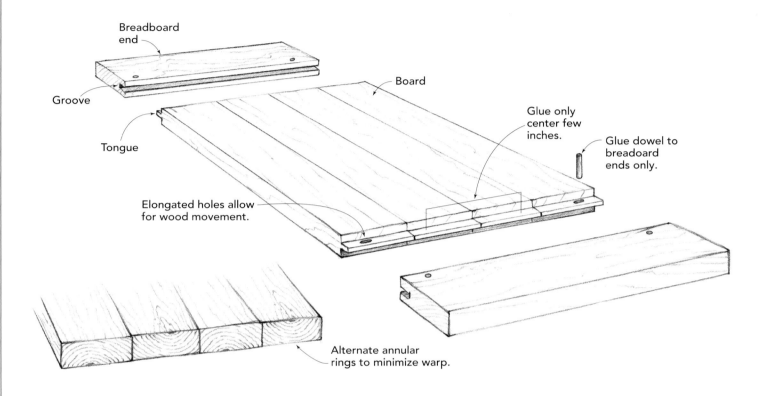

Breadboard end

Groove

Tongue

Board

Glue only center few inches.

Glue dowel to breadoard ends only.

Elongated holes allow for wood movement.

Alternate annular rings to minimize warp.

Photo G: Saw the grooves in the breadboard ends using a dado head set up for a cut slightly narrower than the thickness of the tongue on the pull-out board. Make the first pass, then flip the board end for end and make another pass. This will center the groove in the workpiece.

Photo H: The tongue on each end of the pull-out board should fit snugly into the groove on the breadboard end, but not so tightly that you have to pound it in with a hammer.

5. Cut the opposing rabbets that create the tongue on each end of the board. I saw the rabbets on the tablesaw, using a dado head. Aim for a snug fit (see **photo H**).

6. With the breadboard ends in place, drill two ¼-in.-diameter holes completely through each breadboard end and tongue, 1 in. or so in from the edge of the tongue.

7. Remove the breadboard ends, and lengthen the drill holes a bit with a round file (see **photo I**). Be careful not to widen the holes toward the end of the tongue, or the breadboard end may pull away in use.

8. Attach the breadboard ends by applying just a bit of glue on the center few inches of the tongue and a small drop of glue on the very end of each peg.

9. Sand both faces of the pull-out boards so they are smooth. Sand the ends of the rear breadboard ends so they're flush with the edges of the main body.

10. Belt sand the rear section of the front breadboard end to feather it back to the body of the board (see **photo F** on p. 228).

Installing the pull-out boards

The boards ride on two-piece, L-shaped runners that are attached to the sides of the pedestals. The runners also serve as screw cleats for attaching the desktop (see "Pedestal Desk" on p. 214).

1. Make each runner by gluing and screwing together its side and bottom pieces.

2. Sand the inside faces of the runners so the pull-out boards will slide freely.

Photo I: Elongated holes in the pull-out board tongue allow the board to expand and contract around the pegs without splitting.

3. Drill screw holes through the runners for attaching the top. Elongate the outermost holes about ¼ in. with a round file to allow the top to expand and contract over time.
4. Glue and screw the runners to the pedestal side top rails.
5. Insert each pull-out board into its opening. When fully inserted, the front edge of the pull-out board should be flush to the front rails. Trim or shim at the rear if necessary.

FINISHING UP

1. Place the top on the desk and attach it with screws through the pull-out board runners.
2. Give the entire desk a final finish-sanding.

3. Apply a finish. Paul Wilson sprayed on two coats of a precatalyzed lacquer for the tough finish necessary in a commercial office environment. However, you may simply want to wipe a couple of coats of oil onto the base. The top should get additional protection, though—two or three coats of polyurethane or water-based lacquer would do the trick. It's also wise to finish the underside of the top to help prevent the wood from absorbing moisture unevenly and cupping or cracking.

PART SIX
CHESTS

DOUBLE DRESSER

Furniture makers often are reluctant to depart from tradition. They use solid wood throughout a chest, support drawers with web frames, and avoid using fasteners in favor of intricate joinery. The parts are crafted in ways that require a practiced hand.

Mark Edmundson, of Sandpoint, Idaho, isn't so tradition bound. He isn't reluctant to use modern materials, hardware, and joinery when circumstances recommend them. This dresser was commissioned by a couple with a budget too limited for expensive hardwoods and labor-intensive construction. To fulfill their desires within their means, Edmundson used veneered sheet goods, manufactured drawer runners, and biscuit and pocket-screw joinery.

None of this is immediately obvious. The style is spare and elegant. Though the figure of the wood is not showy, you don't immediately grasp that the dresser isn't solid wood throughout. From the front, it is all solid wood—leg posts, rails, drawer fronts, even the drawer pulls. No fastener or hardware is obvious, even when the drawers are open.

The result is a relatively simple project that can be duplicated with a minimum of shop equipment. You have to make the framework with considerable precision, but you use simple machine setups—rather than a practiced hand—to derive the accuracy needed.

Double Dresser

A CONTEMPORARY TAKE on traditional post-and-panel construction, the double dresser makes use of sheet goods panels, loose tenons, biscuits, and pocket screws.

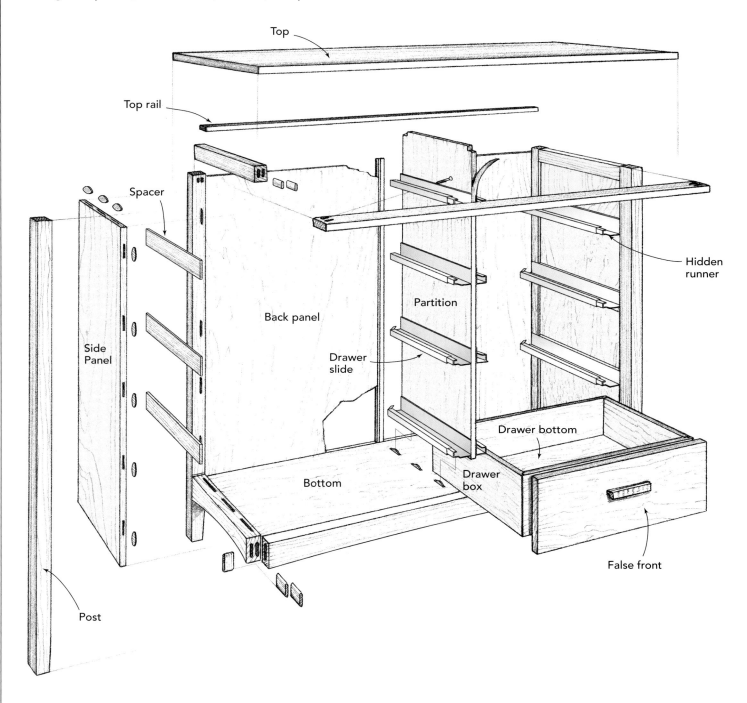

Top

Top rail

Spacer

Hidden runner

Back panel

Partition

Side Panel

Drawer slide

Drawer bottom

Bottom

Drawer box

Post

False front

SIDE VIEW

FRONT VIEW

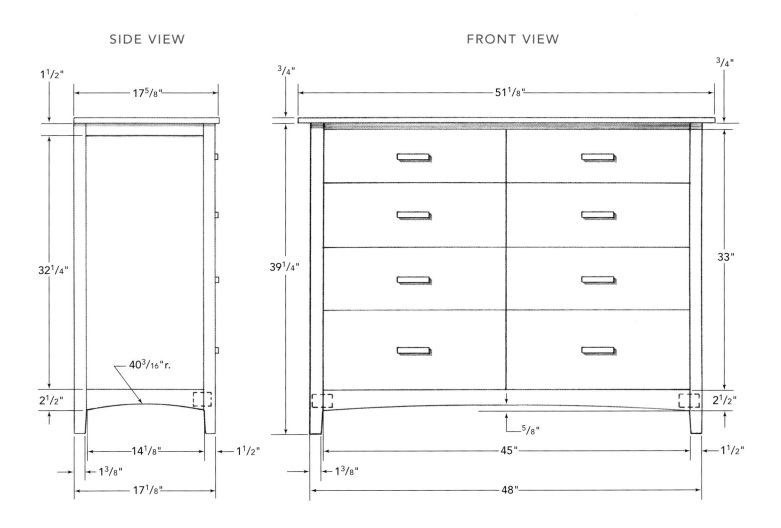

1 1/2"

17 5/8"

32 1/4"

40 3/16" r.

2 1/2"

14 1/8"

1 1/2"

1 3/8"

17 1/8"

3/4"

3/4"

51 1/8"

39 1/4"

33"

2 1/2"

5/8"

45"

1 1/2"

1 3/8"

48"

Building the Chest Step By Step

	CUT LIST FOR DOUBLE DRESSER		
Case			
4	Leg posts	1½ in. x 1½ in. x 39¼ in.	maple
1	Bottom front rail	1⅜ in. x 2½ in. x 45 in.	maple
2	Bottom side rails	1⅜ in. x 2½ in. x 14⅛ in.	maple
2	Top side rails	1⅜ in. x 1½ in. x 14⅛ in.	maple
1	Top front rail	¾ in. x 1⅜ in. x 45 in.	maple
1	Bottom back rail	¾ in. x 1½ in. x 45 in.	maple
1	Top back rail	¾ in. x 1½ in. x 45 in.	maple
1	Partition edge band	¾ in. x ¾ in. x 33 in.	maple
2	Loose tenons	½ in. x 1¾ in. x 2½ in.	maple
2	Loose tenons	¼ in. x ¾ in. x 2½ in.	maple
8	Loose tenons	¼ in. x ¾ in. x ¾ in.	maple
8	Loose tenons	¼ in. x 1¾ in. x ¾ in.	maple
1	Bottom panel	¾ in. x 14⅛ in. x 45 in.	maple plywood
1	Partition panel	¾ in. x 16¼ in. x 33¾ in.	maple plywood
2	Back panels	¼ in. x 22⅝ in. x 33½ in.	maple plywood
2	Side panels	¾ in. x 14⅛ in. x 32¼ in.	maple-veneered MDF
2	Dowels	⁵⁄₁₆ in. diameter x 2 in.	
2	Long top edge bands	½ in. x ¾ in. x 51⅛ in.	maple
2	Short top edge bands	½ in. x ¾ in. x 17⅝ in.	maple
1	Top	¾ in. x 16⅝ in. x 50⅛ in.	maple-veneered MDF

CUT LIST FOR DOUBLE DRESSER

Drawers			
2	Drawer fronts	¾ in. x 6$^{11}/_{16}$ in. x 22⅜ in.	maple
4	Drawer fronts	¾ in. x 8 in. x 22⅜ in.	maple
2	Drawer fronts	¾ in. x 10 in. x 22⅜ in.	maple
4	Drawer box front/backs	⅝ in. x 5 in. x 21¾ in.	alder
4	Drawer sides	⅝ in. x 5 in. x 14¾ in.	alder
8	Drawer box front/backs	⅝ in. x 6⅜ in. x 21¾ in.	alder
8	Drawer sides	⅝ in. x 6⅜ in. x 14¾ in.	alder
4	Drawer box front/backs	⅝ in. x 8⅜ in. x 21¾ in.	alder
4	Drawer sides	⅝ in. x 8⅜ in. x 14¾ in.	alder
8	Drawer bottoms	¼ in. x 14¼ in. x 21 in.	birch plywood
8	Runner spacers	½ in. x 3 in. x 14⅛ in.	plywood
8	Drawer pulls	¾ in. x ¾ in. x 4 in.	maple
16	Dowels	$^{5}/_{16}$ in. diameter x 1 in.	
Hardware			
8 pairs	Tandem single-extension drawer runners	15 in.	from Blum; item #552
8 pairs	Tandem locking devices		from Blum
16	Drawer front adjusters		from Blum

CONSTRUCTION OF THE DRESSER breaks down into two major phases: building the case and constructing the drawers. To build the case, you cut and join all the hardwood members into a framework. You then fill the openings with panels cut from sheet goods, joining them to the hardwood frame with biscuits.

CONSTRUCTING THE CASE

The case for the dresser is a contemporary take on the traditional post-and-panel construction. The legs and rails are made of hardwood, and they are assembled with loose tenons, a modern form of the mortise-and-tenon joint. But the panels are stable, manmade materials, and they are installed with easy-to-cut biscuit joinery.

Preparing the hardwood stock

The legs, the lower front rail, and all the side rails are made from 8/4 hard maple. The top front and both back rails are made from 4/4 hard maple, as is the rear edge band on the partition.

1. Rip and crosscut the maple parts to rough sizes, as appropriate, before dressing the stock.
2. Joint a face and an edge of each piece.
3. Plane the stock to the correct thickness. The legs are all 1½ in. square. If you cut individual blanks from the rough stock, you can make them the final width and thickness using the thickness planer. The bottom front rail and the side rails are 1⅜ in. thick. All the parts taken from the 4/4 stock dress out to ¾ in. thick.

Mortising the legs and rails

Edmundson used mortises and tenons to join most of the rails to the legs. His joint configurations are not entirely what you might expect:

- The front bottom rail has a large single tenon, which penetrates the leg as far as possible (1¼ in.).
- The side rails are joined to the legs with short twin mortise-and-tenon joints. The mortises for them are as deep as they can be (⅜ in.) without penetrating the mortise for the front rail.
- The bottom back rail is narrower and thinner than the front rail, and its mortise is too. But it penetrates the leg the same distance as the front rail's mortise (1¼ in.).

All these joints use a loose, or slip, tenon. To make this joint, you cut mortises in both mating pieces; then join the pieces with a separate tenon that is glued into both mortises. Since you will probably use the same tool to do all the mortises, cut them together. (Edmundson uses a horizontal boring machine.)

"Case Joinery" shows the dimensions and placement of these joints.

1. Cut the mortise in the leg for the bottom front rail. It is ½ in. wide, 1¾ in. long, and 1¼ in. deep. Lacking a horizontal borer, use a router or hollow-chisel mortiser.

2. Cut the matching mortises into both ends of the front rail. The length of the rail makes the staging a bit of a challenge if you do this task with a router, and especially with a hollow-chisel mortiser.

3. Next, change your tool setup to cut ¼-in.-wide mortises.

4. Begin by cutting the deep mortise in the back legs for the bottom rail.

5. Cut matching mortises into the rail ends.

6. Now cut the twin mortises. Positioning the mortises consistently is critical. With the router setup I use (see "Mortising Jig" on p. 242), you can do both of the twins with the same setup. You simply move a spacer to shift the router on the jig.

Tapering the feet

Each leg is tapered slightly. The taper—amounting to just ⅛ in.—extends from the bottom of the lower rail to the foot, a distance of 3 in. It is cut on only the two inside faces (beneath the rails). The adjacent outside faces are straight from top to bottom.

1. Lay out the tapers on the legs. Mark the shoulder of the lower rails on the legs. With a rule and pencil, mark the cut line from the shoulders to the foot.

2. Handplane the tapers. This proves to be much quicker and easier and less risky to do than sawing them.

Shaping the bottom rails

The bottom edge of the lower rails on the sides and the front are arched, rising ⅝ in. from the ends to the center point.

1. Lay out the cut lines on the side rails. This is relatively easy, because the side rails are short. Mark the center point and measure ⅝ in. up from the bottom edge at that point. Have a helper flex a thin batten so it arches from one bottom corner to the center mark and back to the opposite bottom corner. Scribe a line along the flexed batten.

2. Lay out the cut line on the front rail, using the same procedure.

3. Cut to the lines on the bandsaw.

4. Sand the cut edge to smooth it. This is easiest to do with a spindle sander or at the drum of an edge sander.

Grooving for the back panels

The back panels are housed in grooves plowed in the legs, the top and bottom back rails, and the partition edge band. For the best fit, you should cut this groove on the router table so you can reference the cut off the back face (or edge) of each part.

1. Measure the thickness of the plywood you're using for the back panels. If the material is dramatically shy of ¼ in., you may want to use a ⁷⁄₃₂ in. bit to plow the grooves. Just

CASE JOINERY

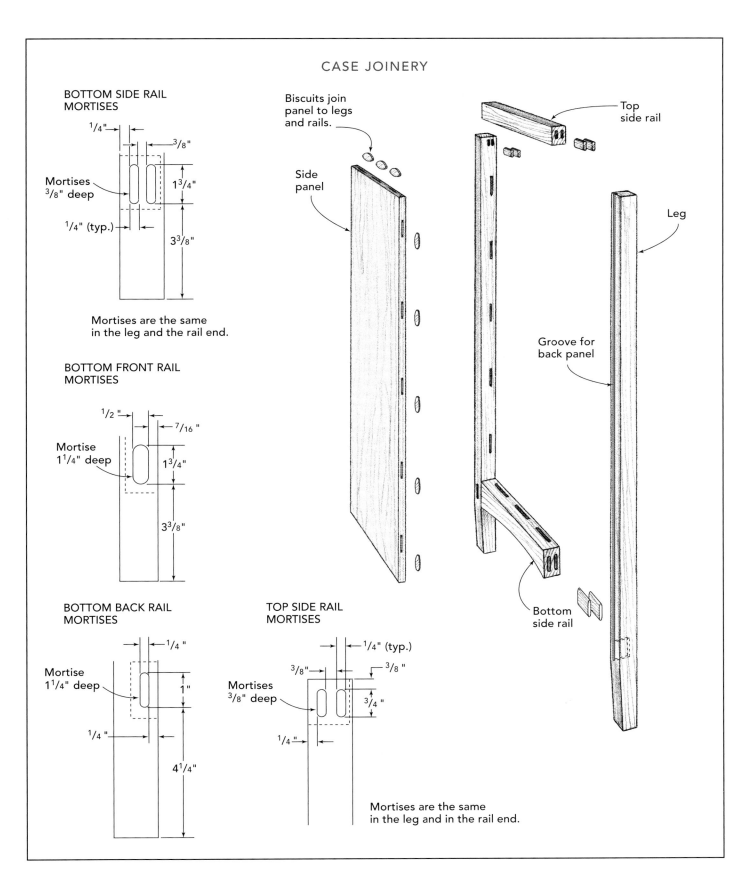

BOTTOM SIDE RAIL MORTISES

1/4"

3/8"

Mortises 3/8" deep

1 3/4"

1/4" (typ.)

3 3/8"

Mortises are the same in the leg and the rail end.

BOTTOM FRONT RAIL MORTISES

1/2"

7/16"

Mortise 1 1/4" deep

1 3/4"

3 3/8"

BOTTOM BACK RAIL MORTISES

1/4"

Mortise 1 1/4" deep

1"

1/4"

4 1/4"

TOP SIDE RAIL MORTISES

1/4" (typ.)

3/8"

3/8"

Mortises 3/8" deep

3/4"

1/4"

Mortises are the same in the leg and in the rail end.

Biscuits join panel to legs and rails.

Side panel

Top side rail

Leg

Groove for back panel

Bottom side rail

MORTISING JIG

This jig is designed for small-scale production mortising. The work holders adjust for different workpiece sizes (and orientations). The bit diameter establishes the mortise width, while the router's plunge controls the depth. The track and adjustable stops control and limit the router's movement. Mark only the midpoint for a mortise; align that mark with the registration line, and the jig and router will produce the mortise.

When cutting the mortise, the router is on top of the jig, with its edge guide riding along the jig's back edge. The stops control the length of the mortise by arresting the router's movement.

Switch to the horizontal work holder to rout side mortises. The setup of the router and the jig's stops shouldn't have to be changed. Moving the spacer in front of or behind the edge-guide facing in the track bumps the router position back and forth for doing twin mortises; no other changes are needed.

Use the vertical work holder when cutting end mortises. Hold the workpiece against the face of the jig with the toggle clamp, but also apply a clamp to cinch the piece against the work holder.

MORTISING JIG PLAN

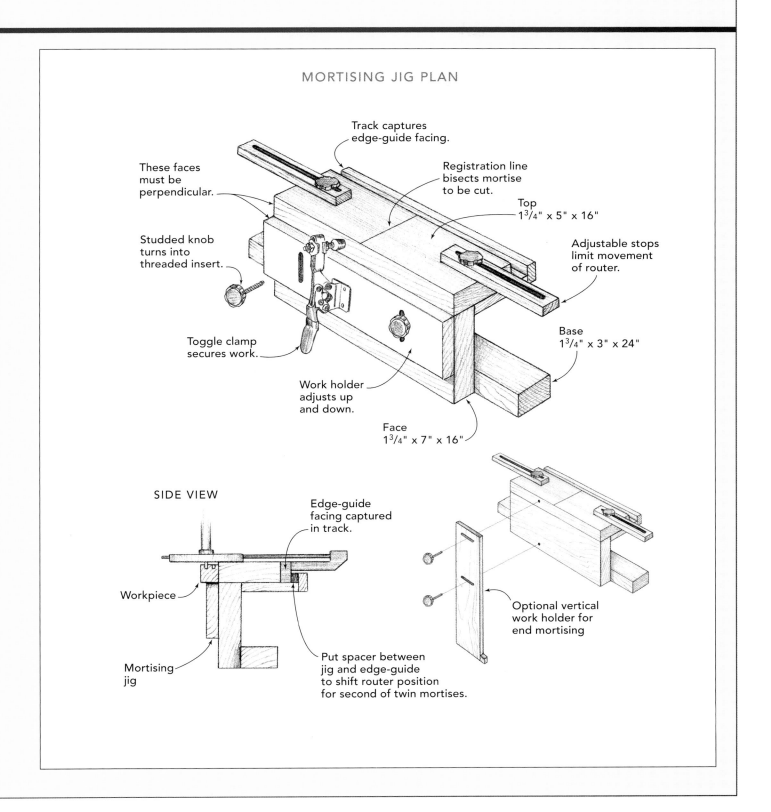

Track captures edge-guide facing.

These faces must be perpendicular.

Registration line bisects mortise to be cut.

Top
$1^3/4$" x 5" x 16"

Studded knob turns into threaded insert.

Adjustable stops limit movement of router.

Toggle clamp secures work.

Base
$1^3/4$" x 3" x 24"

Work holder adjusts up and down.

Face
$1^3/4$" x 7" x 16"

SIDE VIEW

Edge-guide facing captured in track.

Workpiece

Mortising jig

Put spacer between jig and edge-guide to shift router position for second of twin mortises.

Optional vertical work holder for end mortising

bear in mind that you do have to slide the panel into place. Don't let a compulsion to avoid an overly loose fit steer you into assembly problems.

2. Set up the router table. First, secure the bit in the collet. Set the cut depth to about ⅛ in. (The stock is hard and a ¼-in. bit is relatively frail, so cut to the full depth of ¼ in. in two passes.) Position the fence so the groove will be ¼ in. from the reference face of the work.

3. Groove the parts. In all but the legs, the grooves extend end to end. In the legs, they extend from the top down to the mortise (see **photo A**). The partition edge band gets two grooves. Cut each groove in two passes.

Making the loose tenons

1. Mill scraps of the maple to the thicknesses needed. If you use power tools for this, use scraps that are long enough to be machined safely. Be sure the material is wide enough for the applications, of course. The front rail mortises require ½-in.-thick stock; all the others require ¼-in.-thick stock.

2. Rip the stock to the needed widths.

3. Round the edges of the tenon stock on the router table. Use either bullnose or round-over bits.

4. Crosscut the needed tenons to dimensions shown in the cut list.

Dry-assembling the legs and rails

Even if you can't assemble all the frame parts at once, you can join selected ones into sub-assemblies. The point of the exercise is to make sure everything fits, of course, and that the resulting assemblies are square and flat. But you also want to measure for the panels. (You don't want to glue up the bottom panel and rails only to discover that the mortises don't line up.)

1. Slip the tenons into mortises in the side rails (see **photo B**).

2. Fit the legs onto the tenons.

3. Clamp the assembly. If you have metal-jawed clamps that might mar the work, use cauls between jaws and wood.

Photo B: A loose tenon is easy to fit snugly in its mortise. Prepare a long strip to the proper thickness and width, bullnose the edges on the router table, and crosscut individual slips.

4. Check the assembly for squareness and flatness.

5. Measure the panel space carefully and note the dimensions.

6. Assemble the second side in the same way. Note the dimensions of its panel space.

7. Insert the tenons into the front and back rails.

8. Join the rails to the two clamped-up side assemblies (see **photo C**). Apply the clamps so they parallel the rails.

9. Check the assembly for squareness and flatness.

10. Measure the space for the bottom panel and note the dimensions.

Cutting the panels

Edmundson used both veneered MDF and hardwood plywood in the dresser. The MDF was used for the end panels and the top, where the plain-sliced veneer would look best. The plywood was used in the bottom and the back, and for the divider, places that typically aren't seen.

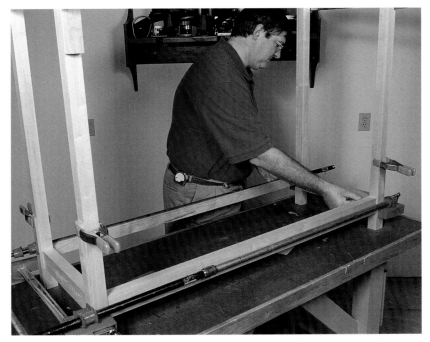

Photo C: A dry run allows you to check the fit of the joints and determine the dimensions for the side, bottom, and back panels. Clamp the sides; then join them to the front and back rails.

1. Cut the bottom panel to the dimensions you took from the dry-assembled case framework.
2. Cut the partition panel from the same sheet of plywood.
3. Cut the two back panels.
4. Cut the two side panels from ¾-in. A1 plain-sliced maple-veneered MDF.

Making the bottom assembly

The bottom unit consists of the bottom panel and the bottom front and back rails.

1. Lay out the biscuit joints between the rails and the panel. The panel is to be flush with the top edges of the rails, so this work is straightforward. Lay the parts upside down on the workbench and butt them together as they'll be in the final assembly. Mark biscuit locations on both rails and panel.
2. Cut the biscuit slots. This is a basic operation. Cut the slots in both the panel edges and the rails with the joiner square on the bench-

top. The rails should be upside down, of course, when you cut them.
3. Glue up the rails and panel with biscuits. Clamp the assembly and set it aside to cure.

Making the side assemblies

Each side assembly consists of a pair of legs, a pair of side rails, and a side panel. The legs and rails are joined with the mortise-and-loose-tenon joints, which have already been cut. The panel is secured with biscuits, and their slots must be cut now.

The only departure from the straightforward is the progression of insets. The faces of the rails are inset ⅛ in. from the faces of the legs. The face of the panel is inset another ⅛ in. from the faces of the rails. All this means is that you have to settle on a consistent way to cut the slots in the rails and legs so they'll align with the slots in the panel edges.

1. Lay out the slot locations on the rails and panel. Line up the parts, faces down, with the ends of the rails flush with the edges of the

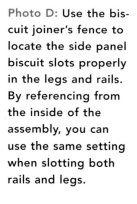

Photo D: Use the biscuit joiner's fence to locate the side panel biscuit slots properly in the legs and rails. By referencing from the inside of the assembly, you can use the same setting when slotting both rails and legs.

Photo E: Glue tenons and biscuits into the legs, and biscuits into the panel ends. Fit a rail and the panel to a leg. Add the second rail, and the second leg.

panel. Don't worry yet about the alignment of the faces. Just mark the biscuit locations on the panel and the rails.

2. Lay out the slot locations on the legs. Don't move the panel and rails. Simply move the legs into place, again with their faces down. Align the legs with their tops flush with the top rail. Make your marks on the panel and on the legs.

3. Cut the slots in the panel. This is a straight-forward cut with the biscuit joiner.

4. Cut the slots in the rails and legs. The backs of the legs and rails are flush, so use them as the reference surface when cutting the slots. Center the slots ⅞ in. from the back edge of these parts. Use the joiner's fence to locate the slots and to orient them square to the faces (see **photo D**). And make sure the rails are face down when you make the cuts.

5. Glue up the side assemblies (see **photo E**). Clamp them and set them aside until the glue cures.

Making the partition

The partition panel divides the case into two bays and supports the drawer runners. The partition, which was cut earlier, is banded on its back edge with a hardwood strip that's already been grooved for the back panels. Its front edge is banded with iron-on veneer tape. That edge is hidden by the drawer fronts in the completed dresser (see "Partition Joinery" on p. 248).

1. Glue the partition edge band to the partition panel's back edge.

2. Cut the notches for the top rails. The edge of the back rail is flush with the back edge of the partition, so the notch must be 1½ in. wide. Cut it ¾ in. deep. Because the partition

PARTITION JOINERY

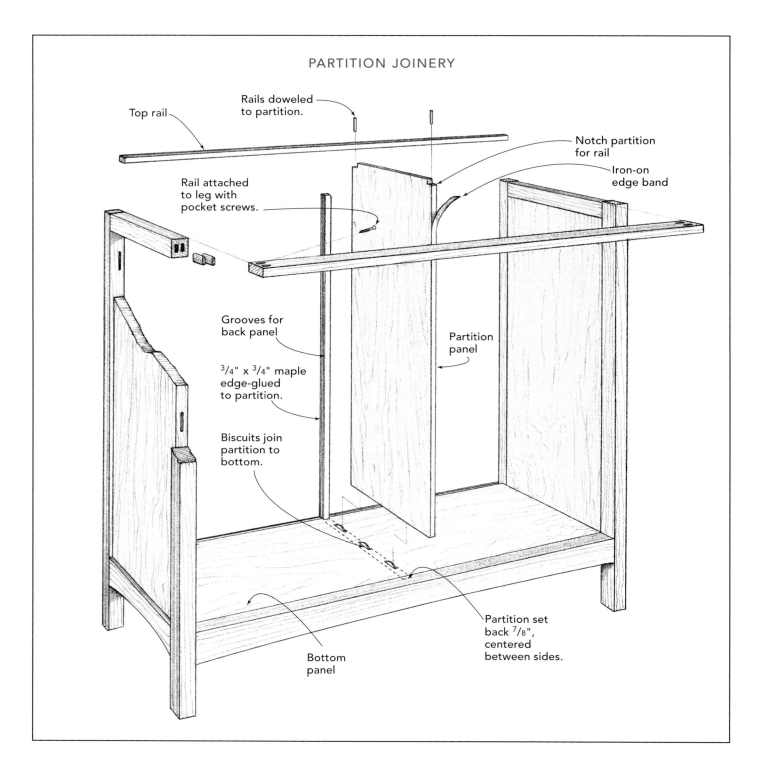

Top rail

Rails doweled to partition.

Notch partition for rail

Iron-on edge band

Rail attached to leg with pocket screws.

Grooves for back panel

Partition panel

$3/4"$ x $3/4"$ maple edge-glued to partition.

Biscuits join partition to bottom.

Partition set back $7/8"$, centered between sides.

Bottom panel

is set in $7/8$ in. from the edge of the front rail, the notch for the front rail need only be $3/8$ in. wide. It too is $3/4$ in. deep.

3. Apply the iron-on veneer tape to the front edge of the partition panel. If you don't have veneer tape, just glue a thin ($1/8$-in. or less) maple ripping to the edge.

4. Cut biscuit slots in the partition panel and the bottom assembly. Stand the partition on the bottom assembly, center it, and align the

Photo F: Glue biscuits in the slots in the case bottom and maneuver the partition into place, nestled under the front rail.

back edge flush with the bottom's back edge. Mark the slot locations. Lay it flat on the bottom and cut the slots in it and in the bottom.

Assembling the case

1. Join the side assemblies and the bottom assembly, using glue. Apply clamps.

2. Attach the top front rail to the legs with pan-head pocket screws. Clamp scraps to the legs to support the rail, flush with the top of the legs, while you drive the screws.

3. Glue the partition panel to the bottom. Glue the biscuits into the slots in the bottom and slip the partition into place (see **photo F**). You need to dip the notched front corner under the top rail as you engage the biscuits. Align the panel flush with the back edge of the case.

4. Drill a 2-in.-deep hole for a ⁵⁄₁₆-in.-diameter dowel through the front rail into the edge of the partition.

5. Glue the dowel in the hole.

Installing the back panels

Although the back of the chest is plywood, it has a more finished look than the usual plywood back. Instead of nailing the plywood into a rabbet, the two panels are housed in grooves in the legs and rails. The panels and grooves have already been cut.

1. Glue the back panels in place. Edmundson used polyurethane glue because it lubricates better than yellow glue. Run a bead of it in the grooves for one panel; then slide that panel into place. Repeat to install the second panel.

2. Install the top back rail. Run a bead of polyurethane glue in the groove in the top back rail. Set the rail in place and drive the pocket screws that secure it to the legs (see **photo G** on p. 250). Working quickly and thoroughly, use mineral spirits to clean any squeezed-out glue from the case.

3. Dowel the rail to the partition. Drill a ⁵⁄₁₆-in.-diameter by 2-in.-deep hole through the

Tip: MDF edges absorb glue readily. So it is easy to get a glue-starved joint. To prevent this, size the MDF edge with glue. Spread glue on the edge and allow it to stand for about 10 minutes. Then reapply glue and complete the glue-up.

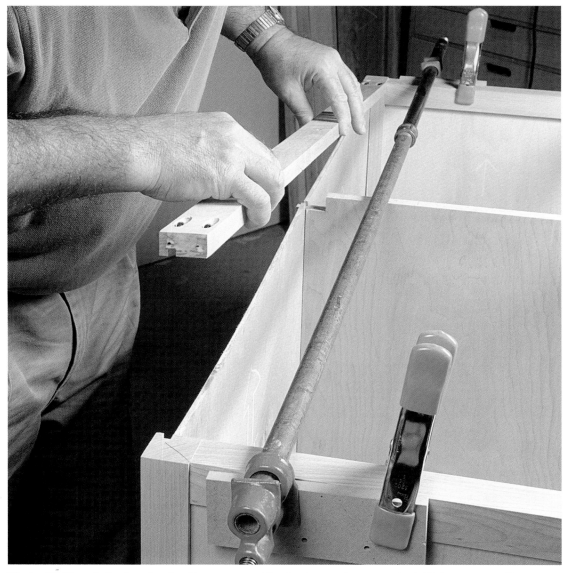

Photo G: **Mount the top back rail as soon as the back panels are seated. Get a corner of one panel started in the rail's panel groove, and lower the rail into place.**

rail into the edge of the partition. Glue a dowel in the hole; then trim it flush.

Making and attaching the top

The top is a piece of maple-veneered MDF to which you apply maple edge bands.

1. Prepare the maple edge bands for the top. Mill 4/4 stock to $^{13}/_{16}$ in. thick and rip $^{1}/_{2}$-in.-thick strips from it.

2. Cut the top panel.

3. Fit the edge bands to the top, mitering the ends of each piece.

4. Glue the bands in place.

5. Plane the edge bands flush with the top and bottom of the panel.

6. Position the top, with its back edge flush with the back surfaces of the legs and back rail. Drive screws up through the top rails into the top.

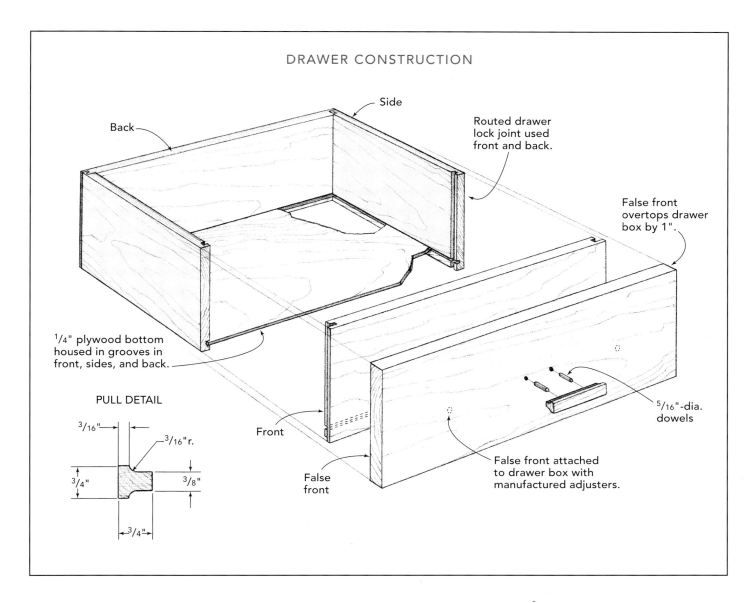

DRAWER CONSTRUCTION

Back

Side

Routed drawer
lock joint used
front and back.

False front
overtops drawer
box by 1".

1/4" plywood bottom
housed in grooves in
front, sides, and back.

PULL DETAIL

3/16"

3/16" r.

3/4"

3/8"

3/4"

Front

False
front

5/16"-dia.
dowels

False front attached
to drawer box with
manufactured adjusters.

CONSTRUCTING THE DRAWERS

All the drawers are solid-wood boxes with enclosed plywood bottoms and maple false fronts attached with adjusters. The pulls are made from tiger maple and mounted to the false fronts with dowels (see "Drawer Construction").

Edmundson mounted the drawers on hidden runners. Key dimensions are affected by this hardware. The length of the drawer boxes is dictated by the 15-in. length of the runners. Beneath each drawer, ⅜ in. of clearance is required for the tracks. The box must be ⅜ in. narrower than the drawer opening. To provide space for the locks that clip the drawer to the runners, a ½-in. space is needed between the drawer bottom and the bottom edge of the drawer sides.

Making the drawer boxes

Any wood can be used for the drawer boxes, including plywood. Edmundson used alder because it is common in his area.

1. Cut the parts. Aim for tolerances of ¹⁄₃₂ in. when working with the hidden runners.

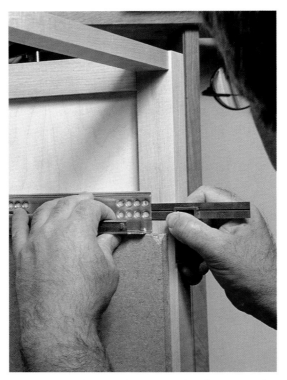

Photo H: **To locate the runner hardware on the case sides and partition, use a plywood jig to hold it at the correct elevation while you drive the mounting screws.**

Mounting the drawer hardware in the case

The drawer runners are integral to the mounting brackets, which you are about to screw to the case sides and partition. To fit a drawer in place (once the hardware is mounted), you set it atop the runners and slide it toward the back. At the drawer back, a hooked tab on the runner is engaged; at the same time, a pair of clips under the drawer engage the ends of the runners. The clips connect the runners and drawer so they move together. To remove the drawer, you open the drawer partway, disengage the clips, and pull the drawer toward you. Comes right out.

To locate the runner hardware so the four runners for each pair of drawers are mounted at the same height, use a simple plywood jig. Begin with the case-mounted hardware.

1. Cut eight spacers for the hardware that mounts to the case sides. You need to have the hardware flush with the surfaces of the legs that face the partition. Thickness your spacers so they will do that.

2. Cut the bottom groove. For the best fit, you want the grooves just wide enough for whatever plywood you use for the bottom. Doing the operation on the tablesaw allows you to fine-tune the groove width. Make the initial cut ½ in. from the bottom edge of each front, back, and side. Adjust the rip fence and make the final pass.

3. Cut the joinery. Edmundson used a drawer-lock router bit in the table-mounted router to cut the joints. Setting up requires a few test cuts to fine-tune the bit height and the two fence settings—one for cutting the sides and one for cutting the fronts (see "Routed Drawer Lock Joint"). Once that the settings are dialed in, cut the joints.

4. Assemble the drawer boxes. The bottom should force the drawer into square, but work on a surface you know is flat to avoid twist.

2. Cut a scrap piece of plywood to use in locating the drawer runner hardware in the case. Cut it to the depth of the case and the height of the top track location. Mark one corner. When you use this jig, always position the marked corner to the bottom and back of the case. That will ensure that all the tracks will be oriented consistently.

3. Mount the first track unit. Set the jig into the case, rest it on the bottom, and hold it against the case side. Fit a spacer between the legs and fasten it. Set a track unit on the plywood and adjust its front-to-back alignment. Screw it to the case (see **photo H**).

4. Move the plywood jig across the drawer bay and hold it against the partition. Set a track unit on top of it, against the partition. Adjust the front-to-back alignment; then screw it to the partition.

5. Install the top two tracks in the second drawer bay in the same manner.

6. Cut down the jig and use it to mount the next tier of runners. Cut it again and mount the third tier. The lowest runners rest on the case bottom and no jig is needed.

ROUTED DRAWER LOCK JOINT

Fast, secure drawer construction is the purpose of this joint. It doesn't have the pizzazz of dovetails, but it can be cut a whole lot faster.

The joint is cut with a single router bit used in the table-mounted router. Once the height of the bit is properly set—do test cuts to dial in the setting—you use it for both halves of the joint. You lay the drawer fronts (and backs) flat on the tabletop to cut them. You stand the sides on edge against the fence to cut them, as shown. Only the fence position changes between these cuts.

The joint can be used with any thickness of stock and any mixture of stock thicknesses. It will produce flush drawers and lipped drawers.

Stand a drawer side on end, its inside face flat against the fence, to rout it. Featherboards eliminate work-piece bobbles.

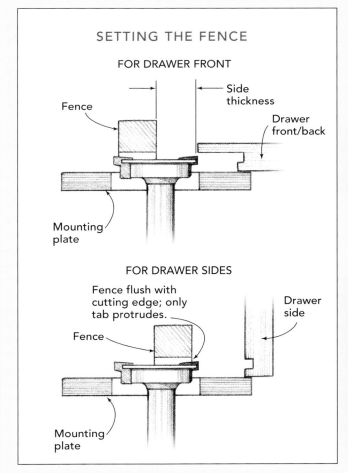

SETTING THE FENCE

FOR DRAWER FRONT

Fence

Side thickness

Drawer front/back

Mounting plate

FOR DRAWER SIDES

Fence flush with cutting edge; only tab protrudes.

Fence

Drawer side

Mounting plate

Lay the drawer front (or back) flat on the tabletop. Guide it along the fence with a push block when making the cut.

The assembled joint has a strong mechanical lock and expanded glue area.

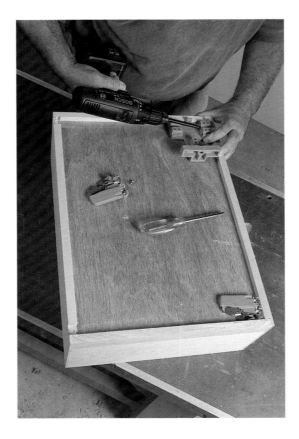

Photo I: Latches fastened underneath the drawer clip it to the runners. A jig from the manufacturer guarantees proper alignment of the pilot holes for the mounting.

Mounting the hardware on the drawers

As noted, the runners can't be removed from the case-mounted brackets. Instead, you extend them, set the drawer onto them, and latch them. Now you are going to notch each drawer back to accommodate the runners, and mount a pair of latches on each drawer that will hook it to the runners.

1. Screw the latches (called "locking devices" by Blum®) to the underside of each drawer. The latch is set on the bottom, tight against the drawer front. Drill pilot holes at the mounting points and screw the latches in place. The mounting holes in the latches can guide the drill bit, but jigs and special drill bits are available, and they do help (see **photo I**).
2. Notch the drawer backs below the bottom for the runners. Follow the manufacturer's

instructions regarding size and exact placement of the notches.
3. If necessary, drill holes in the drawer backs. Some brands of hidden slides have a hook on the runner that captures the back to help stabilize the drawer. If the runners you select have this feature, drill the hole. As with the latches, a jig is available from the manufacturer to make this task easy.

Mounting the drawer fronts

The drawer fronts are mounted to the boxes by way of commercial adjusters, which allow you to fine-tune the alignment of the front after it is attached to the drawer box.

1. Drill shallow, flat-bottomed holes in the backs of the drawer fronts for the adjusters.
2. Work out the alignment of each drawer front on its drawer in terms of the amount of overhang on each side.
3. Attach the drawer boxes to the fronts. Set the front on the workbench, position the box on it with the correct overhang, and drive mounting screws through the box into the adjusters, following the manufacturer's instructions.
4. Put the drawers in the case. Use the adjusters to refine the alignment of the fronts, so you have a uniform grid of fronts.

Making the drawer pulls

Each drawer has a single 4-in.-long pull mounted in the middle. The pulls can be made from scraps of the maple used to make the drawer fronts. Edmundson used tiger maple.

1. Cut several 12-in.- to 18-in.-long strips of ¾-in. by ¾-in. maple.
2. Using a ⅜-in.-diameter corebox bit in the table-mounted router, plow a 3⁄16-in.-deep groove in the center of opposing faces of each strip.
3. Switch to a straight bit and plow a ⅜-in. wide by 3⁄16-in.-deep rabbet into the same faces, trimming away one shoulder of the groove and transforming the section of each strip into a T-shape.

Photo J: Drill dowel holes in the back of each pull. A simple fixture clamped to the drill-press table ensures the holes are located consistently.

4. Sand the pull strips as necessary to blend the surfaces and soften hard edges.

5. Crosscut the strips into 4-in.-long pieces, making one for each drawer.

6. Make a fixture to use in drilling two holes in each pull for the ³⁄₁₆-in.-diameter mounting dowels. Set a pull on a scrap of ¾-in. plywood and nail trap fences all around it. Align the fixture and pull on the drill-press table so the first hole will be exactly where you want it. Clamp the fixture to the table.

7. After setting the drill press for the depth of hole you want, drill a hole in the pull. Lift the pull out of the fixture, turn it around, and return it to the fixture. Drill the second hole (see **photo J**). Drill holes in all the pulls in this way.

8. Before breaking down the fixture used to hold the pulls for drilling, use it to bore holes completely through a scrap of hardwood. Use this as the basis for a jig to guide you when you drill mounting holes for the pulls in the drawer fronts.

9. Lay out the locations for the pulls on the drawer fronts. Lightly scribe a horizontal line across each drawer front—the line on which

you'll center the pull. Bisect the line with a perpendicular.

10. Make a jig with the drilling guide block. Align it on the layout lines and drill mounting holes for a pull on each drawer front.

11. Apply glue sparingly to short pieces of dowel. Drive a dowel into each mounting hole in the drawer front, then press a pull onto the projecting ends of the dowels.

FINISHING UP

The final task is to apply your favorite finish to the dresser. Edmundson used a clear finish on his dresser, and I used a brush-on poly-urethane on mine. For the most thorough job, remove the drawer fronts from the drawer boxes and apply the finish to the back as well as to the front. I left the drawer boxes unfinished. Remove the runners from the case and finish the case inside and out equally. Then remount the fronts and the runners, slip the drawers in place, and fill the dresser with clothing.

Tip: Routing the rabbet that forms the drawer pulls removes most of the support for the work. To support the work, stick a ³⁄₁₆-in.-thick by ¼-in.-wide strip to the tabletop with a couple patches of double-sided tape. Position it on the outfeed side of the bit, against the fence.

Photo B: The post is aligned in the fixture and clamped to its face. When cutting the mortise, use the edge guide to reference the fixture's back edge; the stops limit the router's travel, thus controlling the length of the mortises.

Photo C: Screw a spacer to the fixture's back edge to shift the position of the bit ⅝ in. closer to the fixture. This allows you to rout both mortises in a pair with one router/edge-guide setup.

Tip: To halve the number of times he has to mount and remove the spacer, Burton alternates spacer and workpiece change-overs. He routs the far mortise in the first piece, then he mounts the spacer and routs the near mortise. He switches the workpiece and routs the near mortise. Then he removes the spacer and routs the far mortise. Continue the alternation until all the mortises are cut.

8. Rout the mortises in the posts (see **photos B** and **C**).
9. Switch work holders to do the matching twin mortises in the rail ends. Note that the short twin mortises are cut across the thickness of the rails rather than parallel to the width, as was the case with the side rails (see "Web Frame Construction"). Because the rails and posts are flush when assembled, the mortises are the same distance from the reference edge of both the post and rail. Thus, the router's edge guide doesn't need to be adjusted.

10. Rout the mortises in the rails (see **photo D** on p. 266). Be careful when mortising the bottom rail, which is thicker than the others. The mortises must be located in relation to the top surface. On one end, this is no particular problem. Before mortising the other, you need to shift the position of the work holder so the centerline will align with the jig's register line.

Cutting the grooves and rabbets

The last two joinery cuts to make in the posts are the groove for the side panels and, in the two back posts, the rabbet for the back panel.

Photo D: Switch work holders to use the fixture for mortising the rails. It shouldn't be necessary to alter the stops or the router/edge-guide setup. The mortises in the rails will match those in the posts.

The groove is ¼ in. wide and ⅜ in. deep and is ⁵⁄₁₆ in. from the post's edge. The rabbet is ¼ in. wide and ⁹⁄₃₂ in. deep (so the back panel is ever so slightly recessed).

1. Dog a post to the benchtop.
2. Set up a plunge router with a ¼-in.-diameter straight bit and an edge guide. Adjust the guide so the cut will be properly located in relation to the post's edge.
3. Rout the groove. To avoid the panel being inadvertently glued into the groove, stop the groove just shy of the side rail mortise on each end. Running the groove into the mortise invites glue to escape from the mortise onto the panel.
4. Set up a router either with a rabbeting bit or a straight bit and an edge guide.
5. Rout the rabbet in the inside back edge of the two back posts only. The rabbet extends 43⅛ in. from the top of the post, stopping where the bottom back rail joins the post.
6. Square the inside corner of the rabbet with a chisel.

Shaping the posts

The outside edge of each post tapers gradually from the top to the ankle, where the foot angles out sharply. The face and back are square, as is the inside edge, to which all the drawer rails join. The tapers are completed in three cuts.

1. Lay out the tapers on one post as shown in "Making a Post" on p. 262.
2. Make two tapering jigs to use on the table saw (see "Tapering Jigs"). Using the jigs will ensure you get consistent cuts from post to post.
3. Make the first cut on the tablesaw. This is a stopped cut that begins at the top of the post and extends only to the ankle, from which the foot cants away. Make the cut and stop short of the ankle (see **photo E** on p. 268). Be sure to account for the curve of the blade when establishing the stop point.
4. Turn off the saw. When the blade stops, lift the post and the jig off the blade. Don't mess with the waste. It will come off soon enough.

TAPERING JIGS

These two job-specific jigs are easy to make, do the job perfectly, and can be recycled without remorse when the posts have been tapered. Lay out the cut you want to make on the workpiece, align the work on a plywood or medium-density fiberboard base, and screw a few fences to the base to hold the workpiece in position. Slide the base along the tablesaw's rip fence to cut the taper.

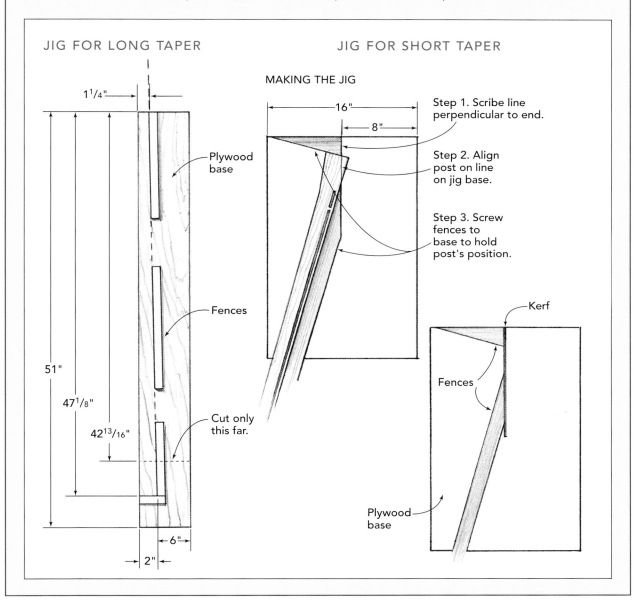

JIG FOR LONG TAPER

JIG FOR SHORT TAPER

MAKING THE JIG

1¼"

Plywood base

Fences

51"

47⅛"

42¹³/₁₆"

Cut only this far.

6"

2"

16"

8"

Step 1. Scribe line perpendicular to end.

Step 2. Align post on line on jig base.

Step 3. Screw fences to base to hold post's position.

Kerf

Fences

Plywood base

Photo E: Cut the post's long taper on the tablesaw, guided by a tapering jig. Stop the cut when the blade reaches the ankle, the point at which the foot splays out sharply.

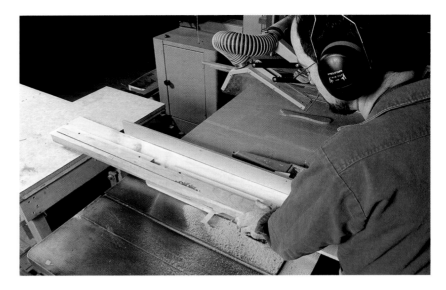

Photo F: A second tapering jig is used to cut the inner face of the foot. To save the jig, stop feeding the work when the waste is severed from the post. Then stop the saw and back the post off the blade.

5. Complete the outside post shape on the bandsaw. Cut from the foot in to the ankle. This is a short cut; and as it is completed, the long piece of waste will separate from the post.
6. Cut the inner edge of the foot on the tablesaw using the second tapering jig. The cut is stopped only to preserve the jig (see **photo F**).
7. Smooth the cut surfaces. Remove the ridge of waste left at the end of the long taper cut. Use a broad chisel. Then shave off the saw marks with a spokeshave or scraper. Sand all four surfaces of each post.

8. Use a block plane to chamfer the perimeter of the foot. This gives the appearance of floating just above the floor and will prevent chipping if the chest is dragged across a floor.

Making the side rails

The side rails have been cut to width and length, and they've been mortised. Now shape them and groove them for the side panels.

1. Lay out and cut the template for shaping the rails (see "Side Assembly Construction"). The shape is an asymmetrical V. Use the same template to shape both top and bottom rails.

SIDE ASSEMBLY CONSTRUCTION

Note that the top rails have the peak toward the back;
the bottom rails are the reverse.

PANEL CONTOUR

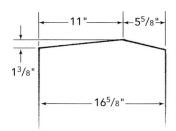

SIDE PANEL LAYOUT

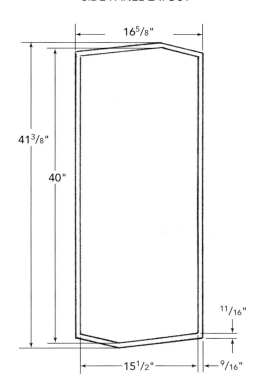

PANEL SHOULDER

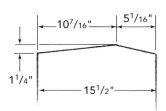

TOP SIDE RAIL LAYOUT

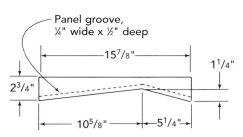

Panel groove,
¼" wide x ½" deep

BOTTOM SIDE RAIL LAYOUT

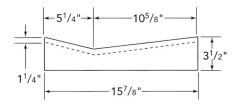

SIDE RAIL TEMPLATE

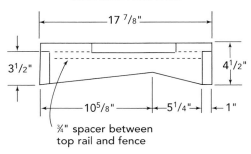

¾" spacer between
top rail and fence

Photo G: Both the upper and the lower side rails are contoured with the same template. Place fences on the template so it can be used on the router table. A second template, derived from the first, is used to contour the top and bottom edges of the side panels.

Tip: Using templates can help you produce consistent, accurate cuts. Make the templates from thin plywood or hardboard and use them to lay out the cuts. Use a router and pattern bit to trim the workpiece flush to the template.

2. Cut the four rails with a router and pattern bit that has a pilot bearing on the shank. This can be done on a router table.

3. Cut the panel groove in the shaped rail edge with a router and slot cutter.

Making the side panels

The 9/16-in.-thick side panel is raised, with the raised field designed to be flush with the faces of the side rails. The contour of the panel—and of the raised field—matches that of the frame formed by the posts and rails.

1. Cut the panels to their final dimensions.

2. Cut the panel contours. Note that each panel is asymmetrical; don't lay out both ends of a panel the same. The cuts can be made with a jigsaw guided by a clamped-on fence.

3. Raise the panels. The shoulder of the panel is square and the tongue is flat (see **photo G**). You want a 3/16-in.-wide gap between the posts and rails and the panel's shoulders. The grooves in the rails are deeper—by 1/8 in.—than those in the posts, so the width of cut from edge to shoulder must be 1/8 in. wider

across the panel ends than along the edges. You can make the cuts on the router table, guided by the fence. With a handheld router, make the cuts using a pattern bit guided by a clamped-on fence or template.

4. Fit the tongues, produced by raising the panels, into the post and rail grooves. Adjust the fit by handplaning the tongues.

5. Scrape and sand the panels to ready them for finishing and assembly.

6. Apply your finish to the panels. Burton used an oil finish. Apply it to both sides and all edges equally. The finish seals the panels and ensures that expansion and contraction of the wood will be consistent throughout the panel. It also makes assembly a bit easier.

Assembling the sides

At this point, parts for both side assemblies are ready to be joined.

1. Make the loose tenons needed for side assemblies and fit them to the mortises. You thickness and rip strips of stock, bullnose the edges to match the radius of the mortise ends,

Photo H: **Assemble each case side by capturing the panel between the rails and carefully engaging the tenons and panel edge in a post's mortises and panel groove.**

then crosscut the strips. You should be able to get a perfect fit with very little effort.

2. First assemble the units without glue (see **photo H**). Don't take this process lightly; it's important. It can steer you around the extraordinary pain and suffering resulting from a glue-up botched by a joint that doesn't quite fit. Think through the glue application, work out the best sequence of assembly, and set up your clamps.

3. Glue up the assemblies. Remember to keep the glue out of the panel grooves, so the panel can expand and contract. Don't worry too much about the alignment of the panel during the glue-up. Since it isn't glued, you can shift it later.

4. After the glue has cured and you've removed the clamps, align the panel so that gap between its shoulders and the posts and rails is consistent. If the gap is more or less than ³⁄₁₆ in. at this point, you can't do anything about it; but you can line up the shoulders

parallel to the posts and make the gap on one side match that on the other.

5. Drill a hole through the inner face of the top rail, equidistant from the posts, into the panel's tongue. Glue a dowel into the hole, pinning the panel in the center. Repeat for the bottom rail. The panel will be able to move in and out from this fixed centerline.

MAKING THE WEB FRAMES

The drawers are supported by web frames, consisting of front and rear drawer rails and two or three runners. The front rails are made of cherry, the runners and rear rails of cherry or maple. The runners are joined to the rails with glued mortise-and-loose-tenon joints. The frames are joined to the side assemblies with twin mortise-and-tenon joints. These latter mortises have already been routed.

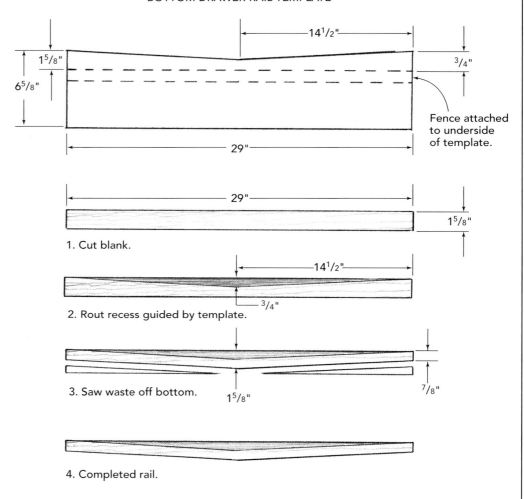

MAKING THE BOTTOM DRAWER RAIL

Cut the twin mortises before shaping the rail. The rail's top surface is flat to support the drawer; its bottom is tapered to parallel the contour. The drawer front will be contoured to match bottom of the recess.

BOTTOM DRAWER RAIL TEMPLATE

14^{1}/$_{2}$"

1^{5}/$_{8}$"

3$/$$_{4}$"

6^{5}/$_{8}$"

Fence attached to underside of template.

29"

29"

1^{5}/$_{8}$"

1. Cut blank.

14^{1}/$_{2}$"

3$/$$_{4}$"

2. Rout recess guided by template.

3. Saw waste off bottom.

1^{5}/$_{8}$"

7$/$$_{8}$"

4. Completed rail.

Tip: If your mortises are not centered across the work, you can get frames that aren't flat. To avoid misalignment, mark the top face of each part. Orient that face against the mortising jig, and the mortises will be consistently located.

Cutting the top rails and runners

1. If you didn't do this earlier, rip and crosscut the top rails to size. Bear in mind that the rails of the top frame are longer than all the other rails, because the top frame is dovetailed into the post tops.

2. Lay out and cut the large tails on the ends of the top drawer and back rails (see "Web Frame Construction" on p. 264). The cutting can be done with a jigsaw or on the bandsaw.
3. Rip and crosscut all the runners to the dimensions given in the cut list. Note that they are the same thickness as the rails.

Cutting the joinery

The rails and runners are assembled into web frames held together with loose tenons (see "Web Frame Construction" on p. 264).

1. Lay out the mortise locations on the rails and runners. The top three rails (both front and back) have three mortises each. To accommodate the dovetails, the top rails—the long ones—have the end mortises located an extra ⅜ in. farther in from their ends. The runners should be identical to one another.

2. Set up the mortising jig and plunge router for mortising the rails. Clamp a rail to the work holder and adjust the edge guide and the jig's stops. Mark the extents of the mortises on the jig itself; then use those marks to position each rail and runner for mortising.

3. Rout the mortises in the rails.

4. Change from the horizontal work holder to the vertical one.

5. Rout the mortises in the runners.

Shaping the bottom rail

The bottom drawer rail has a V-shape to it, giving the face of the chest a pointy chin. The entire rail, of course, isn't shaped, only the underside. The upper surface has a recess cut into it to accommodate the bottom drawer. The rail should already have been cut to size and then mortised for joining to the runners and the posts. Now you must shape it.

1. Make the template for routing the recess (see "Making the Bottom Drawer Rail"). Mount the template to a fence, such as a straight 2x4.

2. Rout the recess. The template is designed to be held in place by clamping both it and the workpiece in a bench vise (see **photo I**). Use a pattern bit (which has a shank-mounted pilot bearing) to make the ¾-in.-deep cut.

3. Chisel the tight inside corner of the recess. Even a small-diameter bit won't produce a sharp corner, which is what you want. So sharpen the rounded corner left by the router bit by paring it with a chisel.

4. Cut the bottom surface parallel to the top edge of the recess. Mark the cuts on the edge of the rail and then saw to the lines on the bandsaw.

5. Plane or sand the cut surfaces smooth and free of saw marks.

Tip: The back rails are ¼ in. narrower than the front rails. To maintain a consistent depth for the mortises without resetting the router's plunge depth, use a ¼-in.-thick spacer under the back rails when clamping them in the mortising jig.

Assembling the frames

1. Make the loose tenons needed for the web frames and fit them to the mortises.

2. One by one, assemble the frames without glue. Apply clamps and measure both diagonals to ensure that each clamps up square. (If the diagonal measurements are equal, the assembly is square.) If it doesn't do that without glue, it isn't going to do it after the glue's been applied. Make whatever adjustments are necessary to ensure all the frames will be square after glue-up.

3. Glue and clamp the frames. Re-check the diagonal measurements, of course, and make sure the frames are flat.

4. After removing the clamps, scrape and sand the frames to remove any dried squeeze-out and smooth the top surface.

Cutting the drawer divider joinery

Vertical drawer dividers are typically joined to the rails with dadoes or sliding dovetails. In this chest, loose tenon joints do the job.

1. Lay out the mortises on the front rails of the top web frame and the two web frames with the center runner. Each mortise must be equidistant from the ends of the rail and perpendicular to the front edge of the rail it is cut into. The middle frame must be mortised twice, in the topside and underside of the rail, to support the dividers above and below it.

2. Set up the plunge router with the ⁵⁄₁₆-in. straight bit. Since one web frame is mortised in both the topside and the underside, the mortises can't be very deep. The cut depth should be no more than ⅜ in.

3. For each cut, clamp a fence to the frame to guide the router (see **photo J**).

4. Rout the mortises.

5. Cut the vertical dividers to size.

6. Mortise the dividers using the mortising jig and plunge router setup.

Photo J: **The vertical drawer dividers are joined to the web frames with mortises and loose tenons. Rout the mortises after the frames are glued up.**

ASSEMBLING THE CASE

With the major subassemblies completed, it is just about time for the case to come together. You need to make all the loose tenons that link the web frames and the side. Then comes a dry fitting, followed by the final glue-up.

Making the loose tenons

The sides and web frames are linked with forty-eight 1½-in.-long loose tenons.

1. Select strips of stock and mill them down to ⁵⁄₁₆ in. thick.

2. Rip the strips to ½ in. wide.

3. Nose the edges with a ⅛-in.-radius roundover bit, so they'll fit the mortises.

4. Crosscut the strips into 1½-in.-long loose tenons.

Joining the sides and web frame

The case, by virtue of all its parts, is a complex assembly. Putting the parts together without glue, and clamping the assembly, is an important prelude to the final glue-up. Dry-fit the case and clamp it tight, just as though you had used glue. Satisfied that everything fits properly and that you've got the assembly routine down, dismantle the chest and reassemble it, but this time use the glue.

1. Set one side assembly on the benchtop, mortises up.

2. Slip a loose tenon in each mortise in the side assembly.

3. One by one, stand all the web frames in their proper positions. The bottom frame should be at the foot end. Set the vertical dividers in place too.

4. Set the second side assembly atop the web frames and work the tenons into its mortises (see **photo K**).

5. Stand the assembly upright on the floor. The tenons should be tight enough in the mortises that the assembly stays together. (If the tenons are too loose, make a new batch.)

6. With a spring clamp, secure a long ripping to the outer face of each post. Apply bar or pipe clamps across the case, aligned with each drawer rail and back rail. Tighten them, just as you will when assembling the unit with glue (see **photo L**).

7. Check over the case. Use a square and diagonal measuring to make sure it is case is square. Be sure all the rails seat tight to the posts.

8. Dismantle the case; then reassemble it using glue.

Photo K: Case assembly begins with the side flat on the bench. After joining all the web frames to it, set the second side in place and methodically start all the tenons into their mortises.

Photo L: After the second side is seated, right the unit and apply clamps parallel to each web frame, across the front and the back. The spring clamps hold pad strips that protect the posts.

Photo M: A large dovetail cut on each end of the top drawer and back rails join them to the posts. This traditional joinery captures the rails in the posts.

Dovetailing the top frame

The top web frame is dovetailed into the post tops. The tails have already been cut. Now you'll scribe the locations onto the tops of the posts and, with the case clamped together, cut the dovetail slots.

1. Set the top web frame on top of the posts. Make sure it is properly aligned.
2. Scribe around the tails with a marking or utility knife. Make sure you will be able to see the marks. Measure and mark the depth of slot necessary, and extend the knife marks down the inner surface of the post.
3. Chisel out the waste.
4. Carefully pare the slots until the frame can be seated. It should be flush with the tops of the posts (see **photo M**).

Making the top

The top is a panel formed by edge-gluing several boards. The front and ends are beveled, to make it appear thinner.

1. If necessary, glue up boards to form the top panel.

2. Scrape and sand the panel to remove excess glue and to smooth and flatten it.
3. Rip and crosscut the panel to final size
4. Lay out the bevels on the front and one end. Note that they are of different widths.
5. Cut the bevels. Do this on the tablesaw by tilting the blade and then standing the top on edge and feeding it along the rip fence.
6. Scrape and sand the bevels to smooth them and remove saw marks.
7. Mount the top with screws driven up through the top web frame into the underside. The pilot holes you drill through the back rail should be sized for the screws; this will fix the top at the back. In the runners and the front rail, the pilots should be oversize or oblong, so the panel can expand and contract.

Making the back

The next logical step is to cut and install the back panel. But you may prefer to have access to the back of the case while you make and fit the drawers. You can cut the panel and install it now or install it later.

1. Measure the case from rabbet to rabbet, and from bottom web frame to top.
2. Cut a piece of ¼-in. birch plywood to fit.
3. Mount the back panel by driving three screws through it into each back rail.

BUILDING THE DRAWERS

The final phase of the project is building the drawers. All are constructed in the same way (see "Drawer Construction"). Although there are eight drawers in the chest, there are only four different sizes.

Cutting the parts

The drawers are built of the usual front, back, sides, and bottom. But these drawers also have slips, which are glued to the drawer sides to broaden the bearing surface and reduce wear on the sides and the runners.

The fronts are made of cherry, the bottoms of ¼-in. birch plywood, and the remaining parts of a secondary wood. Burton used soft maple as his secondary wood.

DRAWER CONSTRUCTION

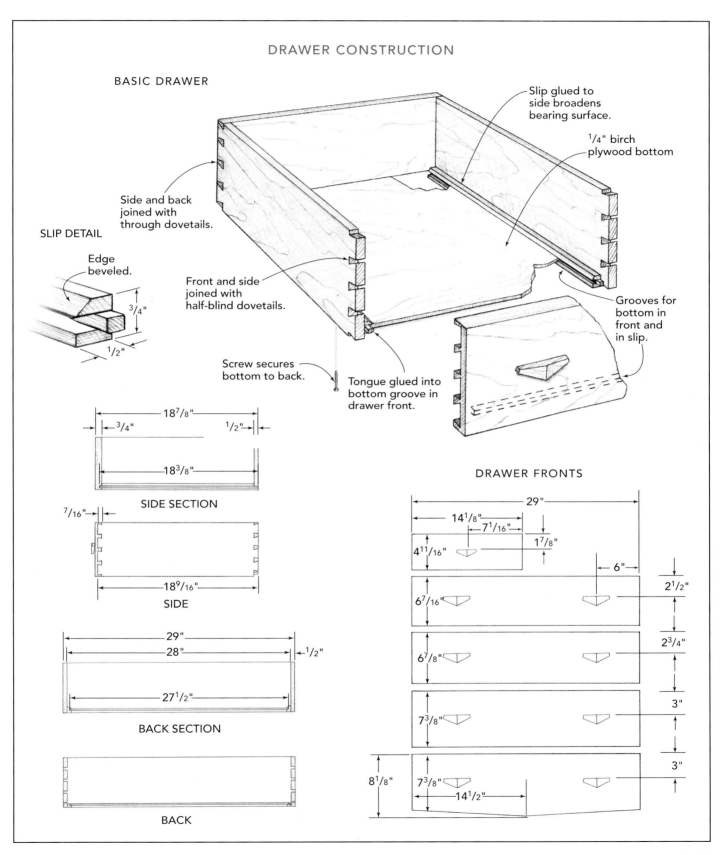

BASIC DRAWER

Slip glued to side broadens bearing surface.

$^1/4$" birch plywood bottom

Side and back joined with through dovetails.

SLIP DETAIL

Edge beveled.

$^3/4$"

$^1/2$"

Front and side joined with half-blind dovetails.

Grooves for bottom in front and in slip.

Screw secures bottom to back.

Tongue glued into bottom groove in drawer front.

18$^7/8$"

$^3/4$" $^1/2$"

18$^3/8$"

SIDE SECTION

$^7/{16}$"

18$^9/{16}$"

SIDE

29"

28" $^1/2$"

27$^1/2$"

BACK SECTION

BACK

DRAWER FRONTS

29"

14$^1/8$"

7$^1/{16}$"

1$^7/8$"

4$^{11}/{16}$"

6"

2$^1/2$"

6$^7/{16}$"

6$^7/8$"

2$^3/4$"

7$^3/8$"

3"

8$^1/8$"   7$^3/8$"

3"

14$^1/2$"

1. Face joint and thickness plane stock for the drawer fronts, sides, backs, and slips. The fronts and slips are ¾ in. thick, while the sides and backs are ½ in. thick.

2. Rip and crosscut the drawer fronts. Before turning on the saw, compare the dimensions specified on the cut list with the actual dimensions of the drawer openings of your chest. As you cut the fronts, fit them to their openings. Side to side, the fronts can be closely fitted. But you need to allow room for the front to expand across its grain; and the taller the drawer opening, the greater the allowance.

3. Rip and crosscut the sides and backs. As with the fronts, reconcile the dimensions specified on the cut list with the actual dimensions of your chest before you cut anything. Cut the parts to fit the openings and label them.

Cutting the joinery

Several different joinery cuts are required. The fronts and sides are joined with half-blind dovetails. The sides and back are joined with through dovetails. The bottoms ride in grooves in the slips and drawer front. As usual, there are a variety of ways you can make the cuts.

1. Cut a groove for the bottom in the front and the slips. Measure the plywood's actual thickness and try to match it when cutting the grooves. Plow the grooves end to end.

2. Traditionally, the front end of each slip is rabbeted across the top and bottom surfaces to produce a short tongue that fits into the panel groove in the drawer front (see "Drawer Construction" on p. 277). Similarly, the tail end is rabbeted across the top surface to accommodate the drawer back and allow the slip to end flush with the back end of the drawer side. Neither cut is essential, of course. But if you make the slips in this way, it's fairly efficient to cut the tongue on the front; then crosscut the slip to fit when its drawer is dry-assembled. Then you can rabbet the end.

3. Before setting the slips aside, cut a 45-degree chamfer on what will be in upper inside edge.

4. Lay out and cut the half-blind dovetails that join the fronts and sides. The dovetails can be

Photo N: Burton saws the margins of the pins; then routs out the majority of the waste. A strip of plywood with a glued-on fence controls the front-to-back depth of cut, and the side-to-side extent of the cut is done freehand.

Photo O: The final paring is done with a pair of custom-ground chisels: one for the left, one for the right.

Photo P: The pins on the drawer backs are routed using Burton's shopmade adjustable pin-cutting template.

hand-cut or machined with a router and dovetail jig. Burton uses a router to excavate the bulk of the waste quickly from the recesses in the fronts (see **photo N**). He then pares them to fit with a pair of old chisels ground with the cutting edges angled to the left and right (see **photo O**).

5. Lay out and cut the through dovetails that join the sides and backs. Bear in mind that the drawer bottoms slide just beneath the backs, so the bottom half-pin of the back penetrates the side ½ in. above the bottom edge. Again, use your favorite approach to cutting these joints. As he does in cutting half-blind dovetails, Burton combines the use of a router and shopmade guide (see **photo P**) with hand fitting.

Photo Q: Another
traditional element
in Burton's chest is
the use of slips to
broaden the bottom
edges of the drawer
sides. The extra
bearing surface will
greatly improve the
life of the drawers
and the runners.

Assembling the drawers

Each drawer is assembled according to the
same routine. Take the time to get each one
square and to fit it to its opening.

1. Run through a dry-assembly before actually
gluing up each drawer.
2. Crosscut each slip to length and then rabbet its end.
3. Next, glue the slip to the inside face of
the drawer side, flush with the bottom edge
(see **photo Q**).

4. Glue up the drawer.
5. Measure each drawer for a bottom. Cut the
bottoms.
6. Slide the bottoms into the drawers. Secure
them by driving a screw through the bottom
into the center of the back.
7. Fit each drawer to its opening. Sand or
plane the sides as necessary to get the drawer
operating smoothly (see **photo R**).

Photo R: With the pins deliberately cut a hair short, the sides are just proud of the pin ends in the assembled drawer. Burton can quickly handplane them flush with the pins.

FINISHING UP

Burton designed his own cherry pulls for this chest and mounted one in the center of each drawer front. You could, of course, use commercially made pulls (see "Sources" on p. 282). If you are using nonwooden pulls, remove them before finishing the chest.

Everyone has a favorite finish. Burton's is oil. It is a great choice for the small-shop woodworker. It doesn't require specialized equipment to apply. Burton finished his chest inside and out with several coats of the oil. The surfaces of the drawer fronts—meaning the face and the edges—are oiled, while the rest of each drawer is shellacked.

SOURCES

GARRETT WADE
161 Avenue of the Americas
New York, NY 10013
800-221-2942
www.garrettwade.com

Woodworking tools and supplies

HIGHLAND HARDWARE
1045 N. Highland Ave. NE
Atlanta, GA 30306
800-241-6748
www.tools-for-woodworking.com

Tools, woodworking supplies, and finishes

LEE VALLEY
P.O. Box 1780
Ogdensburg, NY 13669
800-871-8158
www.leevalley.com

Cupboard locks, knife hinges, hardware, tools, and woodworking supplies

LIE-NIELSEN TOOLWORKS
P.O. Box 9, Route 1
Warren, ME 04864
800-327-2520
www.lie-nielsen.com

Exceptional handplanes

ROCKLER
4365 Willow Dr.
Medina, MN 55340
800-279-4441
www.rockler.com

Hardware, casters, tools, and woodworking supplies

WOODCRAFT
P.O. Box 1686
560 Airport Industrial Rd.
Parkersburg, WV 26102
800-225-1135
www.woodcraft.com

WOODWORKER'S HARDWARE
P.O. Box 180
Sauk Rapids, MN 56379
800-383-0130
www.wwhardware.com

Drawer slides, hanging files rails, casters, hinges, clothes rods, locks, catches, pulls, etc.

WOODWORKER'S SUPPLY
1108 N. Glen Rd.
Casper, WY 82601
800-645-9292
www.woodworker.com

Large dowels, General Finishes Seal-A-Cell and Arm-R-Seal, hardware, tools, and woodworking supplies